Women's Spiritual Leadership in Africa

Women's Spiritual Leadership in Africa

Tempered Radicals and Critical Servant Leaders

FAITH WAMBURA NGUNJIRI

SUNY
PRESS

Published by
State University of New York Press, Albany

For information, contact State University of New York Press, Albany, NY
www.sunypress.edu

Production by Eileen Meehan
Marketing by Michael Campochiaro

Library of Congress Cataloging-in-Publication Data

Ngunjiri, Faith Wambura, 1973–
  Women's spiritual leadership in Africa : tempered radicals and critical
servant leaders / Faith Wambura Ngunjiri.
       p. cm.
  Includes bibliographical references and index.
  ISBN 978-1-4384-2977-9 (hbk. : alk. paper)
  ISBN 978-1-4384-2976-2 (pbk. : alk. paper)
  1. Leadership in women—Africa.   2. Women leaders—Africa.   I. Title.
HQ1787.N495 2010
305.420967—dc22   2009018959

10 9 8 7 6 5 4 3 2 1

Contents

Foreword

By Judy A. Alston

I was honored when Faith asked that I write the foreword for this book.
To be able to see the fruits of my teaching and mentoring labor bear
her own fruit is an awesome experience that makes the past 21 years
that I have spent as an educator so much more worthwhile.

The Road to Leadership

When I consider the concept and reality of leadership, from my own
worldview, I must first situate myself—beginning with who I am, what
I bring, and how I have come to know. In many respects, I respond
to inquiry on every side of this notion of leadership with more questions than answers. So I begin this foreword with some fundamental
knowledge that will assist the reader with an increased understanding
of my perspective as it relates to a (re)visioning of leadership from one
Black woman's perspective—a womanist (Walker, 1983) perspective.

As I have noted in other writings, there is a dearth of research
and writing on women of color and leadership, more specifically from
my view as a Black (African American) woman. The desire and passion
for this area of research came to fruition during my doctoral studies,
but perhaps it was always there in my life experiences as both a tempered radical and servant leader from the beginning.

In August 1996 I received my Ph.D. in educational administration
from Pennsylvania State University. Prior to reaching this goal, I had
been trained in some of the finest educational institutions in South
Carolina. I received a BA in English from Winthrop College, an M.Ed.
in secondary English and an M.Ed. in educational administration, both

from the University of South Carolina. My K–12 parochial education in Charleston, South Carolina, began with a focus on the basics (reading, writing, arithmetic, and religion), with a continued focus on college preparatory curricula and extracurricula leadership opportunities. Since 1987, as a teacher, teacher-leader, and now university professor/administrator, I have committed my life, personally and professionally, to improving educational and organizational leadership—what I believe to be my mission in life.

In addition to my education profile, I am Black. I am a woman. I am middle class. I am a Christian. I am an American citizen. I have a sexual orientation. I have an astigmatism. These "axes of identity," public and private, create the intersections of my selfhood and my view of leadership.

As I matriculated from my K–12 education to the completion of a terminal degree, I was most often in classrooms (usually the only person of color, or one of few, except in K–8) and under the administrative leadership of white, Eurocentric teachers, professors, and administrators. In only a few cases (six to be exact) did I have a classroom teacher or professor who was a person of color—five Black, one Cuban. This educational context and experience, coupled with my training, has led me to a particular meaning making that guides me to think, interrogate, analyze, critique, and (re)act. The epistemological underpinnings, the ways in which I have come to know and influence what is known, have become a critical unit of analysis as I explore the social and political transformation of educational/organizational leadership. It is within this "positionality" (Chavez 2008, p. 474) that the theoretical frame for my discussion, teaching, and research of leadership finds it genesis.

Black and African Women in Leadership

The focus concepts of this book—servant leadership, tempered radical-ism, spirituality, and meaning making—were all formally introduced and delineated in courses that I taught while I was a professor at Bowling Green State University in the leadership studies doctoral program. This text meshes these concepts along with the experiences and knowledge of the marginalized to the center by standing aside to let the community speak for itself (Thomas, 1998). Built upon my research about Black female superintendents as tempered radicals and servant leaders (Alston, 2005), Dr. Ngunjiri extends this research by focusing on African women leaders who are spirited, tempered radicals (a combination of Africana spirituality, tempered radicalism, and servant leadership).

In the context of preparation, practice, and research, a few cornerstones of leadership (power, control, authority, and influence) have historically been used in a negative fashion to marginalize, silence, and erase the accomplishments of historically underrepresented groups, that is, women, African Americans, Latinos, and Native Americans, as well as gays and lesbians. Parker (2005) noted that the "tradition" of African American women's leadership is absent from the literature in general. Often in the field of leadership preparation and leadership studies, the voices of the marginalized are not heard in the discussion or teaching of leadership theories, concepts, and research in general, thus it is a slanted view of the concept. Therefore, in order bring some balance to the field, the perspectives, experiences, and voices of Black and African women leaders are essential to the study of leadership.

I heard once that history is about winners and losers, and the winners get to tell their story. In many ways, the "winners" have told their story about leadership, and their concepts, models, and examples of leadership have reigned supreme and superior. Furthermore, the silencing of some groups while privileging others in the study of organizational leadership has been a product of theoretical perspectives that frame our current understanding of gender, discourse, and organization (Parker, 2005).

Dr. Ngunjiri's new work brings to the fore a new landscape, a much-needed addition to the discourse. It is transformative and powerful research that will broaden and enrich those people who take the opportunity to read and extend their own knowledge and experiential bases.

Judy A. Alston, Ph.D., is director/associate professor of the doctoral program in educational leadership at Ashland University, Ashland, Ohio. Her research foci include Black female school superintendents; the exploration of how the intersections of class, race, ethnicity, gender, sexual diversity, and ability affect educational leaders; tempered radicals; servant leadership; and Black gay, lesbian, bisexual, and transgender (GLBT) issues in educational leadership. She is the coauthor of *School Leadership and Administration: Important Concepts, Case Studies, & Simulations*, 7*th* ed., 8*th* ed. (2007, 2009), the author of *Multi-leadership in Urban Schools* (2002), and the author of numerous journal articles.

Preface

Leadership studies have generally been dominated by theories and approaches developed in the West, by Western scholars who overwhelmingly utilize White males and androcentric models. Various scholars have argued for the inclusion of non-Western and non-White studies of leadership to expand and sometimes counteract the Western hegemony. This book demonstrates how leadership is enacted in a specific social, cultural, and historical context by African women in Kenya. The study is based on leadership and life stories of 16 women from Kenya who lead grassroots, national, Pan- African and global organizations. The study was guided by the work of African feminists, Black feminist and womanist scholars such as Patricia Hill Collins, Judy A. Alston, Khaula Murtadha, Clenora Hudson Weems, Mercy Amba Oduyoye, and others who argue that African and African American women's life experiences are an epistemologically valid standpoint from which to construct theories. In the absence of sufficient studies of African women in leadership, the study was guided by empirical and conceptual work from African American women scholars.

This book will provide a worthwhile contribution to our understanding of women and leadership by contributing the perspective of African women as I have interpreted them. Scholars and the educated publics in the interdisciplinary field of leadership studies will find the explication of tempered radicalism, servant leadership, and spirituality understood through the meaning-making experiences of African women both informative and inspiring. This book demonstrate how context matters in the practice of leadership—a context that has produced critical servant leaders who *rock the boat without falling out,* convicted and guided by their spiritual praxis. Whereas the term "critical servant leadership" was coined by McClellan (2006) to capture how Black men "merge spirituality, servant leadership, and Black identity into a visionary, empowering, and prophetic soul force (pp. iii–iv) that gives voice to the marginalized in their communities, this study expands her conceptualization by contextualizing it to an African demographic. As the witness and interpreter of the life stories that formed the data for this study, a short biography of my life and educational experience will help the reader understand my positionality.

I was born in Nyeri in the Central Province of Kenya (East Africa), the middle child of lower-middle-class parents. My parents were both teachers, so high expectations in academic performance were the norm. I was blessed to have moved from a nondescript primary school in Kirinyaga district to one of the top girls' secondary schools in the country, the Alliance Girls' High School, Kikuyu. Here I interacted with the best-performing girls from all over the country, opening my eyes to the rich ethnic diversity from an experiential perspective.

In 1993, I joined Kenyatta University to study for a bachelor's of education degree with a focus on language and literature. At that point, I had no intentions of becoming a teacher; I thought I would then join a business organization and begin a career in corporate Kenya. However, during my teaching practicum, I came to the realization that teachers have the power to make or break students' lives by the choices they make. At that point, I made the decision to pursue teaching, at least for a short period of time. I did my practicum in a small private school that catered to poor children, most of whom came from the slums of Nairobi. I realized that such students were disadvantaged because the schools they could attend if they did not make it into public schools were often underfunded and understaffed, so their ability to rise from poverty through education was limited. After graduation, I worked in a private Christian school for middle-class children—the exact opposite of my previous school. That experience engendered in me the desire to pursue values-based education as I realized that while the two schools were on opposite ends of the economic spectrum, children in both settings would benefit from authentic values-based education that would prepare them to deal with life, educating them not just intellectually but spiritually to promote character development.

To cut a long story short, I joined Nairobi Chapel, a nondenominational evangelical church situated on the campus of Nairobi University in order to engage in their leadership development program, culminating in my leading the instituting of a Christian school (Logos Christian School). In the four years that I served at Nairobi Chapel, I also engaged in theological education at Nairobi Evangelical Graduate School of Theology (NEGST), graduating with a master's degree in mission studies. One of the defining moments in my development as a leader occurred during that period. In the process of advertising for a principal for Logos, one of the governing board members asked why I was not being considered for the role since I had been serving in a leadership role all along. A pastor who was serving on the board as well replied to this effect: "She cannot be the principal because she is young, she is not married, and she has no children." Suffice it to say that I was flabbergasted. I had not realized that marriage and children formed the basis for credibility as a leader. Only in doing this study did I realize that this issue of denying women positions or the authority due to their positions based on marital status and being biological mothers is actually quite widespread in Kenya—the stories of Esther Mombo and Muthoni Wanyeki in this book affirm that.

A second critical incident occurred at NEGST that helped define my purpose in life as a scholar and as a woman in leadership. During the Biblical Ethics course, one of the men in the class claimed that women should not be in master's degree programs. Instead, the women should be in the certificate "women's program," which was aimed at preparing women to support their husbands in pastoral ministry. This man, a pastor and leader from the Democratic Republic of the Congo, then went on to say that women have smaller brains and therefore less capacity for making ethical decisions!

The third incident at NEGST was more of an eye-opener. I found out that some of the women who had come to the college with their husbands were physically abused right there on campus. The stories that they told of their experiences broke my heart. I could not imagine a pastor and a church leader beating his wife, let alone all of the other abuses that these women faced. That realization made me decide that rather than preach for my homiletics practicum, I would challenge the institution members to rethink their ways by reading and performing a long poem. The poem consisted of five portraits of women who had survived in spite of major challenges—domestic abuse, forced early marriage, widowhood, divorce, and sexist discrimination in organizational contexts. Whereas those poetic portraits were based on my creative imagination, this book demonstrates the reality of the intersecting forces that women face and that are a part of the raison d'être for the women leaders profiled. Even the extreme poem I had created about a Maasai woman forced to marry at age 12, only to be widowed at age 30 and left with children to raise and educate, turned out to be closer to reality than I had ever imagined! Ms. Nangurai's work as chronicled here aims at helping such women and girls access education in order to better their lives and that of the community.

The defining incidents mentioned here led to my decision to enroll in the doctoral program in leadership studies at Bowling Green State University to prepare for life as a woman leader and a professor.

Under the direction of Dr. Judy Alston, I conducted the research that forms the basis for this book in the summer of 2005, intent on demonstrating that even though African women faced a lot of hardships, they were actively engaged in their own emancipation. The portraits illustrate the power of faith and deep spirituality in the lives of women social justice leaders. The portraits further illustrate the choices these women make, regarding their approach to leadership as tempered radicals and critical servant leaders, intent on transforming their communities, organizations, and nations. I wrote this book because I am invested in providing authentic representations of African women to both African audiences and the Western academic audiences of which I am now a part. The conviction that only half the story about African women is told—the half that is deficient, pathological, negative, sad, and sometimes a misrepresentation of the context and the people—led me to engage in this research project to provide a counter-story.

Outline of the Book

Chapter 1 is an introduction to the text, describing the status of women in leadership in Africa with Kenya as an example and offering short introductions to the women participants to show how they fit into the educational, religious, civil society and government arenas as leaders working toward social and economic justice. The chapter also details the rationale for the study, conceptual framework, and design of the study.

Chapter 2 provides a theoretical framework for leadership scholars to place the book within the literature in the field of leadership theory and practice.

Chapter 3 begins with a contextual framework in terms of the geographical, social, political, and economic setting of Kenya, East Africa. Even though some of the women lead Pan-African and global organizations, their most pertinent issues regarding their life history and leadership experiences have to do with the cultural and social setting of Kenya, where they were born, raised, and educated and where they experienced their most significant and meaning-making events as women in leadership.

Chapter 4 contains succinct portraits of nine women leaders plus the liaison who helped in gaining access—it would have required too much space to provide exhaustive portraits of all 16 participants. The nine-plus-one snapshots cover a succinct life story of each woman and her leadership context.

I selected seven participants to provide in-depth portraits based on diversity of experiences, ethnicities, level of leadership (local, national, Pan-African, and global), age, and marital status (single, divorced, widowed and married). I also selected the seven because they provided the most comprehensive stories based on the fact that I spent more time with them than with the other nine-plus-one women. As will become evident in the theme chapters, these seven women are the most often quoted in illustrating the themes. These seven portraits best communicate to the reader what it means to be a woman and a leader in the African context. Chapters 5–11 include seven in-depth portraits; each woman selected for this level of analysis received her own chapter. The purpose of the in-depth portraits is to provide the reader with a profound and multilayered view of women's experiences and expressions of leadership in Africa. Additionally, each of the portraits adds on to the bigger story of what it means to be a woman in leadership—how women's various social identities interact with their experiences and expressions of leadership.

Chapters 12–14 include discussions of the elements of the conceptual framework, using extant quotes to illustrate the themes that emerged in support and/or expansion of spirituality, servant leadership, and tempered radicalism.

Chapter 15 reviews the thematic chapters and reconstructs the conceptual framework based on the themes from the previous chapters. The final section of chapter 15 discusses some of my personal lessons in doing this study and provides implications for practice and future study.

Acknowledgments

I am forever grateful to the many people who have contributed to my development as a scholar, and to the process of writing this book. Many remain un-named, but for all of them I am forever grateful.

To my mentor Dr. Judy Alston (Ashland University): Thank-you is too mild a phrase to fully explain what I feel. You have been the best mentor a graduate student and junior faculty member could ever wish for. Thank-you for directing me toward becoming a professor!

To Dr. Cynthia Tyson (Ohio State University), Dr. Khaula Murtadha (Indiana University-Purdue University, Indianapolis), Dr. Lara Martin Lengel (Bowling Green State University), and Dr. Mark Earley (Bowling Green State University), my dissertation committee, and continuing mentors: You enriched my educational experience—thank- you. When my students appreciate my engagement with them, I thank God for you because I learned how to be a spirit-led facilitator of learning through my interactions with you. I continue to grow as a professor through the guidance of Dr. Alston and Dr. Lengel—may God bless you both.

To Dr. Wairimu Mutai (Loyola College, Maryland), Dr. Anne Christo-Baker (Purdue University, North Central Indiana), Dr. Patrice McClellan (Lourdes College, Ohio), and Dr. Lillian Schumacher (Indiana Tech, Fort Wayne): I thank you for being my sisters in graduate school and my colleagues in the academy. I also thank you for the many times I have asked you to read and review my writing.

To Dr. David W. Miller: Thank-you for the one year at Yale Center for Faith and Culture.

To my brother, John Murigu: Thank-you for your willingness to invest in me, and for giving me Wangari, Wambura, and Ngunjiri to dote upon! I pray that your daughters will grow up to be courageous and committed leaders, and that your son will be a feminist like his aunt! To my entire Mukira family: Thank-you for being the greatest family one could wish for. To my mom, Wangari Ngunjiri, and my aunts, Waruguru Mukira and Rev. Joyce Kariuki: You are the best! To my 34 cousins and counting: I hope I offer a worthy example! And to Grandpa Moses Mukira and my brother Moses Mukira, both deceased: Your memory lingers on.

To my new friends at Eastern University: I am glad to be in an environment where people practice what they preach. Thank-you to Jo Ann Flett, Dr. Sharon Gramby-Sobukwe, Dr. Kathy Ann Hernandez, and Dr. Heewon Chang for being worthy colleagues and critical collaborators.

To the men who create drama in my life: Thank-you for keeping me entertained!

To the 16 women who graciously gave of their time and wisdom: Thank-you for sharing your life with me. And to Aunt Wanjiru (Rev. Joyce): Thanks for supporting me and introducing me to these wise women.

Ultimately, to God be the glory

1

Contextual and
Conceptual Framework

The statement *ex Africa simper aliquid novi*, attributed to Pliny the Elder, is translated as *out of Africa, always something new*. Apparently the saying was often used derisively, because there was little known about the Dark Continent. Through this book, however, out of Africa becomes something new, something worth celebrating. Rather than stories of war and rumors of war, hunger and disease, and corruption and mismanagement of government coffers, herein are stories of women who are working hard at their own emancipation from these and other man-made evils. These are women who lead with courage and conviction, spirit and strength, serving their communities and changing the status quo for the sake of social and economic justice. There is enough bad news coming out of Africa on a frequent basis to make the rest of the world think that nothing good comes out of the Continent. In contradistinction, this book illustrates that there are beacons of light and hope in the women of Africa, beacons of change for a better world. The *Endarkened* Continent can no longer be dismissed as a place of ignorance and disease; these stories demonstrate that there is something the rest of the world can learn from their black African sisters. From these leadership stories, we learn that our African sisters are resourceful problem solvers who collectivize to resolve their common problems, who are not silent in the face of severe challenges but instead are spirited social justice leaders who serve with a servant's heart and a tempered radicalism necessary to achieve their goals for healing community and restoring justice to the marginalized.

Five Steps Forward, Three Steps Back

Africa's women have made tremendous progress in politics, economics, and educational attainments in the last half century. Prior to independence, Africa's women actively participated in freeing their nations from colonial domination as freedom fighters engaged in armed warfare, or by offering spiritual and material support to their freedom fighters, or by keeping the home fires burning while their men fought. In this section, I introduce the status of women in various arenas and how the participants in this study fit as leaders in those areas. As Muthoni Likimani, a prolific writer, indicated, even though the historical canon in many African countries may be silent on women's agency in the anti-colonial struggle, this does not diminish their [women's] contribution to freedom and nation building.

Muthoni Wanyeki, a human rights, women's rights, and development expert, indicated that women's active engagement continued after independence. Women organized themselves into national women's organizations that were instrumental in bringing about rural development in many regions across Africa between 1960 and 1980. Furthermore, Wanyeki noted that in the last 30 years, Africa's women have been at the forefront of the fight for democracy in their nations and for closer unity among African countries through Pan-African organizations such as FEMNET (African Women Communication and Development Network, which she directed for 7 years). Such Pan-African organizations helped articulate the needs of women in the nationalist development agendas. In their native countries, Africa's women organized into civil society organizations through which they agitated for democracy, good governance, and human and women's rights, resulting in more women participating in elected political positions in the new century. Many of the women who now serve as elected members of parliament in many African countries started their activism and engagement through the civil commons.

As of October 2008, when the Inter-Parliamentary Union last updated its records, one African country is leading the world in women's participation in parliament. Rwanda leads the world; 58.3% of Parliamentarians are women—the average for Africa is only 17.9%. The table that follows contains other leading African countries' ranking as of October 2008.

My own native Kenya lags behind at 106th, with only a 9.8% representation of women in the current (as of March 2008) parliament. The stories of Honorable Beth Mugo and Honorable Charity Ngilu, who are members of the cabinet in Kenya, are only the tip of the iceberg when it comes to women's struggles to serve their communities in parliament. Wahu Kaara has tried and failed to get into parliament the last three general elections. Part of the struggle for women in Kenya is that they do not have the financial wherewithal to play the political

Table 1. Representation of Women in Parliaments in Africa, Global Rankings

Country	Global ranking	Percentage of women in parliament
Rwanda	1	56.3%
Angola	13	34.8%
South Africa	17	33%
Uganda	21	30.7%
Burundi	22	30.5%
Tanzania	23	30.4%
Namibia	30	26.9%

Data from Inter-Parliamentary Union website at http://www.ipu.org/wmn-e/classif.htm

games that their male counterparts play, such as giving handouts to voters to "buy" their votes. Furthermore, women wanting to lead in the political arena find themselves facing the threat of physical harm and harassment from male voters who are not ready to be led by women, or hooligans hired by male candidates to intimidate them (*A journey of courage: Kenyan women's experience of the 2002 General Elections*, 2004). As such, political leadership at the national level remains an unequal playing ground in Kenya, as in many other African countries other than those presented in the table that have between 25% and 56% representation. One of Africa's celebrated heroines is Ellen Johnson-Sirleaf, the first African woman to be elected to the presidency, who serves as a source of inspiration to other women as they aspire to parliamentary positions as well as the presidency. Rwanda and Uganda have both had women serving as vice presidents; the hope is that as Johnson-Sirleaf has shattered that political glass ceiling and proven that *the hand that stirs the pot can also run the country*, African nations will move toward a more equitable distribution of political power.

Perhaps the area where women are most likely to be found in leadership positions in many African countries is within the nongovernmental organizations (NGOs) and the Civil Society Organization (CSO). Most of the participants in this study serve or have served in leadership positions in an NGO or a CSO. In the area of human and women's rights, women have been active in advocacy work. Judy Thongori, a lawyer, served as executive director for the Federation of

Women Lawyers (FIDA), Kenya chapter, for 5 years, and during this time she was instrumental in putting into place structures to advocate for economically marginalized women, particularly on issues of property rights. Muthoni Wanyeki served for 7 years as the executive director of FEMNET before she moved to a similar position at the Kenya Human Rights Commission (KNHRC), an NGO concerned with human rights abuses. The KNHRC was instrumental in exposing police brutality and politicians' collusion with hooligans in the chaos that rocked Kenya after the December 2007 general elections. These women are just two of the many women who are involved in advocating for justice in a country where a culture of impunity has reigned supreme for several decades now, so that those in positions of power get away with corruption, abuse of power, and denying those without power their rights.

In matters of economic justice, women in Africa agitate and act toward changing the status quo at the local, national, continental, and global levels. For example, Eunice Ole Marima is involved in helping women in Maasai land to gain some level of economic independence through self-help projects at the grassroots level. At the national level, Jeniffer Riria leads Kenya Women's Finance Trust, a women's credit and loan institution that provides low-income women entrepreneurs with loans and business training—credit facilities that have for a long time been out of their reach in commercial banks (Ngunjiri, 2007a). At the global level, Wahu Kaara is active in the Global Campaign against Poverty (GCAP), the World Social Forum, and debt relief campaigns. As these three women's stories demonstrate, African women are not sitting back in silence; rather, they are actively engaged in their own, their communities, and their nation's economic emancipation.

In the educational arena, women can be found at various levels of leadership, with the highest concentration being at the primary school headmistress level. For example, in Kenya, one study found that 44% of primary school heads in two districts were women (Ombati, 2003). At the university level, though, women are not as well represented, both as tenured faculty and in administrative roles, as demonstrated by studies from Kenya (Kamau, 2004) and South Africa (Chisholm 2001, Mabokela 2003a, b). In Kenya, there is only one woman serving as a vice chancellor (equivalent to a college president) in a public university, out of a total of 12. Among private universities, 3 out of 21 women are serving as vice chancellors. Only one woman serves as the top leader of a religious university in Kenya, even though these institutions form the bulk of the private universities in the country (13 out of the 21 private universities have religious affiliations as theological institutions or church-sponsored universities). In this climate, the stories of Esther

Mombo (academic dean, St. Paul's University) and Faith Nguru (director of research and consultancy, Daystar University) illustrate some of the challenges that women face in religious academic institutions.

In other religious institutions, women do not fare well in rising to the top—in fact, there is still no female bishop in the Anglican Church of Kenya, and no women at the top levels of the Presbyterian Church of East Africa, the Africa Inland Church, and the Methodist Church of Kenya, the four largest Protestant denominations. As such, Esther Mombo's work as a laywoman who has actively advocated for the ordination of women in the Anglican Church in Kenya, and through her involvement in the worldwide Anglican Communion, is illustrative of one woman's untiring agency. Agnes Abuom (vice president, World Religions for Peace) has demonstrated that sometimes women who may not necessarily fare so well in the ecclesial ranks in their own country might still be able to break the celestial ceiling on a global arena. Abuom served as president for the World Council of Churches for Africa for 2 years, the first time an African woman played that role. Both Abuom and Mombo are well regarded on the global ecumenical and Anglican scenes as leaders who are instrumental in bringing about positive changes to these religious institutions. Their stories illustrate some of the ways that women break the celestial ceiling to serve in religious institutions that have global reach.

In local congregations, women often find it difficult to become ordained and to serve as pastors. Sometimes it takes them instituting independent congregations to be able to serve as they feel called. However, Reverend Judy Mbugua (coordinator, Pan-African Christian Women's Association) has served as a trailblazer, one of the premier women to become ordained. Due to her courageous action, the celestial ceiling has cracked minimally, although some traditional denominations now ordain women. However, women clergy find that they are limited to small, rural, or poor congregations and to lower-level positions—the playing ground is still far from equal. That has been part of the story of Reverend Joyce Kariuki, who finds that ordination does not automatically lead to acceptance, nor does credibility transfer from context to context. While serving as the general secretary of the Council of Anglican Provinces in Africa (CAPA), which includes all of the archbishops from the Continent, she found that sometimes she was not allowed into meetings to take minutes because she was a woman! The CAPA headquarters are in Nairobi, where she also serves as vicar of a local congregation. The stories from these women leaders are examples of how biblical patriarchy, Christian patriarchy, and African patriarchy combine to form a potent barrier to women's participation in ecclesial leadership. The stories of Reverend Joyce and Reverend Mbugua serve as illustrations of women's struggles and successes in local congregations and Pan-African religious institutions.

One of the Millennium Development Goals is to have equality of access to primary education by 2015. There has been tremendous success in this area in sub-Saharan Africa, where for the longest time tuition fees formed a formidable barrier to girls' access to primary school education. Various sub-Saharan African countries have abolished primary school tuition fees as a means to decrease the gap between boys' and girls' access to education, including Kenya, Liberia, Ghana, Burundi, Tanzania, Malawi, and Democratic Republic of the Congo. However, in spite of such policy advances, enrollments have risen but have not been sustained to lead to equality in graduation rates from primary schools. In addition, whereas school fees formed a formidable barrier, other issues are at play in girls' access to education. Among the Maasai and other pastoralist communities in Kenya, one barrier has to do with the fact that these communities do not value education at the same level as others in the country do. Living a pastoral existence that is dependent on livestock sometimes means that such communities do not perceive literacy and education as necessary for their children, particularly girls. Forced early marriages and female circumcision (which apparently prepares girls for marriage) are two of the biggest barriers to Maasai girls' retention in primary schools. Euniçe Ole Marima and Agnes Nangurai are two educated Maasai women who have been actively engaged in providing Maasai girls with a safe space in which to complete their primary education and to also ensure that such girls are able to proceed to secondary schools and colleges by finding them bursaries to pay for their education. The two women's stories illustrate the challenges faced and the responses to those challenges by Maasai women in resolving their communities' low literacy rates and economic hardships. At the national level, Shiphrah Gichaga served as the national coordinator for the Forum for African Women Educationists (FAWE), Kenya chapter, which works with the Ministry of Education and the government in ensuring that girls from marginalized communities have access to education.

Defining Leadership

Leadership scholars acknowledge that there are as many definitions of leadership as there are leadership scholars and theorists. As Yukl (2006) argues, leadership is a term "taken from common vocabulary and incorporated into technical vocabulary of a scientific discipline without being precisely redefined" (p. 2). Kouzes and Posner regard leadership as mobilizing people to get extraordinary things done, the most effective leaders according to their research being those who lead by example, inspire a shared vision, challenge the process, enable others to act, and encourage the heart of their constituents (Kouzes and Posner, 2003). In order to be successful, Kouzes and Posner add that leaders have to be credible to their constituents. According to Burns (1978), leadership is "a structure of action that engages persons, to varying degrees, throughout the levels and among the interstices of society. Only the inert, the alienated, and the powerless are unengaged" (p. 2). Further, Burns argues that leadership is distinct from power holding and advocates for transforming leadership where the "transforming leader recognizes and exploits an existing need or demand of a potential follower . . . looks for potential motives in followers, seeks to satisfy higher needs, and engages the full person of the follower. The result is a relationship of mutual stimulation and elevation that converts followers into leaders and may convert leaders into moral agents" (p. 3).

In order to direct my interrogation of leadership among African women, I have defined leadership as a process involving intentional influence upon people to guide and facilitate their activities and relationships in a group or an organization (Yukl, 2001). Leadership is also a process of meaning making among people to engender commitment to common goals, expressed in a community of practice (Drath & Palus, 1994). Furthermore, I think of leadership as more than a position (Burns, 1978); rather, it is the ability of one person to respond to a call to her or his life that necessitates action toward achieving social justice ideals, my area of interest. In seeking participants for the study, I asked several women in the community to recommend those they felt were leaders for social justice, thus the 16 participants in the study. Community nomination assured that the women selected were considered credible in their own communities of practice.

Conceptual Framework

Guiding this study was the following question: What does it mean to be a woman leader in an African context? That is, I was interested in finding out how women make meaning of their experiences as leaders, including how they are able to thrive and be effective in spite of challenges to their authority. The a priori conceptual framework consisted of three elements: Africana spirituality, tempered radicalism, and servant leadership. This was derived from an extensive literature review of leadership studies of Black women in United States and informed by the limited studies of Africa women leaders in the Continent. As with their counterparts in the United States, the participants were likely to be guided by a spiritual focus that would help them as they attempted to lead as active change agents and servant leaders.

The study of women's leadership has contributed to the understanding of leadership in general from various perspectives. Of significance to the study of women in leadership is the recognition that women may or may not lead differently than men, depending on the context in which they lead. Parker and ogilvie (1996) observed that for African American women executives, surviving and thriving within the context of racism and sexism demanded an androgynous leadership style. My conceptual framework will incorporate ideas from the research of Dr. Judy Alston (2000, 2005) and Dr. Khaula Murtadha (1999), both of whom have extensive experience in studying African American female educational administrators. Dr. Sharyn Jones's (2003) dissertation research on African American women educational administrators, especially pertaining to spirituality and tempered radicals, was also useful in formulating this frame.

My conceptual frame is also informed by Black feminist and Africana womanist scholars who posited an epistemology informed by the experiences of Black women in Africa and the Diaspora (Collins, 1996, 1998, 2000; Hudson-Weems, 1997; Ntiri, 2001). According to Collins, Hudson-Weems, and Ntiri, Black feminist and Africana womanist theorizing advocates the use of Black women's experiences in theory building as a valid and constructive scholarly endeavor in the pursuit of an understanding of Black and African women. This framework is developed with the understanding that a study of African women's leadership must be informed by distinctive interpretations of African women's oppression under racism, sexism, colonialism, neocolonialism, and patriarchal culture, as well as African women's use of alternative means of producing and validating knowledge (Alston, 2000; Amadiume, 1997; Bakare-Yusuf, 2003; Collins, 1996; Murtadha-Watts, 1999; Oyewumi, 2002).

The conceptual framework consists of three interrelated components understood within the scaffold of women's experience, which are useful in understanding the leadership experiences of African women: Africana spirituality, tempered radicalism, and servant leadership.

Africana Spirituality

In his seminal work, Paris (1995) described an Africana spirituality that is shared by all people of African ascent:

Africans brought their worldviews with them into the Diaspora, and as a result of their interaction with their new
environments, their African worldviews were gradually altered
into a new-African consciousness . . . *religion permeates every
dimension of African life.* [emphasis added]. In spite of the
many and varied religious systems the ubiquity of religious
consciousness among African peoples constitutes their single
most important common characteristic. (pp. 24, 27)

African peoples all over the globe share a spirituality (not a religion)
that has been recognized as distinctively African in its explanations of
phenomena and its understanding of God as the definitive source and
sustainer of life (Paris, 1995; Shorter, 1974). This spiritual worldview has
been found to undergird the leadership experiences and practices of
African American women (Jones, 2003; Murtadha-Watts, 1999; Reid-Merritt, 1996). Researchers find that a profound spirituality imbued African
American women's leadership experiences and consistently served as
a source of resiliency amidst structural sexism and racism. Murtadha-
Watts (1999) referred to the participants in her study as spirited sisters,
Black women leaders for whom spirituality was a constant source of
inner strength, divine direction, and courage under fire.

Tempered Radicals

The notion of tempered radicals arose out of the research of Debra
Meyerson and Maureen Scully (1995), who conducted interviews and
observations of leaders in different occupations to understand how
those who did not fit the majority mold exercised leadership. According
to Meyerson (2001), tempered radicals are men and women who find
themselves as poor fits with the dominant culture of their organizations: "Tempered radicals want to fit in and they want to retain what
makes them different. They want to rock the boat, and they want to
stay in it" (p. 4). These are people who are intent on leading change
but who also understand that they must tread with care in order not
to endanger their organizational credibility. According to Meyerson,
tempered radicals include women who refuse to act like men in a
male-dominated institution and people of color who want to expand
their boundaries of inclusion in predominantly White institutions. In a
pilot study, I found that the idea of a tempered radical resonated with
my participants as women leading in predominantly male institutions
within a predominantly patriarchal culture. Jones's (2003) study with
African American women educational administrators found that these

women "had strong beliefs about what a leader ought to be, yet their values were often at odds with societal beliefs about what is thought of as leadership" (p. 189). That is, Jones's participants were exhibiting tempered radicalism in order to stimulate change, even while remaining within the organizations they wanted to change. Tempered radicals work from within the system in order to positively change it (Meyerson, 2001). As leaders in organizations where others consider them deviant and different, such women exhibit and utilize certain strategies to survive, thrive, and bring about change. As Meyerson observed:

> Tempered radicals reflect important aspects of leadership that are absent in the more traditional portraits. It is leadership that tends to be less visible, less coordinated, and less vested with formal authority; it is also more local, more diffuse, more opportunistic, and more humble than the activity attributed to the modern-day here. This version of leadership depends not on charismatic flair, instant success, or inspirational visions, but on qualities such as patience, self-knowledge, humility, flexibility, idealism, vigilance and commitment. And, although tempered radicals often act as individual agents of change, they are not lone heroes . . . they are quick to acknowledge they cannot do it alone. (p. 171)

Researchers have found that of necessity, Black women leaders, particularly those invested in social justice agendas, tend to be tempered radicals who attempt to act as change agents from within the structures that are otherwise inhospitable to them as women and as racial minorities (Alston, 2000, 2005; Jones, 2003; Meyerson, 2001)

Servant Leadership

The notion of servant leadership is countercultural as far as traditional leadership is concerned (Greenleaf, 1977); that is, it runs counter to the notions of "powerful, dynamic individuals who command victorious armies, direct corporate empires from atop gleaming skyscrapers, or shape the course of nations" (Yukl 2006, p. 1). Greenleaf posited the idea of servant leaders as leaders who would serve with skill, understanding, and spirit. For Greenleaf, greatness in leadership arose out of being a servant first. Greenleaf considered servant leadership as less coercive and more collaborative than the prevailing notions of traditional leadership. A servant leader does not withdraw from engagement with the system but rather critically engages the system in search of social justice. That is, servant leaders do not merely criticize corruption, injustice, and other structural malaise; rather, they ponder what they can do about it and engage in action and advocacy. As Greenleaf observed, "Criticism has its place, but as a total preoccupation it is sterile" (p. 11). Instead, servant leaders creatively engage with an imperfect world. For Greenleaf, "The servant leader is servant first. . . . It begins with the natural feeling that one wants to serve, to serve first. Then conscious choice brings one to aspire to lead" (p. 13). Scholars in the area of Black women's leadership have found that these leaders exhibited servant leader characteristics, such as deep spirituality, a keen sense of vision and direction, a strong sense of efficacy, a dedication to community building, collaborative leadership styles, and a commitment to their mission or calling (Alston, 2005; Beauboeuf-Lafontant, 2002; Jones, 2003).

Whereas Greenleaf popularized the notion of servant leadership resulting in its being utilized in diverse business and educational institutions, the idea of servant leadership is older than his writing of the Servant as Leader essay (1970/1991). Indeed, servant leadership as understood by Christians derives from Jesus' example to his disciples by washing their feet (John 13:1–13) and exhorting them to not "Lord it over" those they lead, as was the norm in their particular sociocultural context (Luke 22). Greenleaf popularized the notion and dissociated it from its religious underpinnings, although there are still those who are uncomfortable with servant leadership because they feel it has religious connotations. The women participating in this study had no such qualms, except for one who was uncomfortable with any language that reeks of religion.

Alston (2005) created a conceptual framework appropriate in research on Black women's leadership consisting of tempered radicals and servant leaders. Murtadha-Watts (1999) study of Black women's leadership used the lens of spirituality to understand their experiences and tenacity in the face of racist and sexist discrimination. Both scholars used women's experience as a valid tool toward theory creation and understanding of phenomena as explored by Black feminist and Africana womanist theorizing (Collins, 1996, 1998; Hudson-Weems, 1997). I combined and adapted the three sets of ideas for the conceptual framework for the present study, as shown in Figure 1.1 (see next page). The portraits and theme chapters will illustrate how spirituality forms the foundation upon which life and leadership are experienced, understood, and critiqued for the study participants. It is the basis for the women's choice or calling to become leaders, choosing their battles

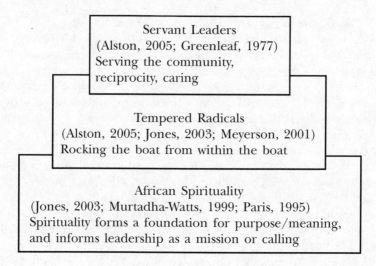

Servant Leaders
(Alston, 2005; Greenleaf, 1977)
Serving the community,
reciprocity, caring

Tempered Radicals
(Alston, 2005; Jones, 2003; Meyerson, 2001)
Rocking the boat from within the boat

African Spirituality
(Jones, 2003; Murtadha-Watts, 1999; Paris, 1995)
Spirituality forms a foundation for purpose/meaning,
and informs leadership as a mission or calling

Figure 1. Conceptual Framework

as tempered radicals, and serving the common good of the race or
the community through a search for social justice.

Studying Women Leaders in Africa

In order to provide the reader with both narratives about the women
leaders and lessons learned or emerging themes that illustrate elements of the conceptual framework, I employed portraiture as the
biographical approach. I aimed at celebrating and learning from the
resiliency and strength of the women leaders in the face of adversities
and challenges to their authority as leaders rather than concentrating
on the deficit or *pathologizing* their experiences. Portraiture as defined
by Lawrence-Lightfoot and Davis (1997) blends several qualitative
approaches, concentrating on a search for goodness that aided me in
producing authentic portraits of the women leaders. Portraiture lays
great emphasis on context (from ethnography), concentrates on the
individual (from biography/life history), attempts to comprehend the
phenomenon as it is experienced by those individuals (phenomenology),
and whereas it encourages a priori conceptual framework, portraiture
leaves it open to change/reinterpretation by the data.

Participant Selection and Research Procedures

To qualify for the study, each participant had to be at least 40 years of age and been in leadership for a minimum of 10 years so that each would have a story to tell. Additionally, each participant's leadership had to be for social justice purposes and had to be perceived as such by the community—this was important because I was interested in social justice leadership that attempts to respond to the many challenges and struggles inherent to the African context. I also ensured that the group was diverse in terms of ethnicity—the women were from Gikuyu, Kamba, Nandi, Gikuyu/Canadian mix, Meru, Maasai, and Dinka (Southern Sudanese). All of the participants were selected through a process of recommendations—the liaison, the oldest participant, and several of the participants let me know who the credible social justice-oriented leaders were. The 16 participants are not part of an exhaustive list of all women who lead for social justice, but they are the ones who were available and willing to speak with me during the 3 months I spent collecting data in the summer of 2005.

The primary data sources were the in-depth, face-to-face conversations I had with the participants, ranging from 1 ½ to 4 hours each. These conversations took place between June 1 and September 4, 2005, in Nairobi and Kajiado. I had interview prompts set around three themes: women's lives prior to becoming leaders (life history), women's lives as leaders, and women's visions for the future. A concluding focus group helped further clarify emerging themes as I had the women discuss topics that I selected based on data from individual interviews. The material was updated in January 2009 to indicate the leadership roles the women play.

In the chapters on themes, it became increasingly clear that the three main components of the conceptual framework intersect in practice. As such, even though I separated them in the discussions, in reality the women are both tempered radicals and servant leaders, and their spirituality impacts and is impacted by both. This is an important redefinition of the relationship among the three elements of the conceptual framework. As such, the three—spirituality, servant leadership, and tempered radicalism—are distinguishable, but in the experiences of these African women leaders, they are inseparable elements that create a gestalt that I refer to as spirited leadership: courageous, committed, conviction-filled, and spirit-inspired leadership.

This book focuses on elite women, that is, women who by their economic status and educational attainments are set apart from the majority. All of the women in this study are educated, ranging from associate to doctorate degrees, placing them within the middle class or higher in social status. This in no way disregards the fact that women have been leading historically and in contemporary society in their families, in rural communities, in urban slums, and in other arenas. As Carli and Eagly (2001) warned, "Focusing on women who occupy such leadership positions should not cause us to forget that women have always exercised leadership, particularly in families and throughout communities" (p. 629).

2
_____

Theoretical Framework

The purpose of this study was to discover, describe, and understand women's leadership in Africa, with illustrative portraits of Kenyan women serving in leadership positions at the grassroots, national, Pan-African, and global arenas. This chapter is a review of the relevant literature beginning at the level of leadership theories and narrowing down to women leading in Africa.

Leadership Theories

The term *leader* often connotes imagery of powerful individuals commanding armies, powerful corporate chief executive officers, noteworthy (or notorious) national leaders, and inspiring individuals such as Mahatma Gandhi, Martin Luther King Jr., and Mother Teresa. Leadership has been a subject of interest across history, even though research on the phenomenon did not begin until the 20th century (Yukl, 2001). Much of the research has focused on determining factors leading to effective leadership, such as traits, abilities, behaviors, sources of power, and/or aspects of a situation and how well a leader is able to influence followers in accomplishing a goal (Hersey, Blanchard, & Johnson, 2001; Koestenbaum, 2002; Kouzes & Posner, 2002; Rosenbach & Taylor, 2001; Yaverbaum, 2004; Yukl, 2001).

Different leadership theorists define leadership according to their individual perspectives and the aspects of the phenomenon of interest to them (Yukl, 2001). Bass (1990) conceptualized leadership as (Kanogo, 2005) the focus of group processes, as a matter of personality, as a matter of inducing compliance, as the exercise of influence, as particular behaviors, as a form of persuasion, as a power relation, as an instrument to achieve goals, as initiation of structure, and as many combinations of these definitions. (p. 7)

These categories encompass traits, behaviors, and situational, transactional, and transformational approaches to the study of leadership effectiveness. However, as Jones (2003) argued, leadership has historically been defined "from a monolithic viewpoint of androcentrically developed models where race and gender have been excluded from theories altogether" (p. 20). All of the seminal studies conducted on leadership used White males as subjects, so effective leaders were assumed to be confident, task oriented, competitive, objective, decisive, and assertive (Heilman, 2001; Hersey, Blanchard, & Johnson, 2001; Wilson, 2004; Yoder, 2001; Yukl, 2001). This necessitated the inclusion of women and people of color in the debates and the theorizing of leadership in the last three decades, with much of the research in the area being done in the 1990s (Adler, 1999; Astin & Leland, 1991; Lipman-Blumen, 1992).

Women in Leadership

Studies on women in leadership have shown that women continue to be underrepresented in leadership positions in government, education, industry, and most other sectors of the economy globally (Adler, 1999; Alston, 2000; Cubillo & Brown, 2003; Eagly & Johannesen-Schmidt, 2001; Giesler, 2000; Heilman, 2001; Weiss, 1999; Wilson, 2004). In this section, I will explore the various theories that have been developed to explain the scarcity of women in leadership positions.

Implicit Theories

In traditional leadership theory, masculine attributes and leadership effectiveness often go hand in hand. Implicit theories that engender leadership as male may have been responsible for years of sex-based discrimination resulting in few women ascending to positions of leadership, a situation often referred to as the "glass ceiling" (Weiss, 1999). However, studies conducted over the last two decades have shown that traits such as interpersonal skills, concern for building cooperation, trust, and use of feminine behaviors such as support, empowering, and caring, even though always relevant for leadership effectiveness, are now gaining currency due to the changing terrain of organizations (Yukl, 2001). Nevertheless, as Yukl and others observed, the belief that men are more qualified for leadership is still normative. Yoder (2001), in her discussion on making leadership more effective for women, argued that leadership is gendered, and it is enacted within a gendered context. Leadership is gendered, so that competence is associated with masculinity, rationality, and whiteness (Chisholm, 2001; Parker & ogilvie, 1996; Yoder, 2001).

Stereotypes and Role Expectations

In the last decade, scholars who were interested in studying women leaders may have been able to find more such leaders in education, government, not-for-profit organizations, and industry. However, as Carli and Eagly (2001) warned, "Focusing on women who occupy such leadership positions should not cause us to forget that women have always exercised leadership, particularly in families and throughout communities" (p. 629). However, women in public positions of leadership have historically been rare. Carli and Eagly noted that, historically, only 42 women had served as presidents of countries or prime ministers, 25 of whom came to office in the 1990s, and almost all of the women in top corporate positions came into those positions in the 1990s. Since their study was published, 13 women have been added to that number, the most recent being the president of Argentina, Cristina FernÃ¡ndez de Kirchner, elected in October 2007, and, before her, Ellen Johnson-Sirleaf, the first African woman to be elected president, who has served in Liberia since January 2006.

    In studies about sex-role stereotypes, researchers found that although women could benefit from positive stereotypes, such as being expected to be more considerate, negative stereotypes would override such benefits by considering them too submissive and emotionally unstable, on the one hand, or iron-maiden, aggressive, and domineering workaholics, on the other (Bass, 1990; Heilman, 2001). Gender stereotypes also affected how women and men were evaluated as leaders. If women exhibited masculine characteristics, such as being "agentic" (Bandura 2001, p. 2), then they were negatively evaluated for violating gender prescriptions (Eagly & Johannesen-Schmidt, 2001; Heilman, 2001). One of the questions that arose from studies of women leaders is whether gender differences exist in the way that men and women lead.

Gender Differences in Leadership

The research on gender differences in leadership compared men and women in various leadership positions. Some compared them in laboratory settings, whereas others studied their leadership behaviors within organizational settings. However, disagreements abound about how to interpret the results of such studies (Eagly & Johannesen-Schmidt, 2001; Yukl, 2001). Bass and Eagly and Johannesen-Schmidt, in their meta-analyses of male-female differences in leadership styles, discussed this disparity in interpretation, noting that even though some field studies showed no discernible differences, others conducted in laboratory conditions showed some differences. Some researchers had found that women are less coercive, less authoritarian, and less able to deal with interpersonal conflicts, and more helpful, affectionate, open minded, and accepting of blame than men (Lipman-Blumen, 1992; Pounder & Coleman, 2002; Ridgeway, 2001; Rigg & Sparrow, 1994). In most studies showing differences, women were reported as being more consideration oriented, whereas men were more task oriented (Bass, 1990). However, Bass argued that even though differences may be expected in the path to leadership, once men and women were in those positions, those differences tended to blur, suggesting that both use the same masculine styles. This seems to have been a general conclusion from many of the earlier studies, suggesting that for women to be successful, they had to *lead like men*. Bass recognized that because of the changing landscape for women and leadership roles, earlier research might need to be discounted. The possibility seems to be that differences between women and men are sometimes present, appearing and disappearing with shifting social contexts (Eagly & Johannesen-Schmidt, 2001; Pounder & Coleman, 2002). However, there was a need to study how women actually lead when they are in those administrative and executive positions.

WOMEN'S WAYS OF LEADING

Perhaps in response to the earlier conclusion that women had to acquire masculine tendencies in order to be successful as leaders, other researchers have explored women's ways of leading, with the understanding that women can succeed as leaders by being themselves and utilizing their natural inclinations (Lipman-Blumen, 1992). Studies have also shown that even though women are in the workplace in large numbers, comprising almost 50% of the working population, they are found in only a few occupations and lower-paid ranks that are unlikely to lead to managerial promotions (Bass, 1990). Women predominate in the teaching profession, but educational administrative positions remain the preserve of men in countries as diverse as the United Kingdom (Cubillo & Brown, 2003; Pounder & Coleman, 2002), Hong Kong (Shum & Cheng, 1997), the United States (Young & Mcleod, 2001),

South Africa (Chisholm, 2001; Mabokela, 2003b), and Kenya (Ombati, 2003). It seems correct to conclude that women are to be found in some leadership positions, albeit in limited numbers, but that they face many constraints to their ascent into any leadership positions.

Other Explanations

Other researchers have looked at these constraints to women's ascent into positions of leadership, ranging from the aforementioned gender stereotypes, lack of mentors, inability to access important networks, and competing demands (Carli & Eagly, 2001; Heilman, 2001; Muscarella, 2004). Yukl (2001), in his review of various studies on women and leadership, also found that other explanations for gender-based discrimination and the glass ceiling phenomena have included

1. lack of opportunity to gain experience and visibility in types of positions that would facilitate advancement;

2. higher standards of performance for women than for men;

3. exclusion of women from informal networks that aid advancement;

4. lack of encouragement and opportunity for developmental activities;

5. lack of opportunity for effective mentoring;

6. difficulties created by competing family demands;

7. lack of strong action by top management to ensure equal opportunity; and

8. intentional efforts by some men to retain control of the most powerful positions for themselves. (pp. 411–412; also see Bass, 1999; Ridgeway, 2001; Weiss, 1999; Wilson, 2004)

Black female scholars assert that being persons of color and women compounds these barriers due to the intersection of gender and race as sources of oppression (Bell & Nkomo, 2001; Collins, 1999; Crenshaw, 1991). Black women face a double whammy and make up a tiny minority in leadership positions (Alston, 2000; Jones, 2003; Murtadha-Watts, 1999; Parker & ogilvie, 1996). It is necessary to study the leadership experiences of Black women and to explore their survival and success strategy against social injustices wrought upon them by the intersection of gender, race, class, ethnic origins, nationality, and sexuality.

Black Women in Leadership

Studies about women in leadership have been comprehensive in both scope and methods, but Black scholars realized that the research leaves out women of color. Researchers have ascertained that Black women represent a tiny minority in leadership ranks within educational institutions as well as in the corporate world (Alston, 2000; Jones, 2003; Morrison & Glinow, 1990; Parker & ogilvie, 1996). Themes emerging from the literature on Black women's leadership styles, practices, and behaviors include androgynous leadership style, tempered radicalism, spirituality, mentoring, and a holistic servant leadership. Prior to elaborating on these themes, Black women's leadership must be understood within the context of Black women's standpoint and the resulting epistemology. This helps to understand Black women's leadership experiences against the backdrop of the intersection of race, class and gender.

Black Feminist Standpoint and Intersectionality

The logic of standpoint theory in feminist theorizing emanates from the notion that women's lived realities are overwhelmingly different from those of men, which results in epistemological consequences (Hartsock, 2004). From this perspective, Hartsock (2004) posited that a standpoint is an engaged position, whereby the ruled or dominated group challenges the status quo and the perverse inhumanity of human relations. Patricia Hill Collins (1996), in her explication of a Black feminist standpoint, maintained that Black women's economic status and experiences stimulate a distinctively Black feminist consciousness: "A subordinate group not only experiences a different reality than a group that rules, but a subordinate group may interpret that reality differently from a dominant group" (p. 223). However, in academic discourse, subordinate voices are hardly ever welcome. In this context, Black women's knowledge claims are obscured and their knowledge production suppressed in order for the dominant group to maintain hegemony (Collins, 2000). Such women are faced with oppression and discrimination arising out of the intersection of race, class, sexuality, and gender (Bell & Nkomo, 2001; Collins, 1998; Crenshaw, 1991). In spite of this domination, African women in the Continent and the

Diaspora have managed to produce intellectual work, often aimed at fostering Black women's activism and a search for social justice (Collins, 2000; Dolphyne, 1991).

Even though African nations are supposedly enjoying freedom from colonial domination, reality suggests that Western domination continues through neocolonialism and Africa's dependency on the West for her economic survival as mandated by neoliberal economic arrangements (Dolphyne, 1991; Oduyoye, 1995; Oyewumi, 2003). As such, African women are a subordinated group as Africans in a White and West-controlled global economy, and as women within neopatriarchal cultures (Collins, 1996; Dolphyne, 1991; Oyewumi, 1997, 2003). Listening for their stories of thriving as leaders within that context becomes an important endeavor that allows African women's perspectives on leadership to emerge. Women in other social, political, economic, and cultural contexts whose experiences mirror those of the participants in this study can learn from and be inspired by the thriving strategies of their African counterparts via naturalistic generalizations (Denzin & Lincoln, 2000; Lawrence-Lightfoot, 1983). Black and African women contribute to knowledge on leadership in context by referencing their experiences as situated *knowers* (Collins, 2000). Their narratives, understood through the lens of intersecting oppressions of racism, classism, imperialism, heterosexism, sexism, and ethnic origins, help the researcher to illuminate theory and the reader to be educated about and enthused by the participants' leadership experiences.

Spirituality

One of the most prevalent themes found in the literature about Black women and leadership is the issue of spirituality. Religion and spirituality have been found to be important meaning-making and coping mechanisms for people of African descent (Dantley, 2003a, 2003b; Mattis, 2002; Paris, 1995). A spiritual foundation undergirds Black scholars' research, teaching, and thriving strategies in predominantly White institutions (Jones, 2003). In her study of Black female educational administrators, Sharyn Jones discovered that spirituality was a running theme emerging from each of her conversations with the participants as a way of life, as well as the driving force behind their leadership (Jones, 2003). Jones's participants described spirituality in terms of the Golden Rule, leading from a sense of calling, and connecting with family, parents, teachers, and students in the school system.

Khaula Murtadha, in her study of Black women superintendents, discussed how such women use their spirituality as a source of sustenance, survival, and resiliency in the face of structural racism and sexism (Murtadha-Watts, 1999). Her participants described their roles as callings, as directed by divine vision, and they talked about the need for their subordinates to exhibit a spiritual centering as well. The spirituality displayed and discussed by Murtadha and Jones's participants involved risk taking and critical evaluation of context and situation, expressed through activism against racism, sexism, and classism.

Mentoring

Another theme in the Black women in leadership literature concerns mentoring; that is, the availability of mentors or lack thereof and how that impacts women's entry into and effectiveness in leadership (Bloom & Erlandson, 2003; Jones, 2003). Mentoring was found to be important in facilitating the professional development of African American women faculty, as well as increasing their representation in predominantly White universities and organizations (Bell & Nkomo, 2001; Tillman, 2001). Presence and promotion in institutions of higher education would be a prerequisite to African Americans' advancement into higher educational administration. Similarly, there would need to be a pipeline of women in senior management who could be promoted into C-Suite positions. Bell and Nkomo (2001) found that there are few such women, Black or White, and the Black women who happen to be in such positions rarely have professional mentors.

In the absence of professional mentors to help them in organizations and institutions, Jones (2003), Bell and Nkomo (2001), and Reid-Merritt (1996) discovered that Black women leaders found life mentors in their female relatives such as mothers, grandmothers, aunts, and *othermothers* who encouraged them to achieve beyond the expectations placed upon them by the racist structures. Black women leaders also found the stories of pioneer Black leaders such as Sojourner Truth, Mary McLeod Bethune, Anna Julia Cooper, and others inspiring them to be strong and to be active in challenging the status quo (Reid-Merritt, 1996). From the African continent, women such as the 2004 Nobel Laureate from Kenya, Professor Wangari Maathai, and political leaders such as Winnie Madikizela Mandela, Ellen Kuzwayo, and Wambui Otieno from South Africa and Kenya, respectively, serve as contemporary inspiring examples of challenging the status quo. However, few such women leaders' stories have been told beyond their national borders, and the experiences of women leaders from Africa as a whole have not received much scholarly study (Bakare-Yusuf, 2003). Additionally, women serving in educational administration positions in universities in South Africa did not have mentors and faced both race and gender discrimination in their context, feeling overused and underappreciated (Mabokela, 2003a). In the next section, we review some of the writings about women and leadership in Africa.

African Women in Leadership

Rewriting History

African women have been missing in the history of the Continent for a long time, due to the incessant patriarchal structures that relegate their leadership activities to oblivion. For example, if Professor Wangari Maathai had not won the Nobel Peace Prize in 2004, then it is unlikely that women outside of Kenya ever would have heard or read her inspiring tales of fighting for the conservation of forests. Similarly, the world knows that there is a woman president in Liberia because that is such a rare occurrence anywhere that it was featured in all media outlets around the globe. Another example is the many women freedom fighters in African nations whose stories have remained untold, whereas men have received recognition and honor for their role in anti-colonial efforts (Baker, 1998; Kabira & Ngurukie, 1997; Otieno, 1998). However, a few scholars have attempted to rewrite history, to include women's stories in the bigger story of the Continent's struggle with external domination (Berger & White, 1999; Coquery-Vidrovitch, 1997; Strobel, 1995; Sweetman, 1984). Sweetman (1984) scoured volumes of works on prehistoric Africa to gather portraits of African women leaders throughout the centuries. He chose to cast 12 portraits on women leaders as far back as the ancient civilizations of Egypt and Ethiopia. His choice was guided by the need to represent women's leadership across the centuries, as well as portraits from all regions of the Continent. Sweetman felt that even though men numerically outnumbered women in the story of Africa, the few stories far exceeded the male stories in their extraordinariness. He concluded that historians underestimated the roles that women played in leadership within Africa's prehistoric, precolonial existence.

One historian who has attempted to demonstrate the agency of women during the colonial period is Professor Tabitha Kanogo. Through oral interviews and a meticulous review of available archival documents, she has exposed how changes wrought upon the Kenyan context by colonialism and missionary Christianity provided women with both opportunities for individual agency and struggle under the hegemony of patriarchy from the clash between modernity (through colonial administrative and missionary policies) and tradition (Kanogo, 2005) Her text illustrates the fact that the chaos, contradictions, and flux provided opportunities for women to rise as individuals and collectives to resolve challenges for individuals, families, and communities. Kanogo also exposed the contradictions inherent in the change process: the worst of African traditions and Western Victorian/Christian gender roles combined to create extreme hardships for African women, such as the domestication of women's roles and the uprising of a new, more severe form of female circumcision in response to missionary and colonial attempts to stamp out the practice (Kanogo, 2005). In the process, women had to rise at the grassroots levels, making use of existing avenues such as missionary boarding schools and education to find a new space for themselves. Education provided women with the power to move spatially from their rural confines to the cities and towns, where they found employment as nurses and teachers, thus earning for themselves a new social status and authority as community leaders. The history of women's agency and victimization during the colonial period provides an important backdrop against which many of the women's narratives in this book are told, because many of these women grew up in the 1950s and early 1960s, toward the end of colonial rule in Kenya.

Biographies of Leading Women

Within the stories of colonial domination, women played an important role as participants and leaders in the freedom movements across the Continent. One such leader, Wambui Waiyaki Otieno, told her story in the form of an autobiography, relating her role as a spy for the freedom movement in Kenya. She narrated the sacrifices she made and the risks she took as she carried out covert operations in order to keep the freedom fighters in the forests informed of the best strategies to take in their armed struggle (Otieno, 1998). Otieno's life story is replete with examples of leadership during the armed struggle and thwarted efforts at leadership post-independence. She would later marry a prominent Nairobi lawyer, the late S. M. Otieno, and would experience the clash of cultures when he died and his clan insisted upon burying him in their rural home, against his legal will and her wishes, demonstrating to Kenyans and the world at large the fact that tradition and modernity in Kenya coexist as uncomfortable bedfellows!

Whereas Wambui Otieno's social status as an upper-middle-class woman allowed her to tell her story in the form of an autobiography, other female freedom fighters were relegated to oblivion (Kabira &

Ngurukie, 1997). In the book *Mau Mau's Daughter*, Otieno complained that she was asked for the names of fellow female fighters at independence, purportedly to reward them for their labors, as had been done for some men, but that list was never used for that purpose (Otieno, 1998). As Kabira and Ngurukie found out when they interviewed six women freedom fighters, these women were not rewarded for their labor, and in spite of their tremendous leadership and risky engagement during the freedom struggle, they lived in abject landless poverty (Kabira & Ngurukie, 1997). For such women leaders of the freedom era, independence did not bring them the promised fruits, due to the fact that the changing of the guard replaced White domination with African class and patriarchal domination (Masinjila, 1997).

In South Africa, the late Ellen Kuzwayo is an example of a woman who served as a freedom fighter, leading the African National Congress (ANC) Youth League in the 1960s and agitating for women's rights throughout her life in politics. Prior to ANC leadership, Kuzwayo was a teacher and then a social worker, but having grown up in a politically involved and educated family, politics and freedom struggle were part of her heritage. In her book *Call Me Woman*, published in 1985, Ellen Kuzwayo narrated her life story, describing the struggles faced by Black South Africans, women in particular, as they fought for freedom from apartheid's inhumanity. South African women showed outstanding tenacity against terrible odds and remained determined, like the women in the African communities of previous generations, until they won the right to enjoy their nation free of White domination (Kuzwayo, 1985). Kuzwayo's autobiography is a story of strength and tenacity through many decades of apartheid and the ensuing economic, political, social, and cultural marginalization of Black Africans in South Africa.

Whereas women such as Wambui Otieno and the late Ellen Kuzwayo are recognized as leaders in the African society, the story that remains to be told is how they survive with resiliency and resoluteness in spite of the challenges placed in their leadership path. Alison Baker (1998), in her study of Moroccan women, who, like Wambui and Kuzwayo, participated in the nationalist and armed resistance movements, chose to approach her study from a celebratory stance. She said, "The book as a whole is unabashedly celebratory. I like and admire these women, and I wrote to celebrate their extraordinary lives and contribution to the Moroccan independence movement" (Preface). That is, Baker was interested in showing how the women leaders' strength and fortitude in the face of national struggles contributed to their nation's eventual independence from foreign domination. Such stories are rare.

Romero (1998), in her study of women in postapartheid South Africa, realized that one of the threads running through all of the narratives she heard was a deep spirituality displayed through religious faith. She was of the opinion that this deep faith displayed by the women was actually typical of Africans as a whole, although particularly evident among the women. Romero observed that it is a source of resiliency and resistance in the midst of appalling economic, social, cultural and political deprivations (Romero, 1998). Women such as Ellen Kuzwayo, Wambui Otieno, and others with them utilized their spirituality and deep religious faith to overcome great hurdles during years of imprisonment, struggling and striving as leaders in the anti-apartheid and anti-colonial efforts. These life stories demonstrated women's ways of leading in the context of African realities. Nevertheless, such stories have remained untold, denying women leaders and leadership scholars everywhere a chance to enrich leadership theories and models. Some examples follow of African women leading in various capacities within different sectors, such as education, politics, and the nongovernmental sector.

Leading in Education Administration

Women in Africa have consistently been underrepresented in educational achievements and access, so few women reach the college level. In her study of female college students in Kenya, Tabitha Otieno found that such women are faced with near-insurmountable obstacles in their pursuit of higher education. These barriers include lack of financial resources, cultural traditions where boys are valued more than girls, and competing demands and gender role conflicts (Otieno, 1995). Once women are marginalized from achieving higher education, this becomes part of the excuse and/or explanation for their underrepresentation in positions of leadership requiring college degrees.

Among elementary school principals, Victor Ombati found that although women make up almost 60% of the teaching force in Nairobi and Thika cities, they represent only 45% of principals in those school districts (Ombati, 2003). His study did not extend beyond the two urban districts, but it would have been revealing to find out how they would have fared in rural districts as well as the national averages. Ombati triangulated data collection methods by employing interviews, focus groups, and observation, and he concluded that patriarchal culture forms the greatest hindrance to women's accent to educational leadership. Favoritism, lobbying, and informal networks formed the methods of accent on the educational leadership ladder, thus excluding women who did not have powerful networks (Ombati, 2003). It is possible that if his study were carried out in rural districts, then the numbers would not be so equal as in these two urban districts. For example, as recent as January 8, 2009, Nation Newspapers reported a story about a school in Northern Kenya that was closed because the parents would not accept a female principal. This was a reminder that even where women are able and capable, local patriarchal culture keeps them out of leadership positions. In her exploration of the experiences of academic women, Njoki Kamau discovered that education was a double-edged sword; it allowed such women to gain social status, but it also created contradictions in their personal lives (Kamau, 1996). Kamau interviewed 24 women academics who assured her that education in Kenya perpetuates gender inequalities. She found that the colonial education system in Kenya served to produce subservience, uncritical obedience, Judeo-Christian moral uprightness, and compliance to cultural gender stereotypes that place women in subjugation to men. This legacy of colonial education that presented women as ignorant gossips in need of moral regulation made it quite difficult for educated women to collectivize and organize to agitate for better working conditions and promotions (Kamau, 1996) Academic women found universities to be harsh working environments, where their gender and marital status continued to serve as reasons for discrimination, and where tenure and promotion into administrative positions were extremely rare. Kamau returned to Kenya 10 years later to revisit the women she had interviewed previously, and she found that they were still struggling as outsiders, attempting to bring about small but significant changes in Kenyan public universities by taking on administrative roles (Kamau, 2004)

In South Africa, Reitumetse Mabokela interviewed six women administrators in institutions of higher education, women who referred to themselves as "donkeys of the university" (Mabokela, 2003a). The image of donkeys sought to describe how these female administrators felt about being charged with challenging responsibilities but denied the respect and recognition due to their positions. The women administrators struggled with being the first or the only woman to hold such a position, so although not necessarily positioned as tokens, they felt their minority status in predominantly male institutions. Their chronic underrepresentation put them under constant scrutiny by men as well as women, creating psychological pressures to succeed that involved working long hours. Similar pressures were evident among the academic women studied by Kamau (1996) in Kenyan universities. Such women have experienced resistance from both men and women, because both have been socialized to expect leaders to be men rather than women. As such, women leaders have complained about what they refer to as the "pull her down" attitude that they experience from other women (Mabokela, 2003a). South African women leaders also have struggled with the intersection of race and gender due to that country's history with apartheid. In addition, African women leaders have struggled under the constraints imposed by class, where they have felt resented by other less accomplished women, yet they have earned their current elite status through academic and professional accomplishments (Kamau, 1996; Mabokela, 2003a).

In her study of gender and leadership in South African educational administration, Linda Chisholm explored the lived experiences of both men and women in order to explicate the conflict between social goals and practices (Chisholm, 2001). After interviewing eight women and eight men educational leaders across racial groups, Chisholm felt that leadership is associated with masculinity, rationality, and whiteness in that context. Many of the Black interviewees experienced race and gender as intertwined and inseparable elements, so those who were both Black and female faced the most constraints to their leadership and authority.

It has become increasingly clear that women in leadership positions in Africa, as represented in the few studies reviewed, have struggled under challenges and constraints to their leadership and authority emanating from the intersection of several variables: African culture and traditions and gender, race, and organizational cultures consisting of invisibility and lack of recognition. Such women have struggled with the competing demands of domestic labor and public life, since women are responsible for the bulk of child care and domestic responsibilities (Chisholm, 2001; Kamau, 1996; Mabokela, 2003a, 2003b). Missing are studies that explore how such women have succeeded and thrived as leaders in spite of all of the challenges and constraints, whether cultural, organizational, racial, gender, economic, or otherwise.

Summary

Studies on leadership theories have explored how leaders lead, and the traits, styles, behaviors, practices, power, and sources of influence they use to engender goal accomplishment (Bass, 1990; Hersey, et al., 2001; Yukl, 2001). However, such theories have been criticized for using White males as their subject of study yet generalizing to all leaders everywhere. That is, most leadership theories are androcentric and miss out on women and people of color from theory formulation (Jones, 2003). As such, women respond to this androcentricity by engaging in theorizing on women's leadership, beginning with differences in styles, practices, and behaviors between men and women (Bass, 1990). However, past studies were not conclusive as to whether men and women do indeed lead differently, with some researchers arguing for differences, others contending for similarities, and yet others recognizing the role of context or situation in moderating women's leadership styles (Bass, 1990; Carli & Eagly, 2001). Other studies on women and leadership concentrated on understanding the role of gender stereotyping on the evaluation of women as leaders, with a recognition that such stereotypes prescribe how women leaders are evaluated by their constituents (Heilman, 2001). These studies focused on the leadership of White women. In response to their being missing in theory, Black women researchers contend that even though they are underrepresented at all levels of leadership, where they do lead, their styles are likely to be androgynous (Parker, 2005; Parker & ogilvie, 1996). In addition, certain elements are evident in their leadership experiences, including profound spirituality, servant leadership, tempered radicalism, and the ethics of care and risk.

Women are underrepresented in all areas of public leadership in African nations, ranging from education, politics, and business and public administration. Common among both African and African American women leaders is the notion of the intersectionality of oppressive forces acting against them, including race, gender, class, ethnicity, and sexuality. Researchers have discussed how women are underrepresented in educational access as well as educational administration (Chisholm, 2001; Mabokela, 2003a, 2003b; Ombati, 2003; Otieno, 1995). The few studies available on women's leadership in Africa have discussed the constraints and challenges that such women face. Such challenges have included: (1) conflict between their private and domestic roles and their public roles as leaders; (2) race and class biases; (3) challenges to their authority as leaders in the context of the patriarchal worldview; (4) lack of recognition and visibility within their organizations; and (5) the paradox of education, where other women resent them for their achievements and attempt to pull them down (Chisholm, 2001; Kamau, 1996; Mabokela, 2003b; Ombati, 2003). Missing in the discussion of African women's experiences is an exploration of the survival and success strategies of existing women leaders within these contexts. The current study explores how select women leaders in an African context transverse gender, traditional culture, organizational culture, and social norm stereotypes as well as other constraints to their authority as leaders. It contributes to theory and praxis about women and leadership in Africa by contrasting the current deficit model with a search for goodness, through stories of resiliency and success in spite of challenges and constraints.

In conclusion, it is imperative to have studies of African realities, in this case, African women leaders carried out by African and/or African-ist scholars, which can be included in the global debate on leadership studies. Theory is used cautiously, because it "almost always privileges a western reading of African realities. This often ends up with a gloomy picture of misery, hopelessness, abuse, mutilation, prostitution, and disease" (Murunga, 2002). This is a risk even when the researcher is African, due to the legacy of colonial education. However, it is necessary "to interrogate gender and allied concepts based on African cultural experiences and epistemologies . . . the goal is to find ways in which African research can be better informed by local concerns and inter-pretations and at the same time, concurrently, for African experiences to be taken into account in general theory building, the structural racism of the global system notwithstanding" (Oyewumi, 2002). For this study, the focus is on the positive stories of resiliency and strength nestled within the complexities, challenges, and contradictions of the women's experiences of leadership in context.

3

Setting the Stage for
Leadership Stories

In this chapter I introduce the geographical location, the cultural,
social, and economic context, and snapshots of participants involved
in this study. The contextual information is necessary for the reader
to get a visual and sensory idea of where the women live and lead,
the conditions under which they exist and lead, and how these help
shape their leadership experiences.

Geographical Location

I conducted the fieldwork portion of this study in Nairobi and Kajiado
(Maasai land), Kenya, among African women leaders. Nairobi is the
capital city of Kenya, and the fifth largest city in Africa, with a population of over 4 million. It began as a trading post and railway station in
1899 and became the capital city in 1905. It is the center of industry,
commerce, education, travel, and entertainment in Kenya as well as the
eastern African region. Being in a mostly peaceful country, Nairobi is
not only home to Kenyans but also to a large refugee community from
Sudan, Ethiopia, Eritrea, Rwanda, Burundi, Somalia, and the Democratic
Republic of Congo. It is also home to many other people from around
the world working as expatriates for multinational corporations; in
addition, several United Nations (UN) organizations have their headquarters in the city. It is a cosmopolitan and multicultural city that is
home to obscene riches as well as extreme poverty; 70% of Nairobi's
inhabitants live in the slums—informal settlements of the urban poor
with no sanitation, no running water, and extremely unhealthy housing—existing on less than a dollar a day. Stories abound about young
girls in the Kibera, Mathare, and Korogocho slums, some who end up
pregnant by age 9, cutting short their primary school education.

Nairobi is also a favorite destination for both local and international visitors: for locals, rural-urban migration in search of greener pastures; for international visitors, work in the many international organizations or leisure, including Nairobi National Park, the only park of its size located adjacent to a city. Nairobi is the center of government business. Geographically, it borders Maasai land to the south, Ukambani to the east, and Gikuyuland to the north and west. It is described as "the city in the sun" because of its moderate rainfall and moderate weather (temperatures range between 54 and 80 degrees Fahrenheit year round). Because Nairobi is close to the equator, the difference in temperature between the two seasons (rainy season and dry season) is minimal.

The only face-to-face conversation that took place outside of city limits was in Kajiado, a town just outside of Nairobi in the heart of Maasai land, where Priscilla Nangurai lives and works.

Sociocultural Context

Africa is a continent that has undergone many cultural changes in the last century. The most important change was precipitated by the dual forces of colonialism and Christianity. Most of the participants in this study were born during colonial times and have memories especially of the emergency period in Kenya when the colonial government issued a state of emergency as it attempted to stamp out a revolutionary war. Fortunately for Kenya, the colonial forces did not succeed and had to give Kenyans their independence. The emergency period was from 1952 to 1960, and the British awarded Kenya self-governance in 1963. As such, several references in the portraits and quotes are utilized to illustrate themes that refer back to this period in Kenya's history, as it was a traumatic experience for the nation. Most of the references to this period are in relation to women's participation in fighting for freedom and their survival mechanisms against innumerable odds.

The colonial period and the changes wrought upon Kenyan society are important to comprehend if the reader is to gain a full picture of women's leadership experiences in contemporary Kenya and the context of some of their activism. Before colonialism, there was no country known as Kenya; rather, the region that was designated a protectorate and later a colony by Britain contained different groups of people that had coexisted peacefully (for the most part) through hundreds of years of history. Colonialism not only combined these disparate groups into one country but, over time, forced them all to begin to meld into a national consciousness. Before this could take place, however, colonialism and missionary Christianity disrupted traditional institutions, creating new ones that were foreign, some welcome and some not so welcome, among the indigenous population. As Kanogo observed, "The effects of the all pervasive ideological shifts that colonialism produced in the lives of women . . . a woman's personhood was enhanced, diminished or placed in ambiguous predicaments by the consequences, intended or unintended, of colonial rule as administered by both the colonizers and the colonized" (2005, p. 1). African men, colonial administrators, and missionaries attempted to control women's morality, sexuality, and physical and socioeconomic mobility; clitoridectomy (female circumcision), bride price, maternity, and education became sites of contestation. Attempts to stamp out clitoridectomy were met with resistance by every community that engaged in the practice: colonial administrators and missionaries found it barbaric and unhealthy, whereas African societies insisted that it was an important rite of passage, enabling women to become full community or tribal members. Only upon successfully undergoing the initiation process with its antecedent teachings as well as the physical cut would a girl be welcomed into full womanhood by getting married and having children.

Whereas in communities that embraced education, mostly boys were educated, but girls also began to seek education in order to change their lot in life. They came to the realization that education provided them with an avenue for mobility, both socioeconomic as well as spatial, as they would move from their rural villages to the towns and cities in search of educational and employment opportunities. However, many African men felt education was a waste on women; after all, they were only meant for childbearing and child rearing, not economic pursuits outside of the home. As such, women began to embrace Christianity, a prerequisite to acquiring missionary education, often in defiance of their parents' and community's wishes. Embracing missionary education also meant repudiating female circumcision, not engaging in arranged marriages, and, oftentimes, not being able to participate in community activities, as such women were considered outsiders.

> These debates emphasized the centrality of women in the crafting of marital, kinship and ethnic cohesiveness and the ways in which modernity was rapidly eroding notions of social order. The interface between gender, ethnicity, customary law, and modernity was conflicted. Forces of historical change during the colonial period thus precipitated a rethinking of the status and role of women within society. Womanhood

thus became a battleground where issues of modernization, tradition, change and personal independence were fought. (Kanogo, 2005, p. 2)

By the time Kenya attained independence from British rule, traditional notions of womanhood and the emerging contemporary notions were still on a collision course. Some women made good use of the ensuing chaos by entering into hitherto unknown public places through employment, renegotiating the marriage arrangements, and reconfiguring what it meant to be an African woman. What emerged as African womanhood was both traditional, with women still taking motherhood and domestic rules seriously, and contemporary, with women engaging in higher education at home and abroad, entering into the professions and public leadership. The effects of the disruption caused by colonialism and Christianity continue to be felt to this day; several of the women leaders reflected on this in their stories.

Upon attaining self-government, the country was led on a path toward success before corruption, mismanagement of government resources, intolerance of government leaders regarding dissenters, and global economic arrangements drove the country toward a path of destruction. In the first decade and a half after independence, Kenya experienced tremendous growth economically, socially, and culturally with the growth of two universities, several mid-level colleges, hundreds of high schools, and thousands of primary schools. However, politically, autocratic leaders were at the helm of government. This period saw the killing of various political leaders because of their anti-government ideology (that is, social justice ideals), including Tom Mboya and J. M. Kariuki. The period also saw the rising of a political class that would do anything to attain power and wealth, amassing for itself large tracts of land in Central and Rift Valley provinces. Upon the death of the first president in 1978, the new government came up with what was called the *Nyayo* philosophy: Nyayo means footsteps—unfortunately, this new government literally followed the negative directions that had been put into place. The period 1978–1992 has gone down in history as one of the worst for Kenyans because of the intolerance of former president Moi's government to any dissent, and the growth of corruption to calamitous levels. The women leaders make many references to this period because the chaos triggered their engagement leadership as they felt compelled to fight for social and political justice. Some of them faced many perils during this period because of their attempts to stand up for what they believed in.

In 1992, after a period of active dissent and political unrest, former president Moi finally assented to the change in the constitution
to allow Kenya to return to being a multi-party state after 10 years of
de jure single-party status. General elections were held at the end of
1992, which saw six women elected members of parliament, up from
two women elected in the 1988 elections. This period ushered in chaos
and uncertainty, as well as hope and jubilation, as the young democracy
emerged, with many in opposition leadership attempting to figure out
what their roles were as critics of government. Now there was freedom
of speech, assembly, and all other freedoms that had been tampered
with during the prior period. It was during this time that the leadership of many of these participants matured. The ruling party, Kenya
African National Union (KANU), managed to remain in power for
10 years, at which time opposition leaders and those in civil society
engaged in an active critique of government leadership, enabling
Kenya to emerge as a democratic nation. In 2002, the then-opposition
parties formed a coalition to enable them to present a united front in
the general elections. The result was that nine women were elected,
eight nominated into parliament. The strategy worked, and the political women leaders in this study became members of the governing
cabinet for the first time.

In 2003, government began a process of constitutional review that
was open to representatives from civil society, grassroots organizations,
educational institutions, and all other important social entities in the
country. Again, most of the women leaders in this study participated
in this process and referred to it severally. However, the draft that
they produced that is referred to as the Bomas Draft, or the People
Driven Constitution, failed at the referendum because members of
Parliament (MP) messed around with it, to the people's dismay. The
MP were apparently afraid of the change in status quo, which might
have resulted in a loss of power for some of them. As such, at the
general referendum, the draft was defeated with a resounding majority, because most people felt it was no longer representative. This
took place in November 2005, after the completion of my fieldwork.
However, it is important in understanding many of the statements
that the women made in relation to their participation in the Bomas
Draft before MP mangled it out of shape and in understanding the
important contributions that these women leaders have made in the
making of Kenya's history.

Since the initial fieldwork for the study was carried out, Kenya
has endured a trying period that saw it lose face in the eyes of the

global community. After a hotly contested general election in December 2007, chaos and fighting broke out as the incumbent president had himself sworn in under shady circumstances. His main opponent claimed that the ruling party had manipulated the process, that the president had rigged himself back into power. The truth of the matter lies in the fact that both sides rigged shamelessly, and that the incumbent did not have the mandate of the people to be sworn in as president in a context where the results seemed to be doctored, in his favor. The resulting bloodshed resulted in over 1,000 people dead, and over a quarter million displaced as the tension turned interethnic. The political situation was amicably resolved 3 months later when the two competitors agreed to form a government of national unity, which includes the largest cabinet ever seen in Kenya's history (44 members, up from 22). Whereas there had been hope that more women would be able to make it into parliament and the cabinet in that election, the number only increased by six, at least two of whom were elected later after their husbands died in a plane crash early in 2008. Whereas this situation is not discussed by the women leaders in this study, as it happened after the field research was concluded, it is still necessary in understanding some of their stories, because it relays the fact that while Kenya has been at peace for more than 40 years, that peace meant the absence of war, not the presence of real national unity and ethnic harmony. At the base of this last conflict was the feeling that certain ethnic groups had been marginalized in the sharing of the "national cake," which resulted in the eruption of chaos directed at the president's ethnic group, which was perceived as having benefited the most because he is the second president from this ethnic group. Kenya has only had three presidents in its 45-year history, two Kikuyu and one Kalenjin. As such, other groups, particularly the Luo and Luhyia from western Kenya, felt that it was their turn to run the country and benefit from having "a big man" in power. The Kalenjin's conflict with the Gikuyu was over land, because the Gikuyus ended up in land that traditionally belonged to the Kalenjin after the colonial settlers hived off large tracts of the most fertile land for themselves. After the settlers left, those who had been moved to Rift Valley to work on the farms remained and through cooperative societies bought the land upon which they had been squatting. Most of the people, though, could not afford to buy back the land, particularly those who did not belong to cooperative societies, sowing seeds of discord that would erupt 5 decades later. Wahu Kaara grew up in that context, as her grandmother was a squatter in a settler farm, whereas Agnes Abuom and Esther Abuom both grew up in Rift Valley as natives of the region.

The interethnic warfare that erupted affected each of them as their families were in the region.

Whereas Kenya is a modern state in a lot of ways, traditions still reign supreme. These traditions have undergone transformation due to the impact of a capitalist economy, such as the introduction of money to communities that originally practiced barter trade. Education, Christianity, traditional religions, and other social constructs play an important role in how women experience life and leadership. Both tradition and modernity coexist as uncomfortable bedfellows, creating a state of flux where many of the norms now adhered to are neither genuinely traditional nor authentically modern (Gyekye, 1997). This is important as a background against which some of the social justice activism of the women leaders can be understood, especially where it relates to access to resources for marginalized populations. In the next several pages, I introduce a short narrative about each one of them, because in the thematic analysis, I used all 16 participants, plus my liaison and myself.

4

Participant Snapshots

This study consisted of 18 participants, starting with myself as researcher, my liaison or co-researcher, and 16 women leaders from Kenya. In portraiture, the researcher brings herself into the study in the role of witness to the events and interpreter of the events and stories presented by the participants. As the researcher, I participated in dialogue with the participants and co-created the narratives from conversations, observations, and documents presented by the participants, through a process of collaborative meaning making. I also engaged in a process of discerning the voices of the participants as individuals, as well as attempting to discover their collective voice. My autobiographical heritage as an African woman who has prior leadership experiences in Kenya prompted my quest to learn from the elders' wisdom and life stories.

In addition, having served in a pastoral role, I was critical of the gender discrimination found in many Christian churches, prompting me to learn from those who have succeeded in that arena. I am also a former schoolteacher, thus the desire to learn from those in educational administration, especially those whose work revolves around equity and justice in schooling. It is apparent that my personal background had an impact on the choice of women who participated in the study, as I was only interested in those whose leadership included a social justice agenda. However, my liaison also had a great hand in shaping the study, because she introduced me to most of the women who were possible participants for the study. We made cold calls of introduction to those participants that Reverend Joyce did not know personally. However, because of the respect given to "people of the cloth," especially those from traditional denominations in Kenya, each time she called and requested a chance for us to introduce the study, they would grant her an appointment. Had I attempted to do this on my own as an unknown young female student, I would have had limited success. I therefore start the introductions of participants with

Rev. Joyce W. Kariuki, my aunt, mentor, friend, and greatest supporter in this research journey.

Reverend Joyce W. Kariuki: Anglican Church Clergywoman, Independent Consultant Gender, Development, and HIV/AIDS

Reverend Joyce participated in the pilot project that I undertook while I was attempting to define the parameters of my study. Through that pilot project, she became excited about the study and began to brainstorm with me on possible participants. The names we came up with covered the length and breadth of women in leadership as far as we could imagine, educational, political, ecclesiastical, and the civil commons. She knew many of the women personally, some we met while in the process of seeking appointments with others. For example, whereas Muthoni Wanyeki and Rev. Kariuki had met in prior NGO engagements, Njoki Wainaina was a new find for both of us. Rev. Kariuki is a sought-after speaker in churches and NGO forums as well as in schools and colleges where she talks about issues relating to HIV/AIDS, women in leadership, and counseling. She has a master's degree in biblical counseling from Nairobi International School of Theology. She is also an adjunct lecturer at Daystar University, where she teaches classes on counseling, leadership, small business management, and entrepreneurship. She worked at the Central Bank of Kenya prior to starting a supermarket and, later on, embarking on the ecclesial path. Her networks permeate the NGO world, where she is involved in women's networks for peace, reconciliation, and HIV/AIDS training, advocacy, and care. After the fieldwork was completed, she served as the general secretary of the Council of Anglican Provinces in Africa, the Pan-African body of bishops, an experience that included exposure to patriarchy at the highest levels of religious leadership. She continues to lecture as an adjunct faculty member at Daystar University, to serve as vicar for a suburban Anglican congregation, and to consult all over Africa. The choice of participants does somewhat reflect her institutional and ministerial backgrounds.

Whereas the leadership positions were current as of September 2005, when the fieldwork was completed, every attempt has been made to update the women's positions and professional movements since then. The 16 participants were distributed across several sectors: two in government, four in education, one in business, and all others in the civil society, including law, human rights, gender, religious, and development areas. Five of the participants were between the ages of

41 and 50, eight were between 51 and 60, two were between 61 and 70, and the oldest was 80, as of September 2005. In terms of experience, most had been in leadership positions for over 25 years. Two of the women leaders were single, three were divorced, eight were married, and three were widowed. All of the women except Muthoni Wanyeki are mothers, and several are grandmothers as well, a social status in which they take great pride. Dr. Esther Abuom is an adoptive mother, having given a home to three children, in spite of being single. In the next several pages, I will introduce the nine women leaders for whom I did not create in-depth portraits due to space and time constraints. I begin the snapshots by introducing the political leaders.

Honorable Beth Mugo: Minister for Public Health and Sanitation

One could say that politics runs in the blood of Honorable Beth Mugo, who at the time of the interview served as Kenya's assistant minister for education. This is because Mugo is the niece of Kenya's first president, the late Mzee Jomo Kenyatta. Her story is riddled with anecdotes from her experiences being connected to the first family of Kenya prior to and after independence. For example, she talked about how her educational experience was marred by discrimination from missionaries because of her uncle's involvement in the freedom movement in Kenya in the 1950s. In the 1970s, while her husband was an ambassador, she and the family traveled abroad for Kenyan missions. At the same time, she engaged in entrepreneurial undertakings and traveled around the world with then-first lady Mama Ngina Kenyatta. In the 1980s, after the family's return to Kenya, she became involved in the women's movement, particularly as Kenyan women prepared for the end of the UN Decade for Women Conference, held in Nairobi in 1985. Afterward, her involvement in women's issues led to engaging in political leadership as the member of Parliament for Dagoretti, one of the constituencies in Nairobi. Her first cabinet appointment was in 2003, when the then-opposition parties took over Kenya's political leadership after winning the 2002 general elections. She was the assistant minister for education in charge of basic education in the Kenya government (2003–2007), a challenging role because the new government introduced free primary education without sufficient human or capital resources to implement it. As of early 2008, she was the minister for public health and sanitation, one of the newly created ministerial dockets in the coalition government formed in March 2008.

Honorable Charity Ngilu: Minister for Water and Irrigation

Honorable Charity Ngilu is referred to as Mama Rainbow because of her role in helping forge an opposition parties' alliance, or Iron Lady, due to her unflinching political stands. Ngilu has been a member of Parliament since Kenya's first multiparty elections of 1992, when she was only 40 years old and with no prior public leadership experience. Her previous experience includes being a secretary at the Central Bank of Kenya and later a businessperson. Her motivation for seeking public political leadership was the conviction that as a woman she would be an effective representative of both women and the poor; she quoted the proverb that says "It is the wearer of the show who knows where it pinches" to justify her decision. By 1997, her leadership star was shining bright; she ran for president as one of the first two women to run for presidency in Kenya (the other one running along with her was Professor Wangari Maathai, the 2004 Nobel Peace Laureate). She came in fifth and established herself as a force to reckon with in Kenyan political circles. She became a part of government in 2003, after the then-opposition parties became the ruling coalition government after winning the 2002 general elections. For the opposition coalition to win, she gave up her own goals of running for presidency instead of encouraging her supporters to vote for Mwai Kibaki. As a thank-you for her support, she was given the docket of health minister, one of the arms of government most riddled with corruption and mismanagement. However, in the 4¾ years that she was minister, Ngilu had experienced both success and failure. One of her most public failures came when her bill for provision of free public health fell through after repeated battles with several political bigwigs. She had been involved in public battles with the then-minister of finance when he said that the bill was too ambitious; the government had no money to fund it. She was of the opinion that the government had money but preferred to spend it on luxury vehicles for MP and weapons of war that the country did not need instead of serving the needs of the poor, who make up 56% of Kenya's population. Eventually the president vetoed the bill just before it became law, publicly squashing any hopes that Ngilu had for providing accessible and affordable health care for the poor. One could say that her bill was shortsighted insofar as resources were concerned—the expense of providing universal health care necessitated a larger tax base than Kenya has at present. On the other hand, she has been able to access funding from the Bill Clinton Foundation and the Global Fund toward fighting HIV/AIDS, and providing affordable anti-retroviral drugs.

Her legacy will include the fact that she reopened several public hospitals that had been run down through corruption and misman- agement in the previous regime. Ngilu was widowed in July 2006, has three grown-up children, and is in her mid-50s. In addition, she is now the minister for water and irrigation, somewhat of a demotion from the powerful health portfolio she held before. She jumped ship in October 2007 by supporting the Orange Democratic Movement instead of her president, which resulted in her being fired from her ministerial position. She returned to the cabinet in the new position and has been barely heard from since, in comparison to her radical and constant criticism of the government since her entry into politics in 1992. Whereas she continues to be considered the most powerful woman in politics in Kenya, that position is slowly fading, and her credibility is slowly diminishing.

Reverend Judy Mbugua: Continental Coordinator for the Pan-African Christian Women's Association

Reverend Judy Mbugua was one of the first women to be ordained within mainstream denominations in Kenya after a long struggle to convince her male-dominated church leadership that it was not anti-biblical to do so. She was born in central Kenya to middle-class parents in 1957, but her story is dominated by both struggle and persistence. In what she described as a foolish move, she quit school at age 16 and then promptly became pregnant. Two years later, she was married with two kids, no job, and no education. Five or six years of struggling and five children later, Mbugua decided that enough was enough. "I was fed up with failure, I was fed up with poverty, I really didn't want to stay there," she said. She completed high school through a correspondence course and undertook vocational training in copy typing, secretarial, and, later, administrative skills. As her career progressed, she felt compelled to begin a fellowship for women like herself, women who at that point in time were not included in church activities because even though they were married, their husbands did not attend church.

Through her own experience of exclusion, she invited women to meet in her home. In a short time, no home was big enough to accommodate them, so they needed to use church facilities. At the time of this writing, they had just acquired land and had built a fel- lowship hall that could accommodate 300 people. Due to her work in this women's fellowship, aptly named "Ladies Homecare Fellowship," she was invited in 1990 to pioneer the Pan-African Christian Women's

Association (PACWA) by the Association of Evangelicals of Africa, where she is the continental coordinator. Mbugua's work and ministry revolve around empowering women economically, educationally, legally, and spiritually so they will be able to uplift their families. She is of the conviction that poverty is not a virtue. She has had many fights along the way—fights with herself, fights with the church, and fights with finding acceptance as a woman leader. She epitomizes a spirited radical servant—humble enough to serve and empower others, yet strong enough to persist through struggles and challenges. Her story is recorded in her autobiography *A Second Chance*, published in 1997.

Professor Faith Nguru: Director of Research and Consultancy, Daystar University

Professor Nguru is a 1995 alumnus of Bowling Green State University (BGSU) (Ohio), my alma mater, having attained her master's and Ph.D. degrees in mass communication from the School of Communication Studies. Whereas some of the other women leaders told elaborate tales of their experiences of gender discrimination, Nguru felt that she hardly faced any. If anything, she felt that being one of the first highly educated women at Daystar University, a Christian liberal arts institution, was a distinct advantage because she was often the only woman in a room fulfilled with men; as such, she would be given many roles to play, and she used these to advance, bypassing the glass ceiling in the process. When I met Nguru, I was struck by her humility and sweet personality. She is one of those people whom others describe as genuinely good, including her former professors at BGSU. However, that sweet spirit belies a woman of amazing stamina, strength of purpose, and tremendous commitment to the mission of education for empowerment. In her professional capacity, she is an associate professor of communication studies and the director for research and consultancy at Daystar. In her personal capacity, she is the wife of the university's vice chancellor, who is also an ordained minister, making her a minister's wife, roles that necessitate a willingness to serve at any time. She and her husband instituted an elementary school in their rural village to provide values-based education to children from the village. When I asked her how she manages all of these roles, she said that it takes a lot of prioritizing and sacrificing—a major sacrifice due to the lack of time for personal social activities. However, these are sacrifices she has been willing to make because she has needed to concentrate on being a professional, a minister's and vice chancellor's wife, a mother (she has a 5-year-old child) a stepmother (her husband's first wife died 8 years ago), and a stepgrandmother. Hers is the epitome of a tempered radical and a willing servant leader.

Njoki Wainaina: Gender and Development Consultant

Njoki Wainaina is nearly 70 years old and has served as the former executive director of the African Women's Communication and Development Network (FEMNET), which she helped pioneer in the late 1970s. She has been involved in gender and development work since the early seventies and was able to narrate the progression of the women's movement in Kenya from 1973 to the present. She attended the global meetings in 1975 (Mexico City), 1985 (Nairobi), and 1995 (Beijing), as well as every regional meeting held during that period. On a personal front, she talked about how she has learned to be more tempered with age, saying that her earlier "independence at any cost" philosophy was flawed. She related that as a young woman leader she had to learn to move from independence to interdependence through the use of negotiation and dialogue tools. Wainaina said her zeal for gender and development work was a result of having been brought up in a family where all children were regarded as equal, a radical idea in those days: "I am the person I am because my parents treated us as equals. I don't know where it came from at their time, [but] we were given equal opportunities with our brothers. And I talk about feminism, and I say my father was the first feminist that I knew. He believed in women, he fought for women . . . as such, my work in gender is not an option; it is a heritage."

Wainaina recognized that patriarchy was so strong that even though she and her siblings grew up in the same home, her brothers treated their wives in more chauvinistic ways. As such, she argued that gender-role socialization has created and sustained the disparities, because both women and men support the status quo. She talked about spirituality being the basis for her enthusiasm for gender equality—all men and women are created equal. Wainaina is a wife, mother, and doting grandmother, even as she now engages in business, her "retirement career," and continues to serve as a gender consultant.

Lynne Muthoni Wanyeki: Executive Director of
Kenya Human Rights Council

When Wainaina retired, she handed over the reins of FEMNET to a young radical feminist named Lynne Muthoni Wanyeki, who at that point was in her early 30s. Six years later, Wanyeki talked about her frustration with being an administrator in a hierarchical institution, one that she found that way and has not been able to change because the board consists of older women who are not as willing to change. She had a very hard time accepting that she is a leader; as far as she is concerned, she is simply an administrator. However, through dialogue, we discussed the fact that her positional leadership has given her a national, continental, and global platform and credibility upon which to express her ideas about human rights, gender equity, and development. She is a highly sought-after speaker in the nongovernmental sector on issues concerning gender, development, and human rights, and she also writes a weekly column for the *East African*, a regional weekly paper. As such, she began to see her role as not only an organizational leader but also as an opinion leader in matters related to human rights, political governance, women's rights, and development. Wanyeki also discussed the way in which racism is experienced in Kenya, arguing that it is so subtle yet so powerful, and that it goes unrecognized:

> I think it is far more than we know. It is something that is so constantly with us that we don't even name it. For instance, the reaction we have towards Kenyans of south Asian descent, very real anger and rage, instead of looking back to how they too as a migrant community here were forced into a colonial setup. The fact that they were in business was a colonial design; they were allowed to be in business, whereas Africans weren't. They weren't allowed to be in agriculture, Africans were. I think we live with that kind of antagonism. . . . In contrast, the people we should have a lot more anger against, the (White) settler community, and yet we don't. Actually we are still trying to emulate them; we don't talk about the fact that huge tracts of land are still under settler ownership and control, we don't talk about how they perceive us . . . yet almost everything about what we aspire to is shaped by our wanting to be like them.

Her values of communalism, collectivity, and dignity for all set her apart as a servant leader, albeit a more radical leader than most. However, she too has learned to become tempered when the need arises in order to succeed in achieving real social transformation. She is also more attuned to racial issues in Kenya, having completed her undergraduate and graduate studies in Canada. Whereas in Kenya she was privileged by her status as a biracial, upper-middle-class woman, in Canada, she discovered her blackness and African identity. The values she espoused are a product of her self-definition as an African woman who has attempted to discover, through working with rural women and in women's development work, what it really means to be an African woman. As the youngest participant in the study, she was more disillusioned than the others, frustrated not only by her status as a woman in a patriarchal culture but also by her position as a woman who is considered young in a society that privileges marriage and children. She, however, still held tenuously to the possibility of social transformation and worked tirelessly to contribute to it in her organizational position and as a media personality. Her training is in political science, and she hopes to spend more time on writing in the near future. As of 2007, Wanyeki currently serves as the executive director of the Kenya Human Rights Commission, an NGO concerned with the promotion, protection, and enhancement of all human rights, including workers' rights, women's rights, children's rights, and the social, cultural, and economic rights of the Kenyan people.

Honorable Eunice Ole Marima: Community Development Expert

Honorable Eunice Ole Marima is the minister for Nairobi North in the Shadow Women's Cabinet, a group dedicated to righting the wrongs in the current government through engagement and critique. For the last 30 years or so, she has been challenging cultural biases against Maasai women and girls, empowering them with economic skills and self-improvement capabilities. She is a formidable grassroots leader who only began to gain some national limelight as the chairwoman of the *Maendeleo* Caucus (Maendeleo is Swahili for development), an organization formed with the aim of reorganizing the largest women's organization in Kenya, *Maendeleo Ya Wanawake* (translated as Women's Development Organization). She is a retired marketing and public relations officer for World Vision, a job she left after 15 years in order to concentrate on community development. Her current work is purely voluntary and unpaid, but she said that she does it because she loves it and enjoys seeing the transformations that empowering women can bring upon the community: "So I have been with those women, which was very easy because I was giving them knowledge, which they appreciate, because I believe in lifting them up. That was not so much of a challenge because the only thing I was encountering was the illiteracy rates. They could not read and balance their books but they are very good upstairs, actually somebody can track her own money."

Marima's work is an uphill battle because of the combination of high levels of illiteracy among the Maasai, social norms that discriminate against women and girls, and limited financial resources. But she is a resourceful woman and a creative problem solver: she started a self-help group, a rescue center for girls running away from forced marriages and female cut, as well as her involvement in politics as ways to solve her community's problems. "*Reto* in Maasai land is help, it's like self-help. I brought in the aspect of self-sustenance. While still at Reto, we are still addressing the issues of health, education, and actually we made education the key thing."

Marima has two diplomas, one in public relations and communication, the other in law (a diploma in the Kenyan education system is equivalent to an American associate's degree). She has made it a goal in life to emancipate Maasai women through increasing access to education. She is married to Hon. Ole Marima, a former MP for Narok, and they have five grown-up children and two grandchildren.

Shiprah Gichaga: Former National Coordinator, Forum for African Women Educationists

Shiprah Gichaga was born in the late 1940s. She recounted her experiences of the emergency period that was instituted by the British colonizers during Kenya's fight for freedom. She particularly remembered how her mother had to single-handedly feed the children, take them to school, ensure that there was food growing in the field, and participate in forced labor, illustrating what Mrs. Likimani describes in her stories of women during the Mau Mau period. She gave credit to her mother for persevering with educating the daughters because she had to fight against so many odds, least of which was community pressure not to bother educating girls. At this time when she was struggling with raising and educating the family, Gichaga's father had been placed in detention, as had most men in Gikuyuland, by colonial forces as they attempted to stamp out resistance to colonial domination. Having observed this phenomenon, Gichaga grew up recognizing the important roles that women played. She made up her mind that she was going to work very hard to get an education, as her mother had given her all she could for a good start in life. She undertook a bachelor's degree in education; only after graduating did she agree to get married and raise a family.

Her career began as a geography and religious studies high school teacher lasting for 16 years, after which she was promoted to the Ministry of Education, Science and Technology (MOEST) Inspectorate Division. Here she rose through the ranks, being promoted four times to senior inspector of schools before she opted to move on to FAWE. She began doing FAWE work at her MOEST gender and guidance and counseling desk for 2 years prior to actually having her own organizational offices. She has been at FAWE officially since 1998. FAWE's mission is to educate women and girls for development. The problems arise from cultural attitudes that degrade women and girls to a secondary status, or, in some cultures, commodities that could be used for barter trade. For example, among the pastoral communities represented by Nangurai and Marima, girls are given in marriage to old men in exchange for cattle. As such, her work at FAWE has revolved around working in such communities where girls are particularly vulnerable to increase their access, retention, and performance in educational settings. In particular, she has been involved in coming up with interventions and programs that reduce the gender gaps in educational access, retention, and performance, especially in science, math, and technical subjects.

Gichaga felt that she faced minimal gender-based discrimination; rather, her biggest struggles revolved around managing being a wife, a mother, and a responsible member of the community alongside her career aspirations. She gave up social pleasures such as attending weddings or having coffee with her friends because she was simply too busy, a sacrifice she was willing to make to ensure that girls achieve their potential by giving them opportunities for their development. In her time as national coordinator, she also squeezed in a master's degree in counseling from the University of Durham in the United Kingdom through distance learning—she does describe herself as a lifelong learner. Her leadership is guided by values such as humility, empowering others, and encouraging and enabling those with whom she works to achieve their highest potential. She retired from FAWE at the end of 2006.

Anisia Karlo Achieng: Founding Executive Director, Sudanese Women's Voice for Peace

The soft-spoken, tall, and stately Anisia Karlo Achieng is a southern Sudanese woman in her mid-40s, a separated mother of two blood children and one adopted son. She resides in Nairobi, having left Sudan due to the 21-year-long civil war that only ended in early 2005.

Her mother died when she went to help a couple who was having a domestic row; her father died later on during the war. As such, she was raised in an orphanage by missionaries, while her other siblings were taken in by relatives. Due to the outbreak of civil war in southern Sudan, the missionaries relocated to Uganda, where Achieng completed her secondary education.

While she was still in school in Uganda, Achieng insisted that the missionaries allow her to return to southern Sudan to look for her relatives; she did not appreciate living as an orphan, because as an African she felt that those who raised her siblings would appreciate reconnecting with her. This served as the beginning of her challenging the status quo by seeking alternatives to the structures that were presented as normative. She said that the nuns were attempting to direct her toward becoming a nun, but that she was not "feeling that." As such, after secondary school, she returned to southern Sudan and tried her hand at police training (too many rules) and nursing (she did not like the sight of blood), eventually choosing to engage in social work with Norwegian Church Aid. However, the war in southern Sudan again forced her out. This time she moved to Nairobi. At first she volunteered for the United Nations Higher Commission for Refugees (UNHCR), which in lieu of a salary paid for her tuition at Catholic University of Eastern Africa, where she pursued a bachelor's degree in social work. At that point, she was a full-time student, a young mother, a wife, and a volunteer for UNHCR, necessitating amazing adeptness at juggling.

Upon completion of her studies, she found it difficult to find a job. Rather than sit on her laurels, she got together with other women to figure out what they could do about educating their own people, as well as other Africans who were struggling with internal conflicts, about war and peace. After studying the conflicts in Sudan and other parts of Africa, the women realized that in all of those cases, the decision to go to war was made by men, leaving women out, yet women paid the highest price: displacement, attempting to support their men at war, war crimes such as rape and physical violence, and so on. With her leadership, Sudanese Women's Voice for Peace was instituted to seek an alternative. She gives speeches, lectures, and consultations to various groups and organizations, including grassroots women's organizations involved in seeking peace for their communities. She undertook various training programs in conflict resolution, nonviolence, women and development, and leadership to become as competent as she could be in her role as a peace builder and peace trainer. She believes that her faith has helped her weather many storms, as she has sought to serve as a peace builder and has given her convictions and values that she uses in being a leader. Her future vision includes graduate-level education in peace building, conflict resolution or nonviolence, and seeking electoral positions in the new Sudan. She also continues to be involved in the peace process in Sudan, as conflicts continue to plague the country, especially in Darfur, and to support the reconstruction efforts in southern Sudan.

Summary

In this chapter, I have given a short description of the geographical context in which the study took place. I have also introduced 11 of the women who participated in this study, including a succinct description of their personal backgrounds and leadership context. In the next seven chapters, I will provide in-depth portraits of seven women whose stories were selected based on the fact that I spent considerably more time interacting with them during the field portion of the study, and they are the most frequently quoted in illustrating emergent themes.

5

Muthoni Gachanja Likimani

Warrior Historian

My weapons are my rights, my spears and my guns are my facts, and I fight to win, as defeat is not in my vocabulary.

—Likimani, *Muthoni Likimani: Fighting without Ceasing*

Honorine Kiplagat, Africa regional chairperson for the World Association of Girl Guides and Girl Scouts, described Muthoni Gachanja Likimani as a "grande dame," a woman of substance whose vision and courage have lit the path for others to follow. Likimani is indeed an admirable if somewhat eccentric character who is always smartly dressed in elegant African attire, Western designer clothing, or even jeans and a T-shirt, depending on the occasion. She turned 80 in September 2005. In spite of her advancing age, she is eloquent about issues ranging from politics and national leadership to family and gender relations. She is a walking encyclopedia of Kenya's history, the women's movement, and women's involvement in fighting for Kenya's freedom from colonial powers. She also is a prolific writer, her most recent work being an autobiography that was published in September 2005, subtitled "fighting without ceasing." I was familiar with her work, having read and thoroughly enjoyed her book on women's involvement in the Mau Mau freedom movement in Kenya. She is well traveled in Africa and around the world and even with her advancing age, she has a sharp memory, remembering names of people, places, and details about events that happened 60 years ago as though it were yesterday.

In narrating her story to me, she recounted her early beginnings as the daughter of one of the pioneer indigenous clergy in the Anglican Church: "It is quite interesting to learn how my father became a Christian and how he met my mother who also converted to Christianity. My father ran away from herding his father's cattle." Her parents were among the pioneer converts to Christianity in their locale, and her father was one of the first indigenous Anglican clergymen.

Likimani had eight siblings, five brothers, and three sisters; she is fond of telling stories about her growing-up years and large family. One of her most critical memories is how the family lived at the periphery of the mission station, whereas the White missionaries, even when they were younger and less experienced than Reverend Gachanja, would occupy the central place of honor. In her young mind, this racial discrimination was inconsistent with the kind of God the same missionaries were preaching about. This would be the beginning of racial awareness for the young Likimani, which crystallized later with her observations during the Mau Mau freedom struggle, her educational experiences in the United Kingdom, and her participation in the postindependent Kenyan women's movement.

Likimani was educated in missionary schools—the only schools available for African children in the 30s and 40s. She recounted how the girls were being groomed for wifely duties such as cleaning, cooking, and looking after children, whereas the boys were being trained for professions outside of the home. She appreciated this education because she found use for it later in life. As she told it:

> One of the very good things our missionary teachers taught us was home economic wit practical lessons. The cookery class was well equipped, not with electricity or gas cookers, but we used wood ovens known as Dover. We were taught [the] western way of cooking, how to roast meat in the oven and cook vegetables. We were also taught how to bake cakes, scones, bread and other goodies; I must say what I know today was taught to me by my missionary teachers. The sewing classes were very thorough. We did embroidery and made fancy baby clothes. . . . Mrs. Soles used to teach us baby care at a small maternity hospital next to our school. . . . As for the home, we learned the proper way to polish wood and do the laundry. Even to this day, what they taught me is what I practice and what I have taught many others through schools, the community and mostly the radio and demonstrations on television. (Likimani 2005, pp. 23–24)

It is interesting to note that Likimani did not consider domestic education "domesticating" or "subjugating," being that it only prepared girls to be wives and mothers rather than professional roles (Kamau,

1996). The women academics interviewed by professor Kamau noted that, to them, missionary education perpetuated gender role stereotypes that limited women to the "private" arena of the home, while preparing men for roles in government, industry, and the "public" arena. Likimani's uncritical acceptance of and appreciation for missionary education may belie her missionary "compound" upbringing, where all things White were considered more "godly" and worthwhile. In fact, she does describe herself as "very muzungu," meaning Westernized and fond of most things Western, partly from having been raised in a mission compound.

After her primary education at the mission school, Likimani could not continue into high school because there were no girls' high schools prior to 1948 that would accept African children. As such, she trained as a primary school teacher, one of three options for girls who did well at the primary level; the other two options were nursing and midwifery, none of which appealed to her. She was enrolled at Kahuhia Teachers College, a stone's throw away from the mission station in which she had spent her entire life. However, as luck would have it, a teachers' college for women was started near Nairobi, and she transferred. For the first time, Likimani was able to get away from the constricting mission environment and attend a government institution. As she recalled:

> This was a good school for me. It was a government school, not a missionary school. Teachers like Miss Dorothy Dodds, Ms. Kirk, and Dr. Parry were very good and understanding. We came from many parts of Kenya and had a chance to mix and befriend girls from other parts of Kenya. . . . This was an eye-opener for me. It was the first time I could talk the way I wanted; dress the way I felt; plait my hair, which I could not do at Kahuhia; wear jewelry on weekends; and attend church if I wanted to. (Likimani, 2005, p. 25)

After her training at Government Girls Teacher Training College, Likimani returned to Kahuhia Teachers College as a tutor. Soon after, she would get married and move away. Likimani was married to a man from outside of her language group, she being a Gikuyu from central Kenya, a farming community; she was married to Dr. Jason Likimani, a Maasai and a pioneer African doctor in Kenya. She recounted her experiences as an African doctor's wife, the racial discrimination that they experienced in the colonial period, when Africans were at the bottom of the racial rung, Asians just above them, and White people at the top. In this context, she and her husband would often be denied the amenities and privileges accorded to Indian and British colleagues.

In the School of Hard Knocks

Likimani's life with her husband was tumultuous, to say the least. She recounted how they traveled to different parts of Kenya due to his frequent transfers as a government doctor. She enjoyed the status of being a doctor's wife and the opportunities it opened up for her children to go to the best schools in Kenya at that time. Behind the high life, the shopping trips to the city, the shopping from UK stores via catalogue, driving cars (a rarity among Africans in the mid-50s), and all of the other good things that came with her life as a doctor's wife, Likimani was deeply troubled. Her husband considered it his "African" duty to carry on extramarital affairs, arguing that Africans were polygamous by nature and that she should be glad he had not actually married a second wife. He was also physically abusing her, in addition to making decisions about the children without bothering to include or inform her. She told her story candidly in the autobiography thus:

> It was difficult for me to be the wife of a famous, well-to-do top medical professional. He was a handsome man who enjoyed socializing; spending time with other people, and coming home at dawn. He would spend holidays with his unknown friends, leaving me at home and of course not informing me where he would be. This kind of behavior would require a special woman to tolerate. Others survive, and many women manage. Indeed, it was and still is a common practice in most African marriages. Many women, especially wives of prominent people, would rather continue holding on to their marriages even if in practice they were already divorced. But for me, I just could not tolerate that kind of life. . . . In addition to this, any question on my part aroused his anger and ended with a fight. In my parents home I had never seen my father beating my mother. Yet with JC I had to say sorry even after being physically manhandled. . . . I quarreled with him about his moving around with other women. . . . My children were already noticing the tension. . . . One of the most painful experiences I encountered during the time that my marriage was undergoing that strain was when my husband decided to take my daughters to Tanzania without

telling me. I did not even know where my children were.
(Likimani, 2005, pp. 90, 91, 92)

Likimani opted for sanity and physical survival. She was afraid that
one day her husband's physical abuse might end in her death. Among
the Maasai community, this would not raise an eyebrow; even so-called
educated Maasai did not think twice about physically beating their wives,
because for many of them, the status of wives is somewhat akin to that
of children. But for Likimani, the emotional hurt and physical trauma
was too much to endure. In thinking back, she said that her husband
was probably no worse than any other man in his age group, but she
was ill equipped to handle real life outside of the mission station,
especially when that included physical and emotional abuse: "I admit
that some of my problems were of my own making, through lack of
advice and inexperience. We were brought up to be straightforward and
truthful. I just wish we were also told that society could be crooked!
We were taught to trust, but little did we know how untrustworthy
people could be! We were taught to be kind and considerate, but our
kindness could sometimes be termed as foolishness!"

Likimani's mission station upbringing, in her opinion, produced
an academically equipped, domesticated, but un-African young woman.
She missed out on the sorts of lessons that she would have learned
by interacting with village women. They would have advised her about
what to do in her marriage, how to treat her husband, not just cooking,
cleaning, and taking care of his children in a Western style, but, more
importantly, what was expected of her as an African man's wife. African
mothers would have advised her on how to question her husband tact-
fully, without arousing his wrath. She complained that she also missed
out even on simple things such as the games that girls played, and the
lessons they learned when they went through initiation ceremonies,
which prepared them for their cultural and gender roles in society. As
such, Likimani was a Western-educated professional woman but a very
poor African. It would take her years to learn how to be an African
woman. As the Swahili proverb says, *Asiye funzwa na mamaye hufunzwa
na ulimwengu*: She who wasn't taught by her mother would learn in
the school of hard knocks. She felt that she might also have passed
on some of those poor lessons to her children:

It is not how I dress, or trying to be an American, or trying
to be Mzungu (British). It is not that. It is who you are, with
great confidence, decency, with good direction, that is what
it's about. And I think me being a mother; we mislead our

daughters and sons of course. *Telling them to be western is what makes you civilized.* . . . It's about learning what to take from *mzungus* and what to leave; I don't hate *mzungus*, I am very *mzungu* myself. But it's to take what is good and leave the rest. You should be confident, you should never be shaken, that's how I look at it.

Here she confessed her Westernization—mzungu is the Swahili word for Anglos/White people, or someone who is Westernized. She felt that one needed to learn how to pick and choose what to take from Western culture and what to leave. That is not always an easy demarcation to create, and it took her many years of experiencing life in many different contexts to be able to finally define what it meant to be a Kenyan African woman. Likimani seamlessly moves among roles as mother, grandmother, community leader, wizened elder, political commentator, gender analyst, and prolific historian.

Personal Uhuru (Independence)

After her divorce, Likimani embarked on a path to personal independence. Having left her children behind, she moved into the city of Nairobi and began to carve out a life as a career woman. Beginning at the Railways Corporation, she used the skills she had acquired as a teacher to work in social welfare. Later on, she left for further studies in the United Kingdom. There she interacted with many African dissidents who had traveled for further studies, or who were agitating for their nations' independence from British colonial rule. She became politically aware through her observations and interactions with them. In addition, she got a job with the British Broadcasting Corporation, in its Swahili bureau service, where she interviewed women leaders from around the world and broadcast their stories. Likimani trained in media, education, and development and health and nutrition studies.

When she returned to Kenya, all of her earlier experiences would prove invaluable in her new life. She utilized her broadcasting skills in her work with the Kenya Broadcasting Corporation (KBC) (then called Voice of Kenya), where she interviewed leaders from Kenya and around the globe. She also traveled around the country observing women's development activities and broadcasting these to a national audience. She did children's programming, collecting and telling stories as *Shangazi*, or auntie. However, after serving for many years in the broadcasting services, she was passed over for a promotion, which was given to a man who had no broadcasting experience, merely because he was (1) a man and (2) a friend of the managing director. Likimani not only quit her job, but on her way out, she deleted all of the interview tapes that she had collected all those years. No way was she going to allow her new boss to use the materials she had slaved over. In spite of this action, KBC used many of her old programs repeatedly for many years: they were that good.

After leaving KBC, Likimani went to work for one of her former clients whom she had served in advertising. Here she worked for several years as a public relations personality, but was once again she was passed over for promotions. The first time a man was brought in from the outside to take a role she felt more than qualified to do. Later on, one of the boss's wives was brought in as a director, and this time, Likimani could not take any more. According to her, this woman never did any work and spent all of her time in beauty salons and spas or shopping. Likimani felt that with all of the business she had brought the company, it should have honored her with that directorship as a matter of course. So she walked out once again, but this time she vowed never to be bossed around by anybody.

Institutional Entrepreneur and Political Leader

Noni's publicity came into being after Likimani's employment discrimination fatigue, and it was a booming success because many of her clients moved with her. It was the first public relations company that was owned by an indigenous African, and a woman at that. Likimani not only represented various companies in their PR efforts, but she also began to engage in publishing her own works. Part of the reason she decided to do her own publishing was because an American researcher took her manuscript and, without her permission, published it in the United States. This was particularly disappointing to her that a woman would do that, and, in addition to publishing the book in the United States, the woman actually put a lengthy introduction in the text, making it seem like she had Likimani's blessings to publish the manuscript. Likimani decided then and there that the safest way forward was to combine publishing with her other PR work at Noni's Publicity.

She was later involved in city governance when she was nominated into the Nairobi city council for a term. As a council member, she came face-to-face with corruption and even more gender discrimination—she was the only woman in a man's world. She fought many battles, eventually getting dropped from the council. She had also tried to run for parliament but could not make it because she would not engage in tribal politics, and she did not have the money to throw around during campaigns like her opponents. She expressed some of her frustrations: "I think the worst thing in this country is fear. I have been a politician and I have been a councilor. I have even been a chairman of a very important department. There are two words I loathed as a councilor, 'to be on the safe side, don't touch that.' To be on the 'safe side' from what? You will never get [a] promotion, you will never get what you want. To be on the safe side, shut your mouth. That's one thing that, my goodness, I used to get so angry."

When Likimani looks back at her 80 years of walking the earth, she wonders whether some of her decisions were too hasty, whether perhaps she could have done things differently. If she had stayed married, would she have survived? Would her children have grown up alright, with both parents, in a "normal" family? Was she too hasty, too intolerant, or just unprepared for the realities of African marriages? Should she have quit her jobs when she did, or should she have waited a little longer? When these moments of second-guessing herself come up, she looks at everything she was able to achieve and decides it was all worth it. If she had stayed married, then she would have remained frustrated and beaten; instead, she was able to get an education and use her knowledge, skills, and expertise in development work and local governance.

Rewriting History

Likimani's greatest contribution has been in the area of writing and repositioning women in Kenya's history. Her most well-known (1985) book *Passbook Number F.47927: Women and Mau Mau in Kenya* is a recollection of anecdotes told to her and her own experiences during the first liberation movement in Kenya. As the wife of a doctor, she was protected from the worst of it. She had participated by helping prisoners communicate with their loved ones through letters. Sometimes she would go and search for them herself and bring them to the hospital, where her husband was treating the prisoners. As a Maasai man, her husband was not considered a threat to the colonial administration, because the Maasai did not participate in the freedom struggle, since the settlers were not interested in their semi-arid land. Likimani, however, had to be vetted; she was a Gikuyu married to a Maasai, and the Gikuyu were the strongest opponents and most active freedom fighters against the colonialists. Later on, Likimani talked with women who had been in the forest and who had experienced the struggles firsthand. Some of the women were involved in the forest, while others were prostitutes in Nairobi who hid ammunition and guns stolen from home guards and colonial policemen in the course of their "business"; these would be passed on to the freedom fighters in the forest. She deconstructed those stories by illustrating that whereas women were left out of the normative discourse on Kenya's freedom struggle, without their participation, the struggle might not have been as successful. She explained this in painstaking detail:

> I thank God for keeping me still alive and giving me the memory to remember the things that were going on 50 years ago; when I was young, we had [an] emergency. Our People rose up to fight against colonialism. They began a guerilla warfare as Mau Mau, fighting in the forest [Mau Mau means *Muzungu Rudi Uraya, Mwafika Apate Uhuru*, which is Swahili for "British go back to your country so Africans can have freedom"], fighting the colonialists. You read so many books. You never see the name of a woman who fought. Have you ever read any? If you have, pass it on to me, and I will return your money. Yet, even as they are missing from the written history, it wasn't because they did not participate. You see, there was a time in central province when there were no grown-up men. Every able-bodied grown-up man was either in the forest fighting or in detention. . . . So others run away and went to hide in Sudan, in Ethiopia, everywhere. There was only a handful who were also fighting not with Africans but as home guards. So the woman and her children were left alone in the central province. Who was feeding those people in the forest and when they came out of the forest they would be shot? It's the women who used their heads. One was working for me later. She told me, "I used to fill bullets in my market basket. Then I would put maize floor or beans and carry it. I would meet these armed forces, and I would say *habari watoto.*" And they would say *habari mama,* because they don't know she is the one transporting bullets. And she will go and will take the stuff to the safe place they had agreed with the forest fighters. Without that barefooted woman who has never been in a classroom, they would not have survived. Some women even went to the forest to fight, like one field Marshall Muthoni.

The woman back in the reservations would be caught up in communal forced labor from seven thirty in the morning to four thirty; by the time she walked back to her hut it is dark. And mzungu [White colonialists] were asking, these maize and beans, when were they planted? Because these women who planted the gardens spent all day at communal forced labor making a road for the armed forces to drive on to get to the forest to kill your brothers, are you with me? There is no road, there were no bridges, it's women who were making them because men were not there. And, they would still see beans growing, potatoes growing, when were they planted? Because they have been at work from seven thirty until four thirty. When did they do it? It's because they would go and organize, I don't have this, and do you have firewood? The one would give wood, the other will give some water, and the other will have collected some food from the garden and dug around a few rows of potatoes. That's what an African woman will do. They only talk about Wangu wa Makeri, what did she do other than dancing naked? I don't praise her and she is from my village. And she is in the archives and the museum, Wangu wa Makeri, what did she do? The woman who did something was called Nyanjiru, who was shot dead at the University of Nairobi when they were following Harry Thuku. When the police started shooting and the men ran away, she asked, are you men? Bring me your trousers I put them on. And then they shot her dead. She was the first to be killed during protests. But Wangu who stripped naked, what did she do for the community? That's what I was saying that a woman is a survivor. Even when she is stripped of her government job, she will still survive. In my area it is the women who put mabati [Iron Sheets] removing the thatch on their roofs. They also decided they wanted piped water at their homes, and they organized and brought it. Communally they buy cows and get milk. If you leave men alone they can't do that, but women can organize. That's what I was trying to say to support you. I am very proud of being a woman.

Likimani historicized women's status from the pre-independence era to the current period in Kenya's history, showing how women had learned survival mechanisms during their colonial experience that they utilized for their social and economic emancipation long after the colonial struggle. They were able to collectivize to deal with the constraints of forced labor in their attempts to ensure that their families survived the struggle. In postindependent Kenya, they formed rotating savings and loans organizations (ROSCAs) through which they were able to build better houses, to pay school fees for their children, to start small enterprises, and to solve other social and economic problems that they encountered. This agency and collective problem solving formed the backdrop against which the micro-credit institutions in Kenya were instituted to help women with financial resources and credit facilities.

Radical Servant Leader

In spite of her many struggles to define herself and to find a place for her to contribute, Likimani has been a spirited and radical servant leader. She is spirited because whereas her missionary Christianity miseducated her on how to be an African woman, her Christian spiritual roots have remained to this day. She has been an astute critic of that Christianity—so much so that she wrote a book about it entitled *They Shall Be Chastised.* In this book, she reflected on the conflict between missionary Christianity and traditional African lifestyles, attempting to show how Christianity disrupted the African way of life. She has continued to be involved in the Christian women's movements and in Christian institutions, including her local church. She also used the stories about African women in colonial Kenya and their agency toward ending colonial domination to help women understand that they have a role to play in public service, political engagement, and family emancipation. Her own service included women and economic development activities as well as extending a helping hand to those in need. She told many stories in her autobiography about helping poor relatives and villagers find jobs or access educational opportunities; she felt that doing this enabled her to contribute to their empowerment so that she need not give handouts; instead, she was giving them a chance at making it on their own. She utilized her position of privilege to help those who had not been so lucky by helping them rise above whatever their circumstances happened to be. In Kenya, providing the marginalized access to quality education is the route out of poverty.

Resonance

Likimani had a lot to say about many things; she had an opinion on everything that came her way, including the then hotly debated constitution review process in Kenya. However, what I took away from her was the idea that African women have been misrepresented in history, because their stories of resiliency and strength in the midst of grave local realities were left out. She explained in detail how women collectivized to solve social and economic problems. She elaborated on women's leadership capabilities by relating how grassroots women led, often without fanfare and glory, in their search for social and economic justice. She showed by her own example, especially in her short stint as a city council member, that it is possible to be involved in political leadership and not be corrupt, as is the norm in Kenya. She modeled for me what it means to be persistent, resilient, and fearless in fighting for what one believes is hers by right.

Perhaps L. Muthoni Wanyeki, who wrote the introduction to Muthoni Likimani's autobiography, said it best: "Muthoni's autobiography cannot be read as though it were only about how broader political struggles informed her personal struggles. It is also about how the personal impacts the political—in every sphere of life. It would be easy, for example, to see her life as being one that was relatively privileged, protected and safe for its time. Christian families had access to education and opportunities that afforded them a relatively good standard of living. Christian families were also less prone to discrimination on the basis of gender within them—female genital mutilation (FGM) was considered both barbaric and heathen, and Christian girls were encouraged to go to school—even if what they were streamed into in school were stereotypically female . . . [hers is] an important documentation of what it meant to be a particular Kenyan woman in particular political times" (Likimani, 2005, p. xvi). Her ability to historicize the experiences of women in Kenya, beginning with the colonial period to the present era, provides a rich backdrop against which all of the other participants in this study locate their narratives. Her rich understanding of the impact of colonialism and Christianity, both the negative and the positive, upon the lives of women in Kenya helps us better understand the experiences of women leaders in Kenya, especially as they lead for social justice relating to women's educational, legal, and economic empowerment.

6

Jeniffer Riria

Economic Justice Advocate

Women need three things: God, money, and courage.

—Jeniffer Riria, interview

Jeniffer Riria, Ph.D., strikes an imposing figure. Even though she is a petite woman, she carries herself with the authority and poise befitting a chief executive officer. Her rapid-fire conversational style suggests a woman who thinks quickly on her feet.

Meru district is located on the eastern slopes of Mount Kenya, an agrarian community most easily thought about in contemporary Kenya as the land of Miraa (Khat), a drug grown widely there. Farmers in Meru grow coffee and tea as cash crops, as well as vegetables, grains, and fruits for subsistence. This is where Riria calls home, having been born half a century ago, the fourth of 10 children born to peasant farmers. Unlike most girls in her generation, she received a primary and secondary school education, and having performed well, she managed to advance to a tertiary education. Her parents believed in educating all of their children, something that was then counter-cultural, because in those days boys were educated past primary school, while girls were encouraged to get married and have families. As she recollected, "Our area where I came from was where the missionaries first came to. People who joined the church began valuing education. My parents had 10 children, we were seven girls, and we all went to school, and we never underwent the rituals of circumcision, because my parents were Christians. Whatever people say, Christianity brought the value for Western education; I believe if we hadn't been a Christian family, we girls would not have been educated. My father sold land and cattle to take the girls to school, and he received a lot of flak from his brothers and other men for bothering to educate girls. I have a lot of respect for him for weathering cultural storms in order to ensure each of his girls was educated."

Early Influences

Riria remembers those early years as being difficult for them as children, but they were also character forming. It was a struggle to go to school, but it was hammered into them that this was their path out of rural poverty. She related:

> For example, my father would go with my sister through the bush to get to Nanyuki, which was the nearest train station, for my sister to get a train to come to Nairobi, because there was no other way to travel to Nairobi. So that was real commitment. My other two sisters who went to school in Chogoria, my father would walk with them through the forest, coz there was no other travel means to get to school. So that tells you my parents' commitment to education of girls. My parents, in spite of being poor, understood the value of educating their children, selling whatever they could to raise the school fees for us.

Perhaps this may not seem like such a major sacrifice, yet Riria's dad was doing the unthinkable—selling land and animals to educate his children, because at that point in history in the 40s and 50s the communities had not yet appreciated the value of Western education, as they were still primarily an agrarian economy.

Riria is a product of Catholic schooling, having attended the Precious Blood Girls School in Kilungu, which she credits with providing her with not only academic education but also the values and principles upon which to build her life. "I went through school based on Christian principles and Catholic doctrine. Some of the things I do today are because I had a very strong [religious] foundation at home and in school. Because we learnt in Precious Blood how to be independent. We also learnt when to call in for help; that is, the difference between independence and interdependence. We were taught to measure ourselves against the task, and figure out what we can do for ourselves and what would require outside help. Most importantly, we were taught humility. These are precious lessons that serve me to this day."

In spite of early challenges, Riria pursued education in Tanzania, the United Kingdom, and Kenya, earning a Ph.D. in women, education, and development at Kenyatta University. She taught at Kenyatta University before she was tapped to work for the United Nations on a special program called "Women Education for Child Survival," from 1989 to 1991.

After her short stint at the UN, Riria moved in 1992 to Kenya Women's Finance Trust (KWFT), assuming the title of managing director, where she remains to this day. Whereas KWFT had been instituted 10 years earlier as a micro-finance institution to serve the needs of low-income women entrepreneurs, its early years were fraught with failure. Riria was brought in to bring it back to life. She remembers her first days there:

> I stepped into my office and what I saw was shocking, papers strewn everywhere on the floor and dust on the walls. The worst sight was that of the employees. Everybody in the office hung their heads and looked at me like "just another passing MD (managing director)!" The dusty records that I could gather revealed that the institution was in great debt. Rent was due, and the salaries had not been paid. Just as I was coming to terms with the shock, someone from a donor institution came and demanded that KES [Kenya shillings]. 840,000 (the balance of the funds the institution had been given as a grant) should be transferred to another institution. The donor was upset with the non-performing KWFT and did not want anything to do with it. I pleaded with him, because this was the only money the institution had, but my pleas fell on deaf ears. The money was transferred to another institution shortly after.

This was the KWFT that Riria walked into, a debt-ridden, mismanaged institution whose lofty charter had somehow gotten misapplied.

KWFT was begun with the aim of serving women entrepreneurs, particularly those who could not access credit facilities from commercial banking institutions because they did not have the necessary property to serve as collateral for loans. Women leaders, including lawyers, academics, and those in governmental and nongovernmental sectors, got together and started the trust in order to serve the economic needs of women entrepreneurs. As stated in the trust's charter:

> The general aim of Kenya Women's Finance Trust shall be to facilitate the direct participation of women and their families in the money economy of the country and in particular those women who have not had access to the services of established financial institutions.

This lofty aim of the organization suffered in the years preceding Riria's leadership, because KWFT was run as a volunteer organization, meaning that it did not have real professionals working there. Additionally, some of the pioneer members soon started to feel the desire to benefit economically from the institution, even though it had been formed with the express purpose of serving low-income women, and they were not low-income women. (For more on those early years and for a case study of KWFT in meeting the needs of women, see Ngunjiri [2007a].)

Rebuilding a Dying Institution

Riria was proud of her achievements as the managing director and later chief executive officer of KWFT, a place where she felt her experience working on women's development and empowerment issues had culminated in excellent results. Even though she was not an economist or a banker by training, she spent time in her first few years at the institution learning everything she needed to learn about micro-finance lending, banking rules and regulations, and financial management. Riria said this:

> All my life I have spent in interventions that empower women. And this for me was a challenge to see that we can empower women through finance. Once you have clarity of mind, you find ways of doing it. Even though I was a social scientist, in two years I had trained and become a banker. I could sit with the Central Bank governor and ask him questions about the balance sheet. It took interest and clarity of vision and commitment. Once I had decided I was going to get into a financial institution, Women's World Banking [WWB], where now I sit on the board as a member and as an executive committee member, provided me with a lot of the training I required. Women's World Banking is a network of microfinance institutions and banks [serving women] around the world. I took every course I could find and read every document I could lay my hands on regarding finance, banking, microfinance, credit, etc. Of course that is based on the fact that already I had the ability to learn. You know when you get a Ph.D. you are told go out and learn. But also the support and learning I acquired through participation in other financial institutions like WWB. For

example, I sat on the NSE [Nairobi Stock Exchange], and I learnt what I could not have learnt in a classroom. I was thrown in on the deep end having come here when this institution was failing; the learning curve was very sharp. But because I was interested in meeting the challenge head on and I have self-drive, I would not allow myself to fail.

Once Riria had become an expert in financial matters and reviving KWFT, growing it into a sustainable micro-finance institution, she found herself serving in a leadership capacity in other financial institutions, such as Postbank, Women's World of Banking, National Bank of Kenya, and Nairobi Stock Exchange. Oftentimes, she found herself as the only woman serving on the boards of other financial institutions, but her desire was to see that change by helping to nominate other qualified women leaders to serve alongside her.

Challenges in the Opportunities

Leading a women's financial institution, especially one catering to low-income women and one that was in dire straits at the beginning of Riria's tenure, was not a walk in the park. Additionally, being a woman in leadership for social and economic justice was not without its challenges. Riria reflected on some of those challenges: "I can tell you right now that there are times I did not know where I was going, there were times I could cry. What did I do? I left a good job. I was a senior lecturer in the university." That was during the initial years when Riria was fighting to save the institution because of the state that it was in:

> I tell you, when I came here, this institution was on its deathbed, but I have been able to revive it and make it sustainable. I began here with minus 2 million Kenya shillings and four staff members. I now have 370 staff members, [and] the outstanding portfolio is 1.7 billion Kenya shillings. The outstanding portfolio is money that is out there with clients. This year alone [2005] we are going to lend over 2 billion to women; we are now at 6 months and we are at 1.4 billion. And I did not know where I would get the money from. The donors who were supporting the institution in its early years had been so disappointed with its mismanagement that most of them pulled out, actually

all except one pulled out. So I had to find new donors and quickly. I was a non-financial manager who had to learn very quickly to become a finance expert. Worse still, the year I started here, we had to clean up the management board to remove some of the women who were causing the institution to fail, and that of course created instant enmity. But it was necessary to remove them in order to revive the institution. Now we have a board made up of professional women who are supportive of the mission and goals of the organization. This institution came from the verge of death, to being run professionally in every department and growing to a countrywide micro-lending institution. And in the near future, we are going to become a regular banking institution serving women's needs.

Beyond the challenges that came with the professional role were also struggles in Riria's personal life. As she confessed, women in leadership sometimes face tough challenges because of the nature of patriarchy:

Now, assertiveness has not been taken very kindly by men. And that is why you see when women assert themselves, and you have heard that if you are a successful woman you are divorced. Most probably it is true, I am divorced. You begin asserting yourself and the men have remained in the 18th century. There are two choices as a woman, you either choose to be put down or you choose to go ahead and you pay a price. This society still does not recognize the value of a woman in the economy. Most of the women that I know would like to have a companion, but it doesn't work that way. And you are left asking, what do I do? So you have to make a choice, it's not an easy choice to make. And you wish you didn't have to choose between what you have to do and your natural role. But that has come for many professional women. And it's tough for women.

As the literature on women in leadership and management also demonstrates, Riria's experience is all too common: women who assert themselves or who find themselves in positions of authority are judged on a different scale from men (see, for example, Carli & Eagly, 2001). As such, assertiveness in women is judged negatively as aggressiveness or behaving like a man, and it is rewarded with negative evaluations. Additionally, women in Kenya face the struggle of asserting themselves as valuable contributors to the economy. As Riria commented, it is a culture that still does not value the economic contributions of women. In fact, as demonstrated by Judy Thongori's and Priscilla Nangurai's portraits, it is a culture that does not place similar worth on women as men, period. It is changing, but it is a slow and painful process. In the meantime, pioneering women leaders such as Riria find themselves facing the painful choice of either staying married and being dehumanized, or getting divorced and facing the ire of a society that believes that women who are divorced are too radical and unmanageable, a blame-the-victim scenario. She reflected further on this dilemma:

> So to begin to support Jennifer who is a professional who is serving the entire country, she is divorced. *That doesn't mean that she is useless. In our society she is useless if she is divorced.* Now it's changing, but a few people have suffered in the process of trying to articulate what you are as a human being in the society. For me, if I can say anything that has been difficult, that is it. That has been it. My work is not a problem because I am committed to it, I have got the skills, I am educated enough, God has given me wisdom to do these things. This [divorce and the social stigma] has been the most single difficult thing. How to combine and balance my professional life and my family life in a cultural space where if you don't do certain things you are not a good person, and I want to be seen as a good person. I am a good person. I know [I] am a good person. But [I] am divorced. Too bad. So women have to learn to accept that. It [divorce] has never become an impediment on my profession.

This was truly as sad a commentary on the state of gender relations and society's expectations as could be, the fact that being divorced places Kenyan women at a social disadvantage. Riria seems to feel the need to exert herself, to assert her humanity, her competency as a professional, her ability to be a productive woman who just happens to be divorced. When she was talking about her status as a divorcee, there was deep pain in her countenance. She has survived, but it seems to have taken a terrible toll on her, and perhaps her children too, because she explained that her daughters were all single mothers and that she was raising her grandchildren to enable them to complete their (her daughters') university education. I felt honored that she was willing to confess to this personal loss, because in our culture divorce is treated as an anathema that most (divorced) women will not discuss, even though it is a matter of public knowledge. For instance, even though Priscilla Nangurai (Nangurai is the topic of chapter 8 in this book) is also divorced, she will not talk about it at all. But Riria walked into that dark and painful place and bared her soul, demonstrating her courage and her human frailty. (In chapter 12, I explore in some detail the issue of divorce as it relates to the status of women.)

Spirituality in Leadership

One of the reasons I enjoyed talking with Riria so tremendously was because she does not dwell on the pathological, nay, her attitude is not "we have a problem" but, rather, "we have a challenge to meet." As such, whereas there are many mountains to scale, she is able to climb them, in most cases successfully, leaving behind a trail for others to follow. She has several spiritual tools in her arsenal for dealing with challenges and opportunities: "I pray a lot. I really believe that if God didn't want me to do certain things, he would have stopped me. So, when I can't go on, I pray, and God hears my prayers so much. Once I do that, I see a way out. I never get desperate. I get depressed, get really challenged, but never desperate, and I have never felt alone. [If] I am really discouraged, I feel that I can stay in bed the whole of the next day. But I pray, and I am telling you, prayer is so powerful, and I have told my staff that and they seem to have taken it in." Here Riria is illustrating how she articulates her spirituality as a source of strength in the midst of the challenges that she faces in her professional life. In Kenya, praying at the office or engaging in other overtly religious practices at work is not a problem, legally or otherwise. That is why people can pray in the office as a normal procedure. Riria actually describes how people pray before they engage in meetings as a matter of normal office protocol. As a nation, Kenyans pray during all national holiday celebrations, in schools, and wherever else they may want to pray, including at work. It is part and parcel of both public and private life to freely engage in religious expression as a demonstration of an African worldview, whereby there is no dichotomy between the sacred and the secular (Mbiti, 1969; Paris, 1995); in fact, those two terms do not exist in Kenyans' native vocabularies. Life in its entirety is a sacred vocation.

Riria talked about organizational structure and culture at KWFT aimed at providing the necessary environment for her staff to thrive at work:

We have developed a culture of caring, the institution has a culture of caring. Because we began as a very small institution, and at that point we worked together, we went to the field together. And as it has grown, we put [a] system in place that ensures that we work as teams. And if a staff [member], for example, loses a staff member, the team here at the unit office takes over, with the regional office. We are able to look after their needs both at the office level and at the personal level. Even as we grow large, now we are building capacity at the regional office to be able to take care of staff with their own personal things, problems, family. We meet every quarter with managers . . . to correct each other, to tell off each other, and to build connectedness with us. We also have very clear policies and procedures that govern how we deal with staff. I only can say that the best system is to deal with staff from a human perspective. Always I tell my staff when dealing with staff to first put themselves in their shoes and imagine you were that person and treat them as you would like to be treated. And it has worked for us; 370 staff is not small. But, even though they are scattered all over the country, we respond to their problems as soon as we are able. And [I] am not saying that it is as smooth as you are hearing me saying, I mean, dealing with human resources is very tough. But that is the approach we use, we try to be fair, we try to be professional, we try to be loving, we try to be family.

Service above Self

Riria appears to be the kind of woman who is aware of her own power, a multi-tasker, carrying on several responsibilities at the same time. She talked about how she manages all of those responsibilities effectively:

You have to be a fantastic manager of your time. You also have to be a manager who is capable of delegating, and once you delegate give responsibility, trust, and authority. You also have to work very hard. That one, you've got no choice. You have to work at overdrive, you don't have a choice. You have to be very clear about what you are doing and a good manager of both time and resources. I work through people.

I am running Postbank from here . . . delegating . . . give
guidance from a knowledgeable perspective. I have [govern-
ing] boards to report to, and I have got to report correctly.
So you have got to give yourself time. The problem is that
I don't find time for myself. That's a problem. And you
know as I grow older I begin feeling it. I wasn't feeling it
before. And you have got to pray hard that the people you
are delegating to see it your way. I don't know how I do it,
I guess it's God who helps me. I don't have any personal
interest other than serving low-income women.

An emerging common refrain is "I have no time for myself." That is,
Riria is so busy playing these roles in the public arena, and she also
talked about bringing up her grandchildren as part of her family role,
that she has no time for herself. Once again, as at the beginning of
the conversation, she credits God with helping her live her life as a
professional woman successfully. But it is also clear from her narrative
that she does not leave things to chance—she prepares herself, trains
herself, and trains her staff to take care of every eventuality.

Maturing into a Tempered Radical

The more I listened to Riria talk about her life, the more I realized
that she has had to learn to choose her battles carefully. Some battles
she has chosen, fought, and won. Others she clearly did not win, such
as the battle to stay married. She explained:

I am a terrible radical, I have been a radical all my life. I
told you all this looks very simple. But it was not easy getting to where I am. Even with my father's support, there
were others. My uncles kept asking, why are you educating
your women? You are educating women for men. They
are going to be married. So no, it was not easy being the
fourth born; by the time I was getting ready to go to high
school, the resources were depleted and the pressure had
increased. So I walked through the night, with my brother
as a chaperon and with my mother's blessing, to the near-
est bus stop 13 kilometers away, in order to find my way to
Nairobi to look for my sister, so that she would escort me
to Kilungu in Ukambani. No small feat for a 13-year-old
girl who had never been away from home. I learnt early to
stand up for myself.

For Riria, a radical is a woman who has the ability to stand up for herself against the social pressure to conform to gender-role stereotypes and cultural norms that negatively impact women's access to resources. In describing herself as a "terrible radical," she affirmed the notion of a radical as a woman who has learned through life experiences to make choices that may not necessarily be popular but that are necessary for personal or organizational survival. She further explained how her radicalism is tempered, depending on the choice at stake:

> If I can avoid a battle, I will avoid it. But if am forced into a battle, I will say, let's get into it. I will fight when I know [I] am correct and [I] am right. Do I have a doubt that I contributed to this war? If I did, [I would] very quickly retreat and apologize. But if you want a war with me on something that I know is justly mine, you will get a war. My wars are straightforward based on principle. And they can be very bitter and very long, but I will fight them. I have to know that I will win before I enter into battle. I choose to fight based on principle and the possibility of winning.

Riria is radical in that she will not let anyone or anything get in the way of her success, but with age and experience, she has become tempered, choosing which battles to fight and which to ignore. Additionally, she has described her struggles with raising KWFT from the dust in terms that made her out to be a radical, one who is capable of understanding the roots of the problem and then solving the problem by uprooting it, such as removing existing "bad apple" board members and ensuring that better ones are elected in their place.

Empowering Women, Empowering Communities

Riria constantly talked about her passion for empowering women, that being her lifelong work and legacy. She explained:

One of the things we have to do is to encourage women to save. Women have to find ways of saving. In an institution like KWFT, we help women move to another level, the level of asset creation. So when she stops working and she can't go to the market to carry that big load they carry on their backs, she has a roof over her head. She has a little savings in the bank. You know, I would tell women they have to know what they are in this world for and believe in themselves. Secondly, women have to realize they are human beings. They are not here by default. They have to realize they are part of this society, a very important part of this society. They need to assert themselves, they have no choice. They must assert themselves. You know, sometimes religion also preaches [the] low value of women. And they use this as the woman was taken from the rib of the man. Thirdly, women need to go to school. Women must attain the highest levels of education that they can so that they can measure up.

Riria recognized three factors that affect women's access to resources: lack of financial resources, socialization from culture and religion that dehumanizes women, and literacy levels. In her institutional capacity, her biggest role has to do with providing the financial resources women need to be effective entrepreneurs, thus helping to solve the first problem. In addition, women can access education loans for their children through KWFT, thus ensuring that the capital raised from their businesses is not redirected to school fees and other subsistence needs. Riria has recognized that if only women are empowered, then that may not be sustainable if the other half of the society is left powerless. More importantly, it may not be sustainable if future generations continue to be socialized in an unequal social system. Her response is to socialize the young people differently: "We have a lot to do with the male population. Mothers, we have a responsibility, because our child must be socialized differently than the norm. What your son is seeing, mom is the one who brings food at home, mom does everything, whereas dad gets drunk all day and all night." Whereas not every man is a nonsupportive "deadbeat" dad, Riria is convinced that many boys and girls grow up watching the inequalities in their own families between their parents, and they learn that these inequalities are the norm. She feels that there needs to be institutions that also help to empower low-income men, recognizing that both men and women should have economic power in order to build sustainable communities.

In listening to her story, it became quite clear that Riria's early life was surrounded by both the Protestant and Catholic religions, as her parents were involved in their local Presbyterian congregation and she attended Catholic schools. It is no surprise, then, that she would have a high regard for religion, even though she confessed to being somewhat of a "church hopper":

> I was brought up to believe that if you trust God, there is nothing you cannot achieve. So everything I have achieved so far, and especially in regards to revitalizing KWFT and making it a sustainable microfinance institution, has been because God has been by my side. There have been moments of doubt, fear, many tears, but in every situation, God comes

through one way or the other . . . something inside of me, something I don't know, which I attribute to God. It's what drives me, it's somewhere, and it's something I don't control. And even when I want to give up, it says don't give up. People don't think that, people think I am so strong that I don't want to give up. But I have my moments, my deep moments.

This "something" that was so difficult to describe Riria ascribed to God as being the guide and source of her strength in the midst of the many challenges she has had to surmount. For the most part, Riria, who is eloquent and articulate, could describe her life experiences clearly, until it came to explaining spirituality. She found, like many researchers into the phenomenon of spirituality, that it is actually quite difficult to fully explain and describe spirituality. But she could say with clarity that "it" gave her the strength to go through hard times without giving up.

Resonance

Riria rose from the position of working with women and development at the university and the UN to being one of the leading financial managers in the country, having successfully led KWFT into sustainability. She is highly sought after to serve on boards of financial institutions, including chairing the board of Postbank and being a member of the National Bank, the Nairobi Stock Exchange, and the international Women's World of Banking. Even though she did not have an MBA, a requisite qualification for most business and financial managers, Riria acquired all of the education she needed to be a successful turnaround CEO of KWFT through her commitment, diligence, and sheer hard work. She has weathered the storm of a broken marriage and the social stigma that went along with it. Like Likimani before her, she has asserted herself as a professional, a woman, a mother, a grandmother, and an effective leader, not just among women but in society as a whole. Her legacy will include the growth and development of KWFT from a minute micro-lending institution to a successful financial institution, soon to become a commercial bank serving women entrepreneurs, whether they are poor or just in need of good credit terms.

The work in which Riria has been engaged in attempting to empower women economically becomes a lot easier once another activist's work, such as Judy Thongori's, is successful. (Thongori is discussed in the next chapter.) That is because the problems that create the economic disenfranchisement of women begin with the low status accorded to women in Kenya through the misappropriation of traditional customs, norms that have come up in society that are not truly traditional but that elders and those intent on denying women their property and human rights claim to be from "our culture" in order to give such norms social acceptance. As Dr. Agnes Chepkwony Abuom (discussed in chapter 10) eloquently argued, women in traditional societies had better social status than women in most contemporary Kenyan communities. However, as the story of Wambui Otieno, referred to in chapter 2, also demonstrates, African men took advantage of the disruption caused by colonialism and missionary Christianity to "create" norms that would not have been acceptable in precolonial societies, norms that have served to subjugate women and to deny them rights to property. As such, in the next portrait, we get a view of women's property rights and women's human rights from the perspective of the law and what women themselves are doing toward their emancipation.

7

Judy Thongori

Women's Rights Advocate

I am not a rebel, I cannot be a rebel. Even though patriarchy is very high in this country, I need the sense of belonging and respectability that comes with certain social structures, such as marriage, in order to be credible in fighting for women's rights as human rights. I respect such structures and remain in them even as I challenge them and seek to change them.

—Judy Thongori, interview

Judy Thongori is an unlikely candidate for the post of fearless defender of women's rights. Do not get me wrong—by no means am I saying that she should not be there, or that she is not fit to be there. Instead, by her own admission, agitating and advocating for women's rights was not her first choice of a career. Corporate litigation was her forte, that is, until she responded to a deep yearning to do something that made a difference to those who needed it most. Hers is a story of a privileged woman who chose to walk in the shoes of the marginalized in order to uplift them.

Being On Top

Thongori remembers her early years as a competition to stay at the top. Having been born the daughter of a teacher, expectations were set significantly high. She remembers her mother insisting that she study, so Thongori was exempt from doing chores as a young girl. As such, it was no major challenge to be at the top of her class during her grade school years. However, as is the case in the Kenyan education system, all of the top girls from all of the districts end up in a select number of "national" schools. That is, the Kenyan system is stratified so that the top students attend national schools, the next level attend what are called "provincial" schools, the next level attend "district" schools, and those at the lower levels of the academic rank attend "local" schools. Many end up not going to high school, because their scores on the Kenya Certificate of Primary Education national exams at the end of Grade 8 are not high enough to gain them entry into any high school. Such students end up in vocational training such as carpentry, tailoring, and masonry. Resources and the quality of teachers are also dependent on the rank of the school, so that the national and provincial schools get the best resources, while the rest get the dregs. As such, making it to a national or provincial school is imperative if a student is going to be able to excel and gain the entry points required for admission to the few public universities.

After Thongori's primary education up to Grade 7 (the system then was 7:4:3:2—7 years primary, 4 years secondary "ordinary level," 2 years "advanced level," and 3 years at the university, until 1985, when this was changed to 8:4:4—8 years primary, 4 years high school, and 4 years university), she was enrolled at Kahuhia Girls Secondary School, one of the best girls' schools in Central Province. After her 4 years and having performed well there, she enrolled for her A level at the Kenya High School, one of the top girls' schools in the country.

Thongori is a tall, graceful, and beautiful woman who speaks very rapidly, as if the words cannot come out of her mouth as quickly as they form in her brain. She is obviously intelligent, judging by the fact that to study law in Kenya is quite competitive, as only the top-performing students from the top Kenyan high schools make it to law school. Additionally, it takes an immensely intelligent and gifted person to have been at the top in every academic venture, especially during both the university and high school years. As Thongori commented, "The first time that I had to work hard to stay at the top was in high school, because there I met girls from other top schools in the country. But I managed to make it to the top by my junior year. At the University of Nairobi Law School, staying at the top was also a major challenge, because these were the top men and women from the best high schools in the country. Once again, I worked hard to get to the top, and to stay there. This was actually when I first realized just how competitive I was."

Upon graduating from the University of Nairobi Law School, Thongori worked at the attorney general's chambers, where she felt wasted because the work was not challenging. She recounted, "I remember praying to God many mornings, God please give me a purpose for life; I couldn't have spent that much time studying only to come and hang my coat behind the door as happens in the civil service." What Judy was referring to here was the way that many civil servants would show up for work in the morning, hang their coats at the door, and go about their own personal business, rather than doing the jobs for which they had been employed. This was the malady of the civil service for a long time, resulting in an inefficient government, which made receiving services nearly impossible. For Thongori, working there wasting her precious time, skills, and abilities was simply not an option, so she prayed herself into a more worthwhile job.

Becoming a Servant Lawyer

That opportunity came when Thongori met a lawyer in town and asked him for a job. Luckily for her, he did have an opening at his firm, and she started the next day. And so began her career in corporate litigation, defending several large companies. She was so excited about her new position that she could be found in the office long after the workday was over, poring over legal documents and preparing correspondence. A year later, Thongori found the job that she credits with helping her figure out her purpose in life. She worked for Lee Muthoga and Company advocates and described it thus: "It was the greatest thing to happen in my life. It has propelled me to where I am because he [Lee Muthoga] taught me a lot in terms of humility, in terms of honesty as you serve your clients and making your clients very central. And even in terms of using the law to change people's lives." As Thongori reflected on her career and professional growth, she credited Muthoga with teaching her things she never learned in law school—that the law can be used to improve people's lives. She said that in law school they learned through the informal curriculum to prepare to work for big money and enjoy prestige. However, Muthoga exposed her to another side of working in the legal profession that she had not known existed, where making a difference is more important than making money.

Thongori made great strides in her career in private practice, becoming a formidable advocate, in her own words, excellent "in cut-throat litigation and commercial law. At that point, I really did not understand; I thought if people did not pay loans, it was because they did not want to pay those loans. It was actually quite pathetic really, my thinking at that point. I was doing great fighting for big companies, especially in the area of trademarks. Anyone who dared compete with our clients was likely to find himself defending a lawsuit." However, rather than going to her head, all of this fame and fortune actually started to prick her conscience. It was not that she did not enjoy making money—indeed, she did. But she began to ask herself the "so what" question, and she was not getting satisfactory answers. When the opportunity came up to lead the Federation of Women Lawyers (FIDA), Kenya chapter, Thongori was ready to make that move. "When I made the decision to move to FIDA, there were some people who thought I was making a big mistake. Even some of my colleagues at the three law firms I had worked in just didn't get it. But I was feeling that I needed to do something different. I was beginning to feel 'so what' if I made all this money? SO WHAT?" Her decision was not made lightly, but she simply had to change her focus in order to feel that she was making a worthwhile contribution with her know-how.

The move to FIDA, though, turned out to be challenging and exciting in ways she could not have anticipated. "When I went to FIDA, it was a move down, not up. I had come from the high court and the court of appeals, but here I was back in the lower courts. And I remember that the first case I took was where the papers had not been properly filed. I was back at the beginning, doing everything from preparing correspondence and filing papers to going to the courts on behalf of my clients. What was even more challenging was that I was not an expert on family law; the learning curve was very sharp indeed." FIDA Kenya is a nonpartisan, nonprofit, nongovernmental organization started in 1985, after the end of the United Nations Decade of Women Conference in Nairobi. The vision of FIDA Kenya is to advance a society free of discrimination against women, which it achieves through legal aid, women's rights monitoring, advocacy, education, and referral. FIDA Kenya is particularly committed to providing legal representation for marginalized and economically disadvantaged women, raising public awareness about women's rights, and improving the legal status of women in Kenya. As such, it is involved in advocating for legal reforms in order to enhance the legal climate for women, who have traditionally not had much in the way of protection, especially in the areas of spousal abuse, access to marital property, and inheritance laws. Kenya's legal system was adopted from British common law, but wherever the law conflicts with traditional ethnic customs, the ethnic customs trump the law. As such, women in Kenya have suffered major injustices without adequate legal protection, especially at the point when Thongori became the deputy director, as there had been several headline-worthy cases involving the clash between customary practices and the law, such as Wambui Otieno's battle to bury her late husband, lawyer S. M. Otieno, referenced earlier (Otieno, 1998).

Thongori's entrance at FIDA was further compounded by the political climate in the late 80s and early 90s. For one, the 3rd World Conference on Women, held in Nairobi in celebration of the end of the UN decade for women, was not well received on the political front. The ruling elite, 99% of whom were men, perceived it as a threat to their supremacy that women were agitating for their rights. But the meeting did culminate in the formation of several women's organizations, FIDA Kenya being one of them (FAWE and FEMNET were also started a few years after the conference). In its initial years, FIDA was considered a feminist organization, feminism being a maligned and highly discredited notion because feminists were considered men haters. As such, leading FIDA would not be an easy matter. In addition to the aftermath of the 3rd Women's Conference, this period also marked active political unrest in the country, ranging from land clashes in the Rift Valley province to massive movements toward democratizing the country. Riots and other civil unrest were commonplace as civil society leaders and politicians alike agitated for a change in the constitution in order to return Kenya to a multiparty state, in place of the de jure single party state it had been since 1982. In 1992, the then president rigged himself back into the top position and began a 10-year period of gross mismanagement of government resources, until that government was finally voted out of power at the end of 2002. As such, to be a woman leading a feminist organization in that time period, one was likely to face a lot of opposition and to risk life and limb in the pursuit of justice.

Thongori loves, nay, thrives on, challenges. She took on this new challenge vigorously and engaged in learning family law, discovering that there were not many laws to protect women's rights. In the beginning, she even wondered whether she had done the right thing, giving up money, prestige, and power to work at the grassroots level. But she remembers one of her friends advising her to get into her new role in family law the same way she had engaged in corporate law—with her whole heart. "I bought all the books necessary and before I knew it, I was writing about women's rights, writing about family law, and I became a respected authority on all things related to women and families. I enjoyed the challenge very much."

Bigger and greater than the challenge of learning family law, and one that profoundly impacted the way Thongori engaged in her practice of law, was coming face-to-face with poverty:

It occurred to me how legal illiteracy had affected people's lives. And especially, just how gifted and privileged we are; we had all this knowledge in our heads, and it didn't cost anything to give it to others. That knowledge given to someone who really needed it literally changed lives. I remember driving upcountry to meet a client, and when she saw me, she started jumping and screaming with joy. Having a competent lawyer was more than she could imagine. Having a lawyer who had driven 3 hours to defend her, all the way from the big city, was like a miracle for her. Now at last, her children had a fighting chance!

Thongori felt that these early experiences with poverty and illiteracy shaped how she invests her energies in legal education, because she realized more often than not that people perish, literally, for lack of knowledge.

Transformed and Transforming through Service

In reflecting on Thongori's story so far, I recognized that even though the lessons about humility and using the law to serve the needs of others came early in her career, it took several years for those lessons to mature into action. That is, it took her becoming successful in corporate law and finding her way to the top for those lessons to start to bear fruit of a different kind—the nudge toward using that success in serving those who could not pay her hefty retainer fees. As noted at the beginning of her story, Thongori grew up middle class and comfortable; poverty was an alien concept to her. But when her own success did not provide her with the inner fulfillment for which she yearned, serving the poor with her skills as a lawyer through FIDA became the avenue to find that fulfillment. She had found a position from which to lead as a corporate lawyer, but she discovered servant leadership as finding fulfillment in serving humanity. As she explained, "I could hardly believe I was the same person who used to practice commercial law; I was a changed person. That has been me."

Thongori found that serving others transformed her and also transformed those she served. As Greenleaf (1977) argued in advocating for servant leadership, the test of whether one is a servant leader is in whether the persons served grow as persons, and eventually became servants themselves. What he did not foresee or foretell is how transforming serving others could be for the servant. Thongori explained this phenomenon thus: "I stayed at FIDA for 5 years, but more importantly, I used that platform to change people's lives, to teach people through the newspapers, talking to them in churches, all sorts of places. The greatest thing was receiving feedback from women and even men who had read what I had written and had used the law to better themselves. When a person is able to change his or her life for the better using the tool of legal literacy, I am fulfilled." Thongori illustrates that servant leadership, finding fulfillment in serving others, brings joy to the servant, transforming her as well as those she serves to be better or to improve their situation. When she observed lives being changed for the better, her own life was changed.

Spirituality in Leadership

In telling her story, Thongori began with how she prayed at the beginning of her career that God would provide her with a purpose for her life. It took several years for that purpose to become clear, when she realized that she enjoyed commercial law and the success she was experiencing there, but she wanted something more than making good money. Her purpose at that point in her career came through serving the needs of those who were marginalized by legal illiteracy and/or economic disenfranchisement. Thongori explained how her spirituality impacted the choices she made in serving others: "For me, humility that is necessary to serve results from the fact that I believe in God and I know that I couldn't have gotten all this information that I have, the capacity that I have, just for me. It is because I must have been meant to serve society. So therefore, I don't think I must charge, charging for me is a by-the-way. When I compare to my colleagues who will not serve clients who cannot pay, for me, God has given it to me so that I can give it to others." For Thongori, becoming a servant lawyer was related to her theistic spirituality, the recognition that she was gifted and equipped so that she could use her skills in service to those who most needed it—the clients who could not pay because they were not able to pay. She related:

> Let me just give you an example. Two weeks ago, I was in the market buying produce on a Saturday morning when this man approached me. He said to me, "Judy Thongori I have known about you for a long time and I have a question for you. Do you mind consultation by opportunity?" That's what he called it, consultation by opportunity. And he said

that he had this issue about his brother, and explained the situation to me and in 15 minutes, I had helped him figure out what they needed to do legally. Now the woman from whom I was purchasing tomatoes, in realizing I was a lawyer, also had a question for me about her own situation, and I was happy to help her too. The reason why I could do that consultation by opportunity without asking either of these two people to come to my office so that they could pay is because of my spirituality. Yeah, it's because of that, I don't know how else to put it. That is what has enabled me to serve. So that whenever people approach me on the streets, in churches, wherever, I have no problem helping them at all. I am not expecting anything in return, that is my tithe, my 10%. I drive all over the country providing legal advice and education in churches, community centers, any place where my expertise is needed. That is my duty, to serve society, and I cannot take it for granted—I am no better than the next person, yet because of what I have been privileged to know, I have to give back. I bring nothing to the table except what God has given me.

Earning Credibility

One of the challenges of being a woman in leadership is the question of credibility—the social norm that leadership is gendered male often means that women are evaluated differently than men, and thus their credibility as organizational leaders may tank, not because they are not competent, but because the standards are differentially applied to the two sexes (Eagly & Johannesen-Schmidt, 2001). For Thongori, earning credibility resulted from both her professional expertise as a commercial lawyer and her character. "I appear to mean what I say, and indeed I do. I am passionate about certain things, and I mean what I say. And, [I] am unlikely to change positions from what I said. So for me, even if one comes to my domestic sphere to people who work for me, you find that I am the same person. The teachers who teach my children can say that I am the same person. And then also, that sheer honesty and staying power. You know what I mean, you maintain a position, taking it and dying with it." As she reflected on her credibility earned by walking the walk, Thongori laughingly commented, "Maybe that's why [I] have remained poor," that perhaps not being deceitful like some lawyers was costing her money! Lawyers tend to have a reputation for being deceitful, even in Kenya. Thongori earning her credibility in this case, then, is based on her personal integrity in carrying out her professional and private roles—she is the same person in each arena. She walks her walk in public as well as in private. This is important, because should a woman be found to have a character flaw related to public or private matters, she is judged a lot more harshly than a man. As such, she has to be a woman of integrity in order to be the kind of leader that can command a following. Thongori also earned credibility because she was a successful wife and mother.

Managing Career and Family

In Kenya, unmarried, divorced, and child-free women have a difficult time attempting to rise to positions of leadership and authority, because culture mandates that women's status is associated with being wives and mothers. However, Thongori has not had to deal with this aspect of credibility, because she is married and has children. She has struggled, however, with the idea that other women who are not married or have no children do not as easily find acceptability, so she is quick to defend their competency as capable leaders. It is an interesting dilemma, as she explained:

> There was an article written about me a few weeks ago in which they seem to have been on a mission to prove there are different kinds of women in leadership. The problem is that a lot of times when they wrote about women in positions of authority, they noticed that most of those did not have children or husbands. And they felt that they were building up an untrue picture of the African woman, because it made it seem as if women cannot combine professional success with managing a home. So they came to me asking that I talk about my family, because in previous articles they had only talked about my professional accomplishments. And I said that I did not mind talking about my family. But the reason why I often did not speak about my roles as wife and mother is because society tends to accept it easier if you are a family person, and they can be able to slot me as a mother and a wife. And I felt no, we need to fight this mind-set, and we need to show people that it's about capacity, not about so-called "natural roles." I did not mind them knowing that I do have a family, but I was wary of them

only accepting me because of those roles rather than as a professional. But nonetheless, I would bring my family to the forefront so that those who are looking up to me can know that we do get *completed by our babies*—we do have marriages that are successful, we do manage both professional and personal roles. So the magazine people took photos of my family and what have you. But then, when they wrote the story, they exaggerated, claiming that I meet my husband for lunch and talking about how I met John, stories they actually fabricated because I never talked about how I met my husband, and we do not meet for lunch—we are both very busy lawyers and have separate legal practices. But I guess it doesn't matter. The bottom line is that the feedback I got from others was that it was great to know I do have a family, that I can balance both. And for me my greatest happiness is the little girl who looks up to me who gets to know that you can manage both. I am proud of my family, because it gives me a sense of belonging, but I do not want people to only focus on that and therefore discredit those who do not have families.

As I listened to Thongori talk in her rapid-fire fashion, I was struck by how much she has accomplished in such a short time. She is only in her early 40s, she has a distinguished public and private legal career, she is a successful wife and mother, she is a member of several governing boards for human and women's rights organizations, and she manages to continue to engage in public legal education as though it were the easiest thing to do. I asked her how she manages to wear so many hats. She responded:

As you can see from the pile [of] papers on my desk and the number of interruptions we have endured in the last hour and a half, it is a heavy load. I have got to tell you, it is not easy, but then I have never shied from challenges. I have to get up at 5 every morning to get some work done before the children get up. By quarter till 7, when the children wake up, I get them ready for school. I sit with them at breakfast, signing their diaries and checking that all homework was completed the night before, sort of maximizing on contact. Then my husband drops them off at school. I pick them up between 4 and 5 in the evening and either drop them off at home or take them to their after-school activities. Sometimes I come back to the office after I take the children home. On Saturday mornings I take them for their Kumon until 9:30, before I come here and do what I need to do. So what am I saying? *Lots of sacrifices and very little time for myself!* I try and sort of focus on when it's the children's time, it's their time. My husband, he gets the least attention. Being a lawyer too, he gets the busy schedule, since his is the same. And I try, we try, to spend time together as much as we can. Sometimes we have people over to our house, sometimes we try and catch a drink together as the children engage in their activities on the weekends—it's a juggling game. But we try. And the marriage, now that I have been married over 10 years, I realize the need to invest in it. I realized that I spent so much time working on others' marriages and absorbing their stress, and so little working on my own. So in the second decade of our marriage, [I] am trying to do better on that, to pay more attention, to expend the same energy on my marriage as I do on my work. Granted, it takes two, but it helps if both people have the same focus. So I hope my marriage will be even stronger in the next 10 years.

I was inspired listening to the fast-talking Thongori describe the lessons she has learned as wife, mother, and professional, because she was not complaining. After providing me with a litany of things to do, which she goes through on a weekly basis, she was quick to note: "I try and find time for everything, and I enjoy everything that I do. It is God's blessing to me." For her, having a busy life and juggling between career, family, and community responsibilities is a privilege and a joy that she cherishes, because she feels blessed to do it all. As a single woman, I think her life sounds overwhelming, but she did not describe it as overwhelming but rather as a blessing, as something that she has enjoyed experiencing. That does not mean that her life has been a bed of roses, and that there were not some stinging thorns along the way.

Challenges in the Opportunities

Thongori related the following regarding challenges being opportunities:

The institutions we work against are a challenge, but I knew that getting in. That is why I am involved, because I want to see changes in the legal system as far as family law and laws relating to women are concerned. The bigger challenge is attempting to change the mind-set of people. That is because mind-set creates a lack of choices, even in the people we are attempting to help. For example, I may give legal advice to a woman who is facing domestic abuse, but she will say she needs a roof over her head, so she will not leave her husband, even though he is probably going to infect her with HIV/AIDS. Poverty does that to people; it dehumanizes them and limits their choices. Poverty reduces people such that they are not operating at a human level—people who do not have the bare necessities of life, who cannot take a bath and have no shelter, people who eat from the garbage dumps, such people are hardly human. These are the type of people who lack a conscience, such that raping a 2-year-old girl is not a big deal. They have become like dogs who scavenge in the dumps. When I think about crime in this country, I think part of the solution has got to be creating an economy that sustains its people so that this dehumanization process can be dealt with. We need to humanize law alongside creating a sustainable economy; the two have got to go together, because having laws will not protect us if poverty continues to dehumanize large sections of society. That for me is the bottom line.

And, indeed, this is a great challenge. Thongori recognized that one system has an impact on the other; in this case, the economic conditions that impact millions of people have an impact on their ability to take advantage of the law. Poor women who need a roof over their heads and bread for their children are unlikely to take their abusive spouses to court, because they feel caught between a rock and a hard place. No wonder Thongori was involved in creating the Center for Rehabilitation and Education of Abused Women (CREAW), which helps women victims of domestic violence in seeking legal redress as well as starting a new life. She is the chairperson for CREAW, which works alongside other organizations such as Women's Rights Awareness Program (WRAP), which provides legal advice and alternative accommodations to abused women, as well as Children's Rights Advisory and Legal Aid Education Center (CRADLE), which provides legal aid and alternative accommodations to abused minors.

Becoming a Tempered Radical

As noted elsewhere in this book, feminism (still) has a bad name in Kenya; feminists are regarded as a risk to community, translated as (extended) family well-being that is dependent on marriage, family, having children, and women maintaining their ascribed "traditional" gender roles. Yet the institution that Thongori was leading, FIDA, is a feminist organization dedicated to alleviating women's legal marginalization and advocating for women's rights. As such, leading FIDA meant that Thongori was often the target of attacks, branded as a radical feminist who (unbeknownst to her detractors) could not keep a husband or be a productive wife and mother. Yet she is a wife and a mother; she has been married to fellow lawyer John Thongori for over a decade, and they have two children. Even though she was only at FIDA for 5 years, her legacy and fame are still connected to her former role as the deputy director of FIDA. And she does recognize that she is a radical, one who stays true to her beliefs and feelings. "If I believe in it, I will die with it," she says.

A radical is one who is willing to critique existing social structures, in her case, legal structures, deconstructing them to show the injustices they perpetrate against women, and reconstructing them for a just society. Thongori is not afraid to challenge the government, the legal system, or ethnic traditions, as long as they invalidate the value of women or cause harm to women in any way, shape, or form. She has been at the forefront of leading the charge in reconstructing the legal system as far as family law is concerned. Even after going back into private practice, she continues to educate the public through the media. Thongori has a national platform on television, where she engages three politicians in debating matters of national interest, such as constitutional review, the Sex Bill, and other issues. The three politicians are also lawyers, so the debates in which they engage would not only be about political issues but also about legal issues of national interest, such as bills being discussed in parliament that could affect changes in the law. Because of the credibility she earned through her leadership of FIDA, and her continued engagement in public legal education, Thongori has become a national thought leader in family law and women's rights issues, something she says she first figured out that she could be while she was still a student in law school and that she has continued to use as part of her repertoire of leadership tools.

Becoming a tempered radical—one who knows the issues to deal with immediately, the fights to pick and die for, and those to let go in order to fight another day—has enabled Thongori to climb onto and stay atop the national platform as an authority on family law. As she noted, "I am not a rebel, I cannot be a rebel. Even though patriarchy is very high in this country, I need the sense of belonging and respectability that comes with certain social structures, such as marriage, in order to be credible in fighting for women's rights as human rights. I respect such structures and remain in them, even as I challenge them and seek to change them." That is the true mark of a tempered radical, attempting to create transformations in social structures or organizations from within. As such, when Thongori speaks about rape and domestic abuse, she is listened to, because those she is addressing, both men and women, can say, well she is married, so at least she must know what she is talking about. As she recognized, "Nothing could be more tempting than to shout from the rooftop, but you know the occupants of the commission, the holders of the law, are men. I think one has got to remember that change is a process. And one has got to start somewhere. For me, understanding the obstacles, adversaries, and working towards changing them is the real test of wisdom."

Resonance: I Am Because We Are

Thongori recognized that she did not reach the heights of success by herself, but that she has received support and encouragement from many sources. She credited Lee Muthoga, one of her previous bosses and currently a judge at the Arusha Tribunal, with teaching her "the humility that ought to attend to the practice of law." She received mentoring and feedback from others, particularly judges who helped her in constructing her professional path. Such feedback prompted her to want to be the best, not just an average lawyer, but the best that she could be. In the same way, she encourages young lawyers to find their niche and to be the best, especially young women lawyers. But the greatest source of encouragement has been her family, both her nuclear family, with husband and fellow lawyer John, as well as her mother and other relatives. One of her greatest joys is meeting young women lawyers who say they want to be like her. She feels a thrill in knowing that she is a source of inspiration to others. As she says, "I left FIDA to younger lawyers to give them space, and even here in my private practice, I will leave after another 8 years and make space for others." She felt that since she is gifted with vision and the ability to see the bigger picture, it behooves her to be a source of light to others along the way. "I like to give encouragement and direction to other people and their projects. I cannot be everywhere, in every board that exists. But I can give leadership by providing advice to those who want to start legal organizations, especially when they are related to seeking justice for the marginalized. I get very excited when I give someone advice, when I can help someone." As she gesticulated and articulated her joy in providing help, I commented on her rising excitement, to which she responded: "I am! I am! I get so excited, I feel so good. I like to solve problems." Hers was an inspiring story of using one's education and resources to serve, and, in the process, finding that serving fulfills the servant leader.

8

Priscilla Nangurai

Warrior for Girls' Education

Only in her own hometown and in her house is a prophet without honor.

—Matt. 13:57, paraphrased

Priscilla Nangurai is the quiet, even shy, but formidable and unyielding former headmistress of African Inland Church Girls Boarding Primary School, located in Kajiado, about 70 miles southeast of Nairobi city. Whereas I had never met her before, I had read and heard about her in various circles due to her unflinching campaign against forced early marriages in Maasai land, and her mission of giving girls a safe place to get their education. Reverend Joyce knew her well and introduced her to me, saying that her story would give a different but necessary spin on the whole question of what it means to be a woman and a leader in an African context. When we got to Kajiado, Nangurai was waiting for us eagerly. I was struck by her simple dress and polite mannerism; it was really difficult to envisage her as the woman who had gained notoriety for her daring to contravene her "culture" by giving Maasai girls a refuge from forced marriages. I was expecting an angry, loud, and fiery warrior. Instead, here she was all shy smiles and open arms.

Defining Moments

Nangurai was born in Ngong on the outskirts of Nairobi in the late 40s. Her father was an employee of the colonial government working in the department of forestry and would later become a Christian due

to the influence of the missionaries in the neighboring Kikuyu Mission.
Nangurai told her story thus:

> I am an old-timer. I am here by the grace of God. I was
> born in this district. I come from a family of eight, and I
> was the sixth born. I have an elder sister, and I learnt a lot
> from her. My elder sister went to Alliance Girls' High School;
> she was one of those girls who went to Alliance when it was
> African Girls' High School, but she was withdrawn and mar-
> ried off. I always remember that day; I was a little girl, [and]
> my father came home and found my sister talking to some
> men. He was very annoyed, because she was supposed to
> marry another man. So he was very annoyed and withdrew
> her from school and gave her away in marriage. When my
> sister was given away, she took me with her, and she wanted
> to give me what she never got. So I went to school around
> here (Kajiado). I did my KAPE (eighth-grade exams in the
> old colonial/missionary education system) and managed to
> join Alliance Girls' High School in 1962. My father had to
> sign a paper to say that he would not withdraw me from
> school the way he had withdrawn my sister. My secondary
> schooldays were not so easy; nobody came to visit me, but
> I think I got used to it, because we were many that were
> not visited. I completed secondary school in 1965 and
> joined Kenyatta University College in 1966 for a bachelor's
> degree in education. After I graduated, I went to teach in
> Olkejuado High School, down the road from here, as I was
> trained to teach secondary school. I got married in 1970,
> and by 1974 I had to move out of Olkejuado to join my
> husband in Mombassa, where I taught at Aga Khan High
> School. Then my husband was transferred again to Nairobi,
> and I decided to come and settle at home, so I came back
> to Olkejuado in 1977.

Nangurai began her story with the statement, "I am here by the grace
of God," setting the stage for the conversation by placing her story in
spiritual terms. Then she went on to describe her early-beginnings story
in a matter-of-fact, even shorthand version—that she had witnessed her
sister being withdrawn from Alliance Girls' School, which was the first
and at that time the only girls' secondary school in the country open
to African children, to be married off. Perhaps this experience at her
tender age set the stage for what would later become her mission in
life—rescuing girls from the fate that befell her sister.

Foundation for a Tempered Radical for Social Justice

The second defining moment in Nangurai's life came while she was a teacher at Olkejuado High School. The governing board had decided to make the school a single-sex one. She explained: "The AIC church started AIC girls in 1959, under the Africa Inland Mission as a boarding school because of the nomadic way of the Maasai people. So I was appointed as head in 1977, but I didn't come then. Olkejuado was a mixed school, but they decided to phase out the girls in order to improve the academic performance of the school. I wanted to quit in protest, and so I came to AIC, where I had been appointed head, this time in 1980."

Nangurai told me this story matter of factly, but later on at the focus group meeting she elaborated on that defining moment as she responded to a question about women in the boardrooms:

> I was in this board for Olkejuado secondary and I get to the meeting, and they are discussing removing the girls from the school to improve the performance of the school. So they are making these decisions, yet when I asked what the background is and how they reached here, he said, "Do you know you have no right to speak here?" And I said, actually I do, I am a member of the board, and we are not in a Manyatta, and I need to talk. And he started cussing at me in kimaasai, "She has no manners." Do you know that night I could not sleep because it was so hurtful. Because there were only two of us women at that board, and our opinion was neither sought nor heard. Later I went home, [and] the matter was reported to my husband. And I told him I am not apologizing, you go and apologize because I won't. And apologize for yourself, not for me. And it really brought hustle at home. So I can understand if you are the only woman and the men are much older; these are the people who want to try to silence you because you are young, so that means unqualified to speak. Interrupt them.

Nangurai elaborated on what had taken place at Olkejuado before she quit and moved to AIC Girls' School. During this conversation, she espoused a bravery and courage that looking at her shy and quiet personality it was difficult for me to visualize her challenging a group of elders; the man in question was her own father's age. In Maasai culture, a woman has no room to speak up; a young woman has absolutely no space, even on a school board, where she was appointed because

of her position as a teacher. She rebelled against the school board
and the elders of her community who reported her "bad manners" to
her husband. This was a defining moment, in that it was the turning
point for her; she quit and moved to AIC Girls' School to attend to
the needs of girls. It may also have been a defining moment in her
marriage, because later her husband would divorce her upon the urging of the elders—they felt she was behaving like a man, challenging
the status quo and contravening her place as a woman by engaging
in her rescue mission.

However, even though she moved to AIC Girls' School because it
gave her the opportunity to serve the needs of girls in Maasai land, it
took another few years before she realized an opportunity to engage
in the battle against some of the cultural malpractices. She explained
how this compelling mission began:

> For three years I tried to find out why the girls were not
> performing well. I noticed that girls were dropping out a
> lot. I was younger then, and I really feared the culture of
> our people, so I did nothing about it. So up to 1986 I did
> nothing, but in that year, one of our girls went home and
> found out she was going to be married off. But she said no.
> She wrote a letter to the district commissioner [DC] asking
> us to find a way of rescuing her. So the DC came, and I told
> him I was afraid I couldn't do it, it's something I would like
> to do, but I can't do it. The DC went to the fathers' place.
> Lucky for her, she had not had contact with her husband.
> Because, traditionally, we stay for 5 days before we move to
> the husbands. Lucky for her she was rescued, and she came
> back here. She is one person who really inspires me. Because
> during the holidays she said, "I cannot go home, because
> they will marry me off." I did not know what to do with her,
> but after talking with my family, they agreed to house her.
> When we succeeded with Charity, I thought to myself, no
> other girls will be forcefully married off if we can help it.
> The beginning was very rough, because the fathers would
> come here and demand to have their daughters back. We
> didn't have a fence here, and they would come to pull away
> their daughters. The district commissioner was kind; he gave
> us protection which when you are given police protection
> it's not very comfortable. It's very disturbing but necessary.
> So we started with one girl, and others began to come.

Nangurai, though fearful of contravening culture, saw an opportunity and grabbed it: here was a girl who had found a way to flee from forced marriage; the district commissioner was willing to help by giving them protection; and now it was up to Nangurai to help Charity get her education, undisturbed. When I talked to Charity, who happened to be visiting the day I was interviewing Nangurai, she said that whereas what she was doing had not been done before, insofar as running away and seeking help from the provincial administration, she was determined to complete her primary education. At the time when she was being forced into marriage, she was only in the sixth grade. She was able to complete primary school, attend secondary school, and train as a nurse. She worked in her rural community bringing much-needed health care to her people. She also said that she had reconciled with her father after she completed her education, because she was able to bring him blankets, seeking his blessings. When her parents died, she took over the responsibility for her younger siblings, whom she has educated. Nangurai's success story is part of what keeps her inspired and motivated to keep fighting to save girls. "When you see your successes, it really encourages you. And I know I have kept saying I will leave. But when you see Charity and others like her, it's very encouraging."

Social Contradictions of a Leading Woman

Nangurai's life as a woman and as a leader is filled with contradictions. On the one hand, she was the principal of a girls' school, where she attempted to help reduce the illiteracy rate among Maasai women by providing a safe haven for them to get their education. This should be a commendable role; instead, she has endured many years of being treated as a cultural traitor. She has struggled with knowing that the community that she has served diligently for most of her professional life has little appreciation for what she has been attempting to do in educating their women. Both the men and the women struggle to understand her mission. She described it thus: "It's very difficult to hammer these things into our people's minds, especially because they are so illiterate. I believe education opens up the mind so one can think further. I keep telling them that's why [I] am giving the girls an education, so as to open their minds so they can see beyond what their mothers see. When I talk to the women, I realize that they don't even realize that they are disadvantaged."

As a Maasai woman herself, Nangurai has been able to see beyond what the rest of her womenfolk could see. In the aforementioned statements, she illustrated what is being echoed by all of the women leaders—both men and women support patriarchy, which is why it is so difficult to change their mind-sets. However, Nangurai continues her mission; in fact, she planned on continuing with the mission even after she retired in December 2005. Her vision was to build a shelter on her property in Kajiado town so that she could continue to offer the girls a place to stay during school recess. Perhaps the greatest contradiction in her story was the fact that the people she was attempting to help did not seem to realize that they were disadvantaged. In most cases, the girls ran away from the forced marriages and FGM by themselves, with no help from their mothers—actually the women are the ones who conduct FGM. However, Nangurai reported that it is not all doom and gloom. Some of the parents whose children ran away (such as Charity) and managed to get an education now appreciate the contribution the girls are making. But this is a rare occurrence, as she explained: "We have received a lot of support, but the community is like, right now you can't tell whether they are for it or still against it. From the year 2001 I started seeing that the men are coming to look for places for their daughters. They will also come in to say thank-you for keeping the girls here and giving them an education after the girl has succeeded and is working and is able to help. So they appreciate that. A few parents have come, and it's very gratifying." Because of their pastoral lifestyle, it is difficult for the Maasai to receive an education—their literacy rate is a mere 18% in a country whose literacy rate is 85%. However, girls are doubly marginalized, as they can be married off in exchange for cattle to add to the herd, limiting their access to basic education.

Cultural Warrior: Spirited, Tempered, Radical, and Servant Leader

For Nangurai to survive, thrive, and succeed in her chosen mission of educating Maasai girls, she has had to become a tempered radical, attempting to change her people's mind-set and cultural norms while living and working among them. She has chosen to serve her people, yet being a highly trained, experienced teacher, she could have taught in any other school in the country. Instead, she chose to contribute to the emancipation of her own people, to help them move along the self-development path. She has experienced what it means to be a tempered radical who is an outsider within her own community. She described some of her survival mechanisms thus: "You have to respect the elders. Even though you know they are against you, [you] still play your part. And to be a leader you have to be a servant. You have to set an example. You have to be a good example. You have to block your ears and be focused. You should not allow people to move you from your goal. You have to have a vision and a goal. You have to be focused on doing something which is empowering Maasai women. You have to fit in with the community; you should not be above them, and you should be with them so that they can listen to you."

In reality, what Nangurai practices is fitting into the culture while also being a radical critic of the same culture. For example, she talked earlier about her experience at the Olkejuado board meeting, where she challenged the elders. Yet in the previous quote, she is advocating respecting elders. She has to manage the contradictions and paradoxes of her outsider position in order to change the status quo. In addition to advocating for respecting elders, she also encourages her girls to learn about their culture. She explained the intricate maneuvering that goes into managing the situation for herself and for the girls as well:

> So these girls, when you listen to the girls, they have different stories. Some of the girls are brought here by these lobby women who are at divisional levels. Some are brought by their mothers. We have a few mothers like that. Some are brought by the chiefs. Many come on their own. They just ran. And when we go to talk to them we teach them some of the skills they can use. We tell them they should not say no to a marriage. But they should then negotiate and say they would like to first complete their education. But if the father[s] insist, you go along with them depending on how far away you are. The girls have to be brought to Kajiado town to do their wedding shopping. Some of the girls run during that shopping trip. Going against the traditions and the culture was not easy. I forgot to tell you that we hold culture talks where old women come and talk to the girls on their culture. Sometimes we hold debates; we go through the cultures and say which ones are good, which ones are not, and some of them walk out in protest. Especially when we touch on circumcision. But it's important. It's important for them to know what is expected of them as well as how to maneuver within the cultural space.

I did listen to four stories upon Nangurai's recommendation, girls who had run away from forced marriages when they were barely 10 years old. One of them had run away from getting the cut and found her way from Transmara district to AIC Kajiado by hitchhiking (that is at least 200 kilometers away). Each of the four girls had a vision for what she wanted to do, which included going to college and engaging in a career that would involve giving back to her community. Perhaps the girls were inspired by their headmistress's story and others who had gone before them, like Charity, and wanted to be like them, as far as giving back to their community and getting a university education.

By having those cultural debates, Nangurai was enhancing the girls' critical thinking and cultural engagement skills, so that they would not become aliens in their community; instead, by comprehending the good, the bad, and the ugly of their cultural context, they would be better placed to contribute to their own and others' emancipation. It is no wonder that girls like Charity and others who were products of Nangurai's gentle prodding had achieved their educational goals and returned to the community as teachers, nurses, and social workers. Their success was her reward, better than all of the awards and bestowals that she had received over the years from various organizations.

Resonance

I was struck by not only the simplicity and shyness evident in Nangurai's demeanor but also her apparent gentleness of spirit and strength of character. Whereas I knew that her husband had divorced her because of her work, upon the advice of the Maasai elders with whom she continued to clash, Nangurai totally refused to talk about this. She simply kept repeating that one had to make many sacrifices, and that her biggest struggle was attempting to manage her mission and her family life. What follows are snippets of her expressions about her situation as a woman and as a leader in her community:

> Going against the traditions and the culture was not easy. . . . In my community women are not recognized. . . . But in the community I am not very much respected, because they take me as someone who thinks she is superior or equal to the men, that being one of the reasons why our people don't educate the girls. They think that if they do the girls will feel equal and they can make their own decisions like looking for a husband for themselves. And deciding not to

get married which is wrong in my community.... I go by the verse in the Bible, where Jesus said a prophet is not honored in his own land.

Nangurai serves her community, whether the people thank and recognize her for it or not. She is convinced that educating girls will enhance the life of the entire community. Hers is a story of quiet determination and persistence in the face of shocking odds, all for the purpose of elevating the status of women in her community, who would in turn emancipate the entire community. She has paid a high price—losing her marriage, losing face in the community that treats her as a cultural traitor, and living in a state of dishonor. As she described it, only in her hometown and in her own house is a prophet without honor. She, however, is not alone in her struggle to assert her humanity and dignity through thankless service. She is not alone in attempting to change the status of women, one girl and one woman at a time.

9

Esther Mombo

Ecclesial Gender Equity Advocate

Righteous Indignation Fueling Action against Injustice

I first met Esther Mombo, Ph.D., when she was visiting New York in March 2005 attending a UN consultative meeting on gender. She and Reverend Joyce had come as part of the Kenyan delegation to the UN meeting. She is a professor of church history and theology from women's perspectives at St. Paul's Theological University, Kenya, as well as the academic dean. She is a graduate of St. Paul's, Trinity College, Dublin, and Edinburgh University, Scotland. She is active in the Circle of Concerned African Women Theologians and is a prolific writer in the areas of women's issues, evangelism, HIV/AIDS, Christian-Muslim relations, and poverty in Africa.

Defining Moments

Mombo was born in Kisii district and brought up by her maternal grandmother, who supported and encouraged her to become a "woman preacher" in a culture where women continued to be demeaned and undermined. As she was telling her story, it was evident that she greatly admired and respected her grandmother, who had broken with tradition and gone to school, something that was very rare in the 20s, when her grandmother was a girl:

> I was her first grandchild, so she was happy to be with me. I went to school from that home. She is the one who taught me the Bible, she ensured I went to Sunday school and actually taught me a lot of our history through stories that had a moral implication. Because she was among the first girls in

her village that broke with tradition and went to school, she
ensured that I went to school. So she told me orally a lot of
the Bible stories. She also was a preacher in her own right.
She was among the ladies who went to preach to women
in prison. When I look back I think I did theology perhaps
unconsciously not realizing she had a very big influence on
my decision. She had a passion for those women in prison.
In the village she was known as the preacher.

As Mombo thought back to her upbringing, she realized that she
might have chosen to study theology and work in Christian institutions
because of her grandmother's influence. Mombo attended primary
and secondary schools in Kisii before she moved to Nairobi to attend
high school, and after high school, she moved in with a relative who
promised to send her to college. However, the promise was not kept,
and she ended up serving as a nanny to her uncle's children for a
year. This infuriated her to no end:

An uncle of mine said to my grandmother and my mother
that he would take me and would help me to continue with
school. But I ended up in his house working as the house
girl. I was a relative, yet they turned me into their house
girl! I helped to bring up two children. I woke up at 5 [a.m.] to
go get milk, then get back and prepare breakfast. The house
wasn't hers, she shared with another family. I couldn't sleep
in the sitting room, since that wasn't theirs. Me and another
girl for the other family we slept in the kitchen. So I slept in
the kitchen next to the fridge, and I did that for a year. One
thing that was said while I was with them was that I cared
for the children as if they were my own. And other women
would come and say how come you have such a good house
girl. I did that coz these were my uncle's children; even if I
was being paid, they were still his. At the end of the year I
decided I was going to go to my own home, rather than my
grandmother's. My father was very angry with my mother
coz he said here your brother took our daughter that he
was going to help her go to school instead he made her a
house girl. I remember when I left that home, I told my
aunt that I have taken care of your children while you did
your degree, but I will get more degrees than you. I came
from a home that was very poor where we have the house
for parents, and the other house that has chickens, calves,

and goats is where we children slept. So I was sitting there with my mother, the goats, and the calves feeling really angry coz I felt that I had wasted a whole year when I could have been in school. My mother was very good in cooling me down. But I felt really cross. I kept telling my mother one day I will even drive to my aunt's house. I told her I wasn't just meant to be a house girl. At the time you could get a job as an untrained teacher. My father did not want me to go back to school coz now he wanted me to contribute economically to our family upkeep. So I went and was hired as an untrained teacher.

The anger that Mombo expressed at the injustice she suffered under her aunt's hands is a defining factor in her life. It propelled her to want to succeed and surpass her aunt's one degree, and to make sure she would not be at anyone's mercy ever again.

Gender Discrimination in Religious Institutions

After her experience with her relatives, Mombo was hired as an untrained teacher, a defining factor that would determine her later career goals. She amused me to no end when she talked about her inspiration in theological school, that fear of her grandmother made her keep on the straight and narrow:

When I accepted Christ, I felt that God was calling me, but I couldn't be exactly sure where. I wanted to teach adults not children. But I felt that there was a whole area of struggling to convince my father. My father had thought I was going to get married to someone they had chosen, and they felt that because he had a job he could look after me. But they didn't realize there was no way I was going to rely on a man to look after me when I had nothing. So I joined theological school against my father's wishes. But my mother got the wrath of it. I remember him telling her that the day I came home pregnant, my mother and I would both be thrown out of the home. So I feared men, because I did not want my mother to be thrown out. As I went to theological school, my grandmother also told me that I need to remember that the men in there may be Christians but they are real men. So I operated from two sources of inspiration: fear

and the knowledge that I shouldn't trust the men in the
school merely coz they were Christian. And how true my
grandmother's words turned out to be!

Mombo went to theological college against her father's wishes but
with her grandmother's blessings, because she felt a calling to serve
within ecclesial circles. It was amusing to realize that even within her
community, which is not particularly traditional, merely 2 decades ago
fathers still expected to choose spouses for their daughters. But Mombo
would have none of it.

When she joined theological college, Mombo faced a new challenge, that of attempting to fit into a decidedly male and clergy-filled
arena:

> I entered through the gate, and the men asked me, are you
> sure you are coming to this school? Are you sure you are not
> going to KTTC [Kenya Teachers and Technical College] down
> the road? At the time we were six women in a community
> of 80 students, one married woman [and] the others were
> single. But in theology we were not welcome. Two women
> in the class with 20 men; every derogatory remark was made
> against us. We felt we were in the wrong place. The college
> was particularly male—male in structure, male in the content
> of teaching. Male even in the cafeteria, it was just a male
> place, and we were made to feel like intruders.

Mombo's story resonated with me because it was my experience when
I entered a graduate seminary in Nairobi; it was the same feeling of
being unwelcome, and more often than not, men, whether lecturers,
students, or staff, would tell us women that we were in the wrong place.
I guess little had changed between the early 80s and the beginning
of the new century: theological institutions were still male dominated.
Mombo's struggles were only just beginning; her experience while in
training was merely a harbinger of things to come. In her first day
on the job in a theological school, her entire class—including one
current bishop, walked out on her, this after she had struggled to get
that posting:

> Job hunting became difficult. So I went back to teaching,
> I went to a school that belonged to the diocese. I still felt
> that I wanted to teach adults. So I tried to get a job in a
> Bible school. While the bishop said that he wanted to hire

me, the council wasn't ready to hire a woman. But after a
while he called me for the job. But, a, they couldn't give
me my own house and, b, some of the students said they
couldn't be taught by a woman. They couldn't give me my
own house because I was a single woman, and how could
they control my morality? So my morality was questioned. I
had to live with a local parish priest. And [in] this house I
was treated as one of the women; if it [was] to cook or clean,
I did it. They were very conservative people theologically.
People whom if you plaited your hair or dressed in a certain
fashion you were not born again. I decided I wasn't going
to change my outlook. I had my earrings and I plaited my
hair and dressed not in an overly dressy manner, just in the
way I could afford. And the parish priest was my student coz
they had been ordained before training. And I just took the
job, and the first day I went to class, the students said they
couldn't be taught by a woman. Only three students remained
in class, and actually I taught the whole class period. I said
to them I had been given a job and I was going to do it. If
they refuse to come to class that is up to them. Because the
tribe in which this school was situated had a very low place
for women; they regarded women as children.

In spite of her educational attainments, Mombo would soon learn that
sexual discrimination did not end in her theological college, but that
it was alive and well in other theological institutions and in the church
as well. The students who walked out of her class were local priests;
one can only wonder how they treat women in the churches.

Becoming a Tempered Radical and Servant Leader

Mombo attempted to fit in as best she could in order to carry out
her mission of educating church leaders. She cleaned and cooked
alongside the other women in her new home, humbling herself to
live under a student's roof just so that she would accomplish her mission. She was rewarded from an unlikely source for her thankless and
unrecognized work:

Because I was the top student in my graduating class at St.
Paul's, I received an award to do a master's program in the
UK. So I went to my dad and told him I would be leaving

for UK. My dad was very proud of me and he put together a going-away party for me. My uncle came; by this time we had made up, and he gave a very good speech. I went to Ireland, [and] I did my masters degree and wanted to stay on, but I chose to come back. Also, because I couldn't get an extension, I couldn't get more money to go on with school, and I didn't want to hide around like many people do.

Higher education did not end Mombo's problems with gender-based discrimination:

So I came back with [a] master's degree, thinking I would be treated differently, like at least I could get a house on my own. They still didn't want to give me a house of my own. The available house was next to the living quarters for male students, and they didn't want to give it to me. I remember one of my colleagues asking "if they could trust her to teach the men, why couldn't they trust her to live with them?" But it was decided that now *where will she hang her underwear*? You have grown as an African woman and you know we do not hang our underwear outside, so how could this be the deciding factor as to whether I could get a house next to the men's hostel? But that was a big thing in the council meeting. So here I was, with a master's degree. I taught in various places as an adjunct. But actually for some strange reason I chose to work in that particular school. I felt a call to work in this school, even though I earned less than my students. The church and that diocese had very few clergy, but by the time I left, my colleagues and I had trained about 60 clergy. But back then, the support I got was from male colleagues, who had been in Europe, who treated me as a colleague not as a woman. And they made sure that the students understood I wasn't a woman, I was a colleague. Even when I was being treated as a child and my morality [was] being scrutinized, my focus was that God had called me here.

Mombo was discriminated against on several counts: age, gender, and marital status. Within Christian institutions in Kenya, age is revered; being married with children is next to godliness—her experience with age and "childlessness discrimination" resonates with my own. This is a product of both African traditions, where family is of paramount importance, and mission Christianity, which advocates for women's most important work being wives and mothers. As such, even though Mombo had a master's degree, getting a job and obtaining suitable living quarters was a struggle. But Mombo was convinced that what she was doing was important—it was a compelling and divine mission to help train clergy for the church in that region of the country. Her relationship with God gave her the strength to persevere through the many struggles. Whereas she is not ordained at present, Mombo felt that it was necessary for the church to ordain women to enable them to become effective and credible leaders in the church. As such, she undertook a crusade to convince the diocese to begin ordaining women, and since she was not asking them to ordain her, she became a credible campaigner: "While in that diocese I initiated the whole dialogue on the ordination of women. Between 1985 and 1995, I spoke about it in every synod. And at first they would chase me and tell me to go away and get a husband. I made a lot of mistakes back then, coz I was young and didn't know how to play the game. I began politicking coz I realized you had to find ways to gain the men's trust. By 1990 they had agreed in principle that they would ordain women, so it was working. By the time I was leaving to go and study for my Ph.D. I knew change was inevitable."

In spite of her many mistakes, perhaps because zeal *without knowledge is a dangerous thing*, Mombo managed to get the diocesan leaders to consider ordaining women. Eventually, she succeeded in convincing them, and the Anglican Church in Kenya was among the first mainline denominations to ordain women. In addition to her success with this vision, she had also managed to elevate the status of her family by building them a good house and supporting her siblings in accessing educational opportunities. Afterward, Mombo managed to get another scholarship, this time to undertake doctoral studies at Edinburgh University, Scotland, where she undertook research on women's contribution to the growth of the church in Kenya. Upon her return, she faced the challenges she had left behind; how to get a fitting job within church-related institutions: "When I returned, again, I couldn't get a job. Because I have been within the church and I wasn't one to go back to public universities, coz I felt that I had been with the church and I wanted to contribute to the church, I want[ed] to critique the church from inside. I job hunted and taught in various places for a while. Then I saw a job advert in St. Paul's and I applied for it."

Eventually Mombo got a job at her alma mater, St. Paul's University. Her drive toward working in church institutions was the desire to contribute to the church by critiquing it from within, the mark of a tempered radical. In spite of knowing the struggles awaiting her in church circles, she chose to serve where she felt she could have the most impact. Her struggles intensified, because not only was she back in a theological institution, but soon she became the academic dean. She recounted her struggles:

> In some ways I have had colleagues [who] are supportive, and others who say we are being ruled by a woman. So I have to find ways to survive, coz one side says it's wonderful we have a woman; others said "she is just a woman." So what exactly is just a woman? We have students who feel you can't deal with them because you are a woman, not just a woman but a laywoman in a heavily clerical environment. She is just a woman in a context where a woman has to be identified with her husband at my age. So since I don't have [a husband] that is a problem but for me, they serve me just fine. But for them it's like [an] oddity. So if I become assertive, I am not motherly, if I become motherly, I am not assertive. So both ways you are a loser. So you better do one thing.

In this context, it seemed like Mombo could not win, however much she tried. If she was assertive, then she was not motherly, if she was motherly, then she was not assertive enough, a struggle faced by other women in leadership. In addition, her being single was working against her. However, some of her colleagues once again appreciated her and her work. Students she taught in her earlier college teaching position felt that they did not have to listen to her because she was merely a woman. In most cases, the students who attend theological training tend to be middle-age men who have been in clergy positions and who have decided to get training, and in most cases, they also come from rural settings, where opinions about women in leadership are still unfavorable. However, Mombo was not going to give up. She served as best she could, taking upon herself the names they threw at her and turning them on their heads:

> The first management meeting we had, I learnt that a woman was being sacked because she was suspected of having done an abortion and she is a single woman. So I come to the management meeting, and I am sitting there with six men and [I am] the only woman. I quickly look at these papers, and being a leader, it clicks on me. I couldn't tell

you who she was, but I knew I had seen these two women and she was probably one of them, both were single. I did not know them personally. I had nothing to say about them. So I raise my hand and I raise a point of order, could I be given a little bit of the story about this one. One man there says, "We finished that." And I said no, it's matters arising. And this man in management kept saying I am his daughter. And I said to him no, I have no father here. The relationship I can have with you is that of a brother, you are my brother, and you can be either my elder brother or my younger brother. And what I was resenting then, when he said a father, then I cannot question anything they say. So I demand that I be told. So they said she had bled and the clinical officer had confirmed. Have we found out who made her pregnant? They are all shocked. Why? I said, she did not make herself pregnant? Then the chairman decided we have a feminist in our midst. So they start calling me a feminist. So, students are calling me a feminist, these men are calling me a feminist. I figured I might as well capitalize on this label, do everything feminists are known to do. I shall ask the odd questions here. So I insist the man who made her pregnant needs to be known. And I said, [I] am single, I have just accepted this job; I haven't signed anywhere that I am not going to be pregnant. Neither have I signed that I am going to get children from a husband. Neither have I signed that I won't abort. I know it is illegal in this country, but this woman, it's true she aborted. She did it because she could not afford a baby. In this country, there are women who can afford to have a proper abortion, but she did it the way she did because she was poor. So it shows that you pay poorly, so she had to take whatever concoction she took to help her abort. The White guy on the management committee went home and told the wife, hey, here we have an African woman who is telling off these African men. She went home for 3 months on suspension and she was reinstated. Unfortunately she died, because whatever she had taken, she never got proper medical attention. So my fame was going on, both negative and positive. Because they had called me a feminist, I just said I was going to capitalize on that. So I continue[d] on the management committee, and I made sure I read all the information beforehand, because as a woman, I really needed to know what is going on so

that when I asked questions or whatever, they couldn't say
it's just a woman.

Here Mombo figured out that the best way to deal with her situation was to take upon herself the terminology that was being used
to describe her and to use it to her advantage, to do whatever they
believed feminists do. She thus decided to crusade for the betterment of the women on campus, both students and employees. She
also learned survival tactics that she utilized in handling the board,
being very prepared for every meeting so that she would contribute
from knowledge instead of ignorance. In addition, she attempted to
stand up for women; even when she was aware that the woman was
in the wrong, she felt the need to stand up for her because the man
was not being punished, yet the woman in this case had not gotten
pregnant alone. She was not justifying the woman's actions as much as
explaining those actions in relation to the bigger structural injustices
and institutional culture. Changing the culture required many smaller
changes, as Mombo related:

> The Rentokil woman who brought the services said when
> she first came to ask about it, she was told that the college
> had no women. I realized I needed to mobilize the women,
> so I invited them to my house for fellowship. In my classes,
> if I was doing history, it had to have a component about
> women. If I was doing theology, I would even start with a
> quote by a woman theologian. So the feminist thing is going
> on. It didn't go well with the hierarchy of men. My leader-
> ship is challenged; for some people, it's a breath of fresh
> air, for others you are still a woman. I remember my first
> graduation charge, as the academic dean, to the effect when
> they went to serve in the community, don't tell women to
> persevere when they are being battered, ask why they are
> being beaten and rescue them. I was not going to apologize
> for being a woman.

The Rentokil woman about whom Mombo is speaking came to provide
sanitary disposal in women's bathrooms. In this quote, she illustrates
the paradox of her situation: on the one hand, there were those
who appreciated having a woman's touch in leadership; on the other
hand, the majority did not like having a woman in such an important
position. But Mombo had come to serve the community, and she was
determined to prepare clergy, both men and women, who would serve

the communities they represented and who would be sensitive to gender relations in those communities. Like the other women leaders in this study, Mombo found a way to use her skills and competencies to serve the institution and the community, to be a change agent. To increase the number of women in the college, she had to raise funds for their tuition and living expenses and be sensitive to women in their roles in church and the advantages of acquiring theological training. She also admitted women who would otherwise not be welcome in the college, such as single mothers; ultimately, it meant challenging the norms and customs that barred women from enrolling at the college.

In addition to supporting her family, Mombo also decided to extend her mothering by fostering three children, boys between 9 and 15 years old, whom she educates and provides a home to. This was a counter-cultural move on her part, because society expects her to get married and then have children, and after having her own blood children, she can then go ahead and provide a home to children from the extended family who for one reason or another need a home. Instead, Mombo decided that she had the financial capacity, the nurturing instincts, and the commitment to go ahead and foster these children and give them a safe home. Her servant leader stance extended from her public roles to her private one as a foster mother. An unmarried, child-free woman, especially one over age 40, has low status in the African community. In fact, Mombo talked often about being "seen as a monster" for not being a mother and enduring outright insults from men in management, such as "Go get yourself a husband." By choosing to provide a home to needy children, she was both giving herself the opportunity to play the role of a mother and going against the cultural grain that dictates that the only way for women to be socially acceptable is to be wives and (biological) mothers.

Deconstructing Patriarchy

Mombo comprehended the contradictions in her personal situation as a woman leader, as well as in the wider social construction of gender in general. She argued that both men and women had been socialized into patriarchal constructions of gender, so that in advocating for change, oftentimes she found resistance from both men and women. As such, her work involved helping women understand the roots of their worldview and behavior, even as she advanced change strategies such as increasing their numbers in the theological college and supporting them financially through scholarships. In her advocacy and action, she was not pro-women or anti-men; rather, she felt that it was necessary to bring about change for the betterment of the entire college as well as the communities that both men and women clergy would be serving.

To illustrate the social construction of gender in Kenya's highly patriarchal society, Mombo explained by deconstructing some of her experiences:

> Gender is not just a women's problem; patriarchy affects both men and women, and even men suffer under its effects. . . . But being single, it's the mystery of who sleeps in your bed rather than how well you perform. You have no identity unless you are Mrs. And even when you are reverend, you should be reverend Mrs. And a doctor, you should be doctor Mrs. Why can't they use just one of them? Using both means that those who only have one title are not reverend enough or doctor enough. And that second title sometimes is used against me. They would stand up and the one who has doctor Mrs. is given more room to speak, more voice. And this doctor without, someone would say, I wonder how someone can serve in this ministry without a husband.

Mombo's experiences with discrimination based on her marital status meant that even though she was fully qualified for her role as academic dean (she won the job by merit), she often faced resistance to her authority as a leader. Men as well as women questioned her ability based on her lack of a husband. But this did not stop her from doing her best to serve a community resistant to her authority. One of her sources of support has been the Circle of Concerned African Women Theologians, a network of women theologians from across the continent of Africa. Upon her arrival at St. Paul's, Mombo helped inaugurate a circle chapter, bringing together women students, faculty, and staff from the college as well as other women theologians, pastors, and priests who work in churches and para-church organizations. The activities of the circle have resulted in St. Paul's offering the first-ever master's program in HIV/AIDS pastoral counseling in Africa, a very timely preparation program to help deal with the scourge of the pandemic. In addition, it has offered support and networking opportunities for all of the women concerned and a place where they can discuss and come up with strategies for survival in their male-dominated religious work settings. The St. Paul's circle birthed what they metaphorically called the "square of concerned male theologians," a group of male priests, pastors, and theologians that is willing to join in the struggle toward making religious institutions more gender sensitive for the betterment of society.

As the highest-ranking woman in theological training circles in Kenya, Mombo represented the country and continent in several important international commissions, such as the Eames Commission, which produced the Windsor Report; the commission was charged with producing a report and recommendation for the Anglican Communion worldwide after the New Hampshire Diocese appointed a gay bishop. Mombo was of the opinion that whereas homosexuality is a hot and divisive topic in the church and in social and political circles, in 10 years' time, it may not be an issue.

Resonance

Mombo's life has been fueled by righteous indignation against injustice, beginning with her own experiences under the hands of a relative and continuing through her many years of work and leadership in Christian institutions. The anger that she felt against the injustices perpetrated against women in Christian institutions and churches energized her action to level the playing ground and change the modus operandi of the organizations within which she worked. For example, she contributed to the ordination of women in the church by her constant activism for the same, and she proved that she was not doing it for selfish reasons by not seeking ordination for herself. She also managed to increase the number of women in theological training to ensure that the excuse for not giving them positions of leadership in the churches would not be that there were no theologically qualified candidates. She has demonstrated by her life and example that persistence pays: it took many years for any of the changes she was attempting to bring about to actually take place, but she never gave up. She also demonstrated deep resiliency in the face of amazing challenges, some extremely personal and humiliating, yet she went on unflinchingly, doing what she believed was her calling: serving Christian institutions to prepare leaders for the church in Africa.

In her personal walk, Mombo chose to take a difficult path by fostering three children in a society where that is considered counter-cultural. Her faith is thoroughly actionable, and her beliefs are evident in all of her words and deeds. She is a mentor to many others, helping women persist in spite of the challenges they face in Christian institutions and churches by coaching them and leading by example. Whereas she herself had no mentor when she was coming up in the ranks, she recognized the importance of mentoring others. She also recognized the place for networks, and so she worked in collaboration with other women theologians to fight injustices in Christian institutions and churches in Africa, as well as to provide direction for difficult issues such as HIV/AIDS counseling and care. Her story would make any leader, man or woman, think seriously about quitting or giving up in realization that persisting may actually be the wiser though more difficult course of action. Whereas her work is primarily leading a Kenyan institution, some of Mombo's engagement has been on the Pan-African (such as with the Circle of Concerned African Women Theologians) and global scene (such as the conferences she attends and participates in at the UN and for the Anglican Communion).

10

Agnes Chepkwony Abuom

Peace Advocate

The question of bread for myself is a material question, but the question of bread for my neighbor is a spiritual question.

—Nikolai Bordyaev

Agnes Chepkwony Abuom, Ph.D., likes to quote the above saying in her many speeches about social justice. She was another participant whom I did not know and had not heard about until I started making inquiries about possible women leaders to interview. Reverend Joyce recommended her, because at the time, she was the (lay) African president of the World Council of Churches (WCC), a position of ecumenical oversight and direction for all Christian churches that are members of the WCC. Abuom is also the executive director of Taapco, a human and an institutional development consulting firm, although she hardly has any time to spend there because of her busy schedule. In the time I was in the field, Abuom was out of the country more frequently than she was within the national borders. For instance, we met for the first time in early June to set up an appointment; this could not take place before mid-July because she was away during the intervening period. After our first appointment, she traveled to Sudan and then to Nigeria before our second appointment a few weeks later. She could not participate in the focus group because she had to be present at the memorial service for Dr. Garang, the Sudanese revolutionary leader who had served as vice president for just a month before his sudden death.

When I met with Abuom for our first conversation, I was impressed by how easily she jumped into the meat of the study. I had earlier given her all of the documentation supporting the study, but unlike everybody else, she seemed to have perused through the consent letter. Our conversation began something like this: "When you look at the continent and in this country in particular, I can see the resilience of the African women in terms of economic survival and ensuring that in spite of all the bartering of the family structure, she holds the unit together. She becomes the pillar. To leave her at the pictorial image of a beast is not telling the whole story."

This was the part of the conversation that I got into the tape recorder after I stopped her to seek her permission to audio record our conversation. She launched into deconstructing the history that has been provided in textbooks (she has a Ph.D. in history) and the dominant discourse about the status of women in Africa by attesting to the resiliency of the African woman, which became sort of the theme of the whole conversation. Thirty minutes into this discourse, I was able to steer her back to her early beginnings.

Defining Moments

Abuom was born and brought up in the Rift Valley province of Kenya. She remembers her African Christian upbringing with nostalgia: "I grew up in the hills of Nandi, and I come from a very strong Christian family, two girls and one brother. My mother had basic education, but she couldn't continue. She trained to be a community development assistant. We are only three, but I have sisters who are not biological. In terms of schools, I went to a missionary boarding school, in the border of Nandi and Western Province. It was a Canadian Pentecostal boarding primary school. Then [I] came to Limuru girls, and found the Australian missionary ladies."

Abuom talked about her family structure, including sisters who are not biological, suggesting that her family included children who had been added to the family, perhaps poor relatives who were adopted into the family. This is quite common in African families, whereby one finds biological children, as well as near and distant relatives, all living as children of that family. After her primary and high school education in Christian schools, Abuom proceeded to the University of Nairobi, whereupon she embarked on a short-lived student leadership and political engagement career. Short lived because she was soon expelled: "I was expelled from Nairobi for leadership reasons; that's how come I went to Uppsala, Sweden. We had the first peaceful demonstration in the universities in this country organized by [the late]

Ooki Ombaka, myself, and four others; I was the only woman. We led a strike. Actually it started with the faculty of architecture where the Danish dean would pass only Indians and not Africans. These Africans would go outside to Europe and pass. At one stage of marking there was a problem. And we staged this peaceful sit-in, and it coincided with an election year of 1974."

Abuom's retelling of her expulsion from the University of Nairobi was as a matter of historical fact, but this was actually a defining moment in her life. In those days, there were only two public universities in Kenya, Nairobi and Kenyatta. As such, to be expelled from one meant that one's chances to acquire higher education would be curtailed. There were no private universities in the country back then. Her expulsion indicates that Abuom was known for being a radical student leader, and she was thus targeted for discrimination by the government, which was intolerant of dissent. After expulsion from the University of Nairobi, she and her comrades embarked on campaigning for their leaders of choice for the 1974 parliamentary elections, choosing leaders whom they felt supported their social justice goals. Her comrades are all historical figures in terms of fighting for social justice in Kenya, both within government and as activists within the civic commons. During this period, she was also involved in the National Council of Churches of Kenya's "Solidarity with South Africa Movement," a group whose focus was on supporting South Africans' efforts at freedom from apartheid. She got a job with a local Christian publication, titled *Target*, and she worked there until she left to complete her studies in Uppsala. She said that the *Target* editor gave her a job because no one else would touch her with a 10-foot pole because of her political and social justice activism.

During her university education period in Sweden, Abuom enjoyed the exposure she experienced by being in an egalitarian political system and student-centered learning system. As such, what had been meant as an evil act, Abuom's expulsion from the University of Nairobi, would later turn out to be a blessing; a chance to travel abroad and pursue her education as well as being exposed to a different social system. She explained: "The Swedes were a very good solidarity nation with various countries. So I was exposed to solidarity and what people can do about the oppressed and marginalized. I was also exposed to a small but democratic country. I got involved with the Lutheran church. So my education is basically from two cultures, the Swedish culture and the Kenyan-British culture, which are very different cultures. The British, you are pushed through the system, (whereas) the Swedes you are left to organize yourself."

Critical Ecclesial Leadership

Abuom was of the opinion that how she got involved in church work would interest me, so she explained:

> My coming into church work will interest you. I went to Zimbabwe as a research fellow for 2 years. And most of the exiles were there, I found Micere Mugo again over there [one of her comrades from the University of Nairobi, who was also expelled and who is a noted author, forced into exile in 1982 due to her political activism]. I wanted to be part of an academic fraternity in Kenya, so I applied to Kenyatta and was taken on in the faculty of history. And so I came and before I could settle down, I was put behind bars in Nyayo house here. I had been fighting for justice for a long time then and didn't stop when I came back to Kenya. It was a woman who sold me out, you can't believe it, you know. So I was put in a cell; it was a false accusation so they entered into a *nole prosequi*, but I then couldn't get a job.

In essence, Abuom ended up in church circles because she was considered "too hot" because of her social justice activism and would not be safe elsewhere; she was too radical to fit into the system, especially in the higher education arena of the early 80s. At this period in Kenya's history, there was a lot of unrest on university campuses, with students rioting and throwing stones as they dissented against government excesses. The government did not tolerate dissent and criticism, and lecturers who dared speak against the system were detained for lengthy periods without trial. Notable scholars such as Professor Ngugi Wa Thiong'o ended up being jailed without trial and, upon release, had to leave the country and go into exile. As such, with her history of activism as a student, Abuom was deemed unacceptable to teach in the university setting, in spite of her excellent qualifications. However, she could fit into the church, because the church has been, since the mid-70s until the current period, the most vocal critique of government corruption, human rights abuses, and mismanagement of resources. Abuom found a ready home within the Anglican Church circles utilizing her training in history and development studies to serve the church and local communities and as an active critic of the government.

Abuom not only critiqued the government for its abuses, but she also critiqued and sought to change the church for its failures too:

If you look at the struggle for liberation, it does not profile women leaders. Look at this dispensation and look at what women did, but listen to the names, listen to the stories, look at the papers. They will not profile women. Even in the church, when the church was struggling, it wasn't only Bishop Gitari and Bishop Muge and Bishop Okullu [Anglican Church primates who actively dissented against the government, advocating for release of political prisoners and for multiparty democracy]. I wrote a paper sometime back where I said the struggle for democracy by the church was good, but the prophetic voice was only limited to a few [male] voices. Yet the struggle was a broad-based struggle. Again when you want to look honestly at political leadership, even where women have contributed, [when you] listen to Mau Mau and pre-Mau Mau, you will find that our history has gaps, and they [women] are not spoken about.

In this conversation, Abuom sounded much like Muthoni Likimani in her claim that, though replete with women leaders from as early as the 1920s, the recorded historical canon is only about men's participation in the freedom struggle.

Abuom went on to explain this lack of gender representation in Kenyan history texts: "There were women actively involved in every community. I mean, must Wambui (Otieno) fight for herself? Irrespective of her personal life, she was a freedom fighter. Why did she have to speak for herself? Why do we only speak of the Onekos and whatever?" At this point, I mentioned that the book that Wambui Otieno had written, detailing her life as a Mau Mau agent, her marriage to the late S. M. Otieno, and the cultural/legal wars that ensured from his death, is not available in Kenya. Abuom continued:

That is it. If it was a man's book and whatever, it would be available. If you look at the church, look at the women who have struggled as deacons and priests, you would be surprised by how many of those we have. But the creative things they are doing are never told. They are taken over by the men. So, you can go whichever side, we have to really claim, it's reclamation, and it's a restoration process. I would say we need to deconstruct church structures so that they become people structures, and build others we need to reconstruct because they have been broken. I would use the same analogy for leadership, because there is certainly the things that need to be deconstructed and others to be reconstructed. And at the heart of it is the mind-set of the people.

Abuom critiqued the abuses, excesses, and gender-related injustices that existed not only in the government but in the church and in society as a whole. She opined that before the broken-down gender structures could be reconstructed, they needed to be deconstructed, to be understood as the product of a social mind-set. Most critical in her view is the gender gap that exists in social discourse about men's and women's contribution to development, social justice, and community. Women had been left out of the discourse. When stories of social justice activism were told in the church and in the nation as a whole, only the stories of men were told, leaving out women's contributions. That could explain why I had never heard of Abuom prior to beginning the fieldwork for this project, yet I knew about all of the men she mentioned. That is, all of the bishops who had constantly critiqued the government, some to the point of being killed in freak accidents, and the men who had been detained by the colonial government due to their freedom-fighting activities. Nowhere in this discourse and written history did we ever hear the stories of women such as Agnes Abuom, Wahu Kaara, Muthoni Likimani, or even Wambui Otieno, to whom they all refer in relation to their freedom-fighting activities in the first or second liberation movements. The first liberation movement in Kenya was the Mau Mau freedom struggle to gain Kenya's independence from British colonial rule. The second liberation struggle was the movement to free Kenya from despotic leadership, to change the country back to a multiparty political state, to bring about human rights such as freedom of speech and association that had been seriously curtailed during the regimes of Kenyatta and Moi (1963–1992). This second liberation struggle really began in the 60s, soon after independence, but it gained urgency in the 70s during the second half of first president Jomo Kenyatta's rule, when young politicians and University of Nairobi students often engaged in active critiques of the regime. Some of the results of the era were the killings of J. M. Kariuki and Tom Mboya. Moi's regime perfected this reign of terror, especially after the coup attempt in 1982, resulting in several young politicians and university professors being detained, with others fleeing the country for long periods of time. Abuom was actively involved from the 1970s. She knows from personal experience what the torture chambers at Nyayo house looked like. The church provided her with a (relatively) safe haven from which to continue her engagement with social justice activism. Anglican Bishop Muge was killed in a freak accident after a particularly public disagreement with a politician, so being in the church did not ensure one's personal safety.

Deconstructing Patriarchy

Abuom recognized the social structures that keep women down, that hinder women's ascent upon the corporate, ecclesiastical, or government ladder: "We are waiting for women to become leaders after they have nurtured and sent the children out of the home. But that would be too late, it is too late. But it's because of the models. Look at the church—when do we convene meetings, now it's the time to start going [it was about 7 p.m.]. Are you not making it difficult for that woman who has a family? Where will she grow her leadership style, where will she be pointed out, where will she be recognized?" The social norms and organizational cultures inhibit women from accessing leadership positions because they are structured in favor of male participation.

Abuom also considered the many struggles for women after they have bypassed the social, cultural, political, and economic glass ceilings to arrive at a leadership position. Using her own story and those of others that she knows intimately, she discussed the struggle to have their authority recognized:

So leadership cannot be nurtured in a vacuum, there has to be a platform, there has to be space. The spaces we have today, if I didn't have the example of my mother, if I didn't go to school, and as I was telling her, even now as the African president (of WCC), I have to fight for my recognition. And you know what they say. That bishop said, "When it comes to sitting, that one we know she will represent." It's like grudgingly accepting the position of a person, the space of a person. I give you the example that women will go through in the church. When I became the Africa president, the first for this region of Eastern Africa, West Africa has already, but men not women, I came to the national council, and I told them, we were having an executive committee meeting. Normally we pray for people who are in leadership. So I asked them, could you also pray for me? They never did. They never did. Why? Because I am a woman. . . . It's a big struggle. Not just a struggle of recognition but where possible even the spaces get narrowed for you. It's like it's automatic when archbishop has a function for the general secretary of NCCK [National Council of Churches of Kenya] to go, but it's not automatic that you have a president of WCC in your church. It's not automatic that you will be invited. So that creates problems. And that's why you see it pushes women into this fighting mode that also ends up being counterproductive, because you only affirm what their prejudices are. And because they control media, they just portray you as an aggressive female. The politicians keep blocking the 30% representation in parliament, because they can't handle even the few that they have 6% currently. You see, the Kenyan woman, in the midst of struggle and survival has become so strong that the man is threatened. We have got to break this cycle of imbalance, because women's leadership is not to repeat the mistakes of men['s] leadership.

The aforementioned struggles and contradictions that Abuom has discussed are evident in most areas: church, the political arena, the human rights arena, and every possible space that women occupy as leaders is riddled with these contradictions—they have positions, but not authority. In addition, Abuom credits her upbringing, her parents, with modeling for her a culture of complementarity, where her father could and still does what are otherwise considered female roles, such as cooking, when the need arises. For Abuom, this culture of complementarity has been irreparably altered to a culture of competition:

The second one is the culture, the identity, the African women was always consulted. We don't have kingdoms in Kenya, but whatever the case, when decisions were made, the women had their say, perhaps at home before the men went out to make decisions, but they did have their say. So when we look at the African palaver, the men would be in the middle, the women would be at the back. But the discussion doesn't start in that palaver, the discussions were already done in the house, and the second sitter has already stated her position. And when they notice that the men are off [on a] tangent, then you will observe how they relate. When they say the power behind the throne, the British talk about the power behind the throne, but in Africa the reality is that the power resides behind the throne with the woman. Even when you look at marriage, look at the *muthoniwa* processes, even in ensuring that immortality and continuity of life goes on. Who else will you look at except the kikuyu and the Luhya? Look at the child festivities; it's the women who lead. Look at the Kikuyu and Luo homesteads. In the polygamous setup, every homestead that exists, who is the pillar? It is the woman. Look at the property division. Take the Maasai. *People say, o the Maasai are not gender sensitive. It is not until we got the commercial economy that the Maasai woman was completely destroyed* [emphasis added]. The Maasai woman, all the milk products were hers, all the hides were hers, she determined what to do with them. All the animals she got at the wedding were hers.

Again, Abuom deconstructs social structures as they exist today by returning to history, to the precolonial and pre-Christian eras, when many ethnic cultures in Kenya and Africa were constructed along dual-sex or complementary gender role setups.[1] Her comment about the Maasai came as a complete surprise to me; having spoken with two Maasai women (Ole Marima and Nangurai) before I met with her, I had heard a different story about cultural practices that subjugated women. Instead, Abuom, with her clear understanding of African history, was telling me that the current status quo is not, strictly speaking, cultural; rather, it is the result of traditional culture's violent interaction with a capitalistic, money-based economy. The same could be said of some other traditional cultures in Africa that are critiqued for being gender insensitive and abusive to women. The changes in social structures have created the conflicts and contradictions, yet this discourse is missing from our history books—it is not the story that is told about our traditional cultures. Abuom was attempting to help me understand how this came to be, that what we call traditional culture today is actually the confluence of real traditional culture with a market paradigm that supports competition instead of cooperation. What we have is confusion and contradiction,[2] as Abuom explained: "We are cultureless. We are actually cultureless in the sense that we are aping everything. Because, look at today's draft constitution which says division of property should be equal between the two genders of children. I tell you, in the [real] Nandi culture, if I was unmarried and a woman, I would inherit part of my father's property. In this context, the boys are saying no, because they have taken on something they don't know. But [traditionally] that was uncontested."

The flux state in the cultural transition from traditional to contemporary has left the African communities at the point where they are neither traditional nor contemporary; the norms now practiced are not sanctioned by modernity or tradition; that is part of the source for the social norms and gender relations that we see now, because people behave as the "market" dictates, or anything goes. It is no wonder that Maasai is the worst example of commoditizing women into an expendable good, but only the worst; each ethnic group, to a varying degree, subjugates women in Kenya. This is especially visible in the bride-price process, whereby women are essentially "sold" to their husbands, an abuse of a tradition that was supposed to demonstrate the family's appreciation for the woman's natal family. During the colonial period, this practice changed into an almost commercial transaction.[3]

The alternative, as contested by Abuom, is to deconstruct and reconstruct social structures, to decolonize our mind-sets, to free ourselves from mental slavery and begin the process of self-emancipation and self-definition necessary in creating a just community. Thus, Abuom says:

> That is why we need to decolonize the men. We need to decolonize the men from the prison of wrong/false notions and ideas about themselves and about their own communities Reason being: Number one, these very men are not able to actually exercise power and authority fully in the context they are in, because they are also captives of another force. Neither can they do it in the family fully, because they have lost it and are living a false reality. So we need to look at decolonization as a process to change several realities. And that is what the women were saying during our initial gender training in the Anglican Church. Women in Nairobi and Central were saying, we know what the problem is. It is not us, it is the men. Secondly, the other decolonization that is critical is of the woman herself, especially those of us who have been alienated through education. The higher up in education you went like me, the more alienated you became. So you don't belong and in the modern so-called culture that we are in, we cannot exercise authority and leadership, can we? We can't, so we are worse off than my mother and my grandmother. You see, my grandmother was an evangelist. And she moved beyond community. She had more power than I have. Yes. She had more leadership. More voice than I do. Because the way they related with her husband. For me, now we are in this competitive enemy-like culture. So we are both losers. Because in the competitive culture that we are in, my husband becomes

envious, it becomes conflictual because the woman cannot go beyond (the man). Whereas in the traditional culture, you could lead, as long as your leadership traits [were] evident and there were clear boundaries. So anyway, for me decolonization is of the mind, and that's why I started by looking at Pan-Africanism particularly as social cultural liberation. As one Ghanaian young person told me today, slavery is not political. Slavery is of the mind. And some of us educated women are offering our minds to be enslaved because of the leadership patterns we are attempting to utilize; why should she, if she becomes an archbishop, go into that leadership mode which is not constructive, it is not inclusive, it is not transformative, it is not a change-friendly leadership model?

Abuom advocated for a complete social overhaul, the decolonization of both men and women, because patriarchal structures are kept in place by both genders. This is the same argument advocated by Dr. Mombo and Reverend Mbugua. Abuom further advanced the notion that unless there is a complete overhaul, the possibility constructing a more complementary culture where men and women lead because they are capable rather than because they are men or women will not be feasible. As such, men need to be decolonized, women need to be decolonized, and society needs to be decolonized and reconstructed along socially just lines.

Spirited Tempered Radical and Servant Leader

Listening to Abuom, reading the transcripts, and reading other articles that she has written on the subject of women and development, I was struck by the fact that she is the epitome of tempered radicalism. She has been engaged in initiating change within the church, starting with the Anglican Church in Kenya, then the National Council of Churches of Kenya, and eventually to the World Council of Churches. Her interest and engagement with development and justice issues have been consistent throughout her adult life, beginning with her campus activism. In addition, Abuom represents the women leaders who believe in serving their community, their nation, their continent, and humanity at large by utilizing their skills, knowledge, and expertise. She articulated her view of leadership as she gave me advice on how to lead and how not to lead: "Desist from the leadership models of men, because that is the killer assumption, the killer factor today for most of us, because we want to show that we are strong, we are powerful. The world needs caring leadership and nurturing leadership. It doesn't want this killing, cutting each other's feet off. The world needs the consultative kind of leadership, not the solo approach, the hero. We have gone beyond the stage of heroism."

Abuom advocates for an ethic of care, and the use of negotiation and consultation rather than the heroic, lone-ranger approach. As far as she is concerned, caring and nurturing leadership is needed the world over, and it is a distinctively African womanist style of leading, although few women leaders in positions of authority actually practice it. In the previous quote, Abuom also connects her style of leadership to God: "God made me into what he wanted"; that is, both her tempered radicalism and servant leadership are because God has used the experiences in her life to mold her. In addition, since God made her as a woman, she has no need to attempt to become a man in her style of leadership. She figured, what she has as a nurturing, caring, ethical, humanistic leader is what society needs, especially African societies that are in such desperate need of healing and reconciliation. She feels that her leadership, and the kind of leadership she would teach others, is a combination of biblical, feminine, and cultural traits. Abuom says:

> But my view is to look at leadership biblically, but also seek out [appropriate] cultural traits, some of which I have told you, including the transformative leader, the leadership that can manage change. One of the characteristics that you can see in women is their adaptability. They are able to adapt. You look at situations today. The man loses a job and becomes depressed. The woman loses a job and sells *sukuma wiki* (collard greens) on the street and keeps moving. Life goes on. Life goes right on. Women do not operate from a rigid point of view. When change comes, women adapt as necessary; instead of breaking, they are malleable, not brittle.

Resonance

Abuom practices and advocates for a leadership that is transformational, adaptable, relevant, biblical, cultural, nurturing, caring, consultative, and just. She feels that the church, the political arena, government, and other social institutions are all run on a leadership approach that is counter-productive, that does not meet the needs of the community or nation. She is of the opinion that a thorough look at traditional African culture, the Bible, and women's survival mechanisms could breed a new form of leadership that is needed in Kenya, Africa, and the world as a whole, that is, a leadership that would result in meeting the justice and development needs of the world's marginalized, as well as running institutions, corporations, and governments to meet real human needs.

11

Wahu Kaara

Critical Prophetic Leadership

The spirit of the Lord God is upon me, to preach provision to
the poor, to proclaim liberty to the captives, to procure the year
of the Lord's justice.

—Isaiah 61:1–2, paraphrased

Before I embarked on this research journey, I had never heard of
Wahu Kaara. I knew I was not alone in my ignorance, because every
time I told my friends and even some of the other participants that
I was interviewing Wahu Kaara, they would ask me who she was. This
was in contrast to people like Muthoni Likimani, Muthoni Wanyeki,
Charity Ngilu, and Beth Mugo, who were in the public limelight. Just
before I met with her, I found that Kaara had just participated in
debt and poverty relief campaigns in the United Kingdom, the most
recent activity being campaigning at Gleneagles during the 2005 G8
leaders' summit. When I went to interview Dr. Abuom, she also talked
about Kaara's activities and engagement with human rights, debt relief,
and poverty eradication, indicating that I should definitely speak
with her.

I met Kaara at her office at the All Africa Conference of Churches,
where she was the ecumenical director of the Millennium Campaign
and coordinator of Global Call against Poverty (GCAP). Kaara is very
simple in her dress, perhaps a legacy of her many years teaching in
high schools in Kenya. However, when she opens her mouth, there is
no mistaking the zeal, knowledge, and passion for social and economic
justice spewing forth.

Defining Moments

Kaara talked about her early beginnings:

> I was born and brought up in the Rift Valley, and that's
> where I interacted or was confronted with the dynamics of
> social contradictions. You remember our history very well;
> even Kenya had an experience of what I would call apartheid.
> And RV is part of the White highlands, so I interacted with
> those racial contradictions observing my grandparents and
> parents and me. And one very critical time I don't forget,
> I think I was about 6 or 7 years old. I saw a young White
> boy coming to my grandparents who were squatters. And
> we had gone there for a family celebration. And when this
> White boy came, he put everybody into disarray. I could
> see my grandfather and grandmother, old people running
> around from him, and he came and broke the calabash that
> held the local brew, a sacred brew that was used for sacred
> purposes. To me he was just a child like me. So I asked him,
> why doesn't he have respect for the old people, and why
> would he break that calabash? And my grandmother and
> my uncle were frantic, they couldn't believe it, including
> my parents; it's as if I had done the worst. But at least the
> young boy got very shaken, and subsequent to that, ironi-
> cally, the White settler had such respect for my grandmother.
> And he would even come to my grandmother's hut to eat
> with her and want to know where I came from, and really
> whether I was the grandchild, and what I do. So that set
> the ground for my questioning the social dynamics in terms
> of social relationships.

Indeed, Kaara's penchant for questioning social realities began at that
early age and has continued to date. She talked about questioning and
critiquing the subject matter that was taught to her in primary school,
challenging the status distinctions in high school, and soaking in the
wisdom and experiences of her professors at university, many of whom
wrote some of East Africa's greatest books about the region's colonial
experience. She described these developmental experiences:

> When I went to school, it was even worse when we were
> learning about slave trade and slavery and who discovered
> what. I remember as early as primary school when I inter-

acted with who discovered Mt. Kilimanjaro and Mt. Kenya, and we would be told it was so and so. And innocently I would ask my teachers, discovered? And I would look in the dictionary what discovery meant, then I would say, but you want to say that the African people, who even gave names to those mountains, how come Mt. Kenya needed Rebmann to come and discover it? My A-levels history and literature and at university perfected that kind of thinking, constantly questioning the canon that had been handed down. And I went to the university at a time when real learning for making critical minds and critical thinking was enhanced. I was a student of Ngugi wa Thiongo, Maina wa Kinyatu, and Okot P'Bitek at the university, where I found my space and developed a clear ideological stand. I made a decision that I also need to study so that I can contribute in making history during my lifetime.

These defining moments, beginning very early and continuing through her educational experiences, set the stage for the social and economic justice activist that Kaara would later become.

Leadership for Social Justice

These early educational and life experiences perfected in Kaara the kind of critical thinking and engagement with social realities that has been the cornerstone of her life as a leader for social and economic justice. After university, she taught history and literature in several high schools, always aiming at preparing students as she herself had been prepped, to be critically engaged with the realities of life in postcolonial Kenya. She would later become a principal before she lost her job, due to her engagement with Kenya's second liberation movement, the movement that would result in the entry of a multiparty democracy and increased political involvement among women.

Kaara was married to a fellow social justice activist, who died a few years ago; they have four children. At one point, her husband was in exile in Tanzania because of his involvement in the second liberation, particularly his activism in demanding for political freedoms. Kaara herself could have been an exile were it not for the actions of an elder and a board member of the school she was heading, who defended her against accusations of treasonable activities. She spent some time at Freedom Corner—a place where wives, mothers, and supporters of political prisoners gathered for several months agitating for the release of political prisoners.

Kaara is totally committed to fighting for economic justice from both a national and global platform. To this effect, she has been involved in a series of social forums, movements whose priorities relate to agitating for economic justice, especially for Global South nations. She explained: "Globally, I have been a key debt campaigner through a platform here in the country called Kenya Debt Relief Network, and in total the question of economic justice. And that's how I perhaps modestly call myself [a] global, social, and economic justice activist. Currently I am very instrumental in the process of the World Social Forum through the African Social Forum, Kenya Social Forum, and our local Huruma Social Forum."

I had never heard of the World Social Forum (WSF) prior to my interactions with Kaara, so I asked her to explain what the organization was all about. She explained:

> The World Social Forum is involved in looking for another world; build a just world because in the current world everybody is quite unjust. And the social forum tries to critique the liberal paradigm as it exists and tries to engage in alternatives that people creatively are coming up with, like you are trying to argue from your observation here; what the ordinary people do is never documented. And the social forum is keen in trying to build synergy of the emerging alternatives for sustenance of life. Because the current paradigm it's clear is serving the interest of finance capital only for profit, and at the level we are in, it is actually a great danger to life sustenance. So the World Social Forum emerged as a platform to begin to build that synergy, and it was motivated by wanting to critique what happens every beginning of [the] year at the World Economic Forum in Switzerland, which perfects the current paradigm in terms of the economic models that serve the neoliberal agenda that facilitates finance capital for profit. So that is the process, and the key thing is that people are agreeable that another world is possible.

Kaara's excitement about the possibilities inherent in the paradigm shift offered via the channel of the World Social Forum mechanisms was palpable, because she felt that this could be the beginning of an alternative model of social and economic relations between the Global

South nations and their rich counterparts in the northern hemisphere. She was of the opinion that here was the chance to change the status quo, and whereas the World Social Forum is not a religious movement, it offered her a spiritual platform, a platform to turn the world back again into what God intended. She explained:

> So for me this is a lifetime achievement; now I can rest in peace because the World Social Forum is a platform that articulates nothing other than justice, economic justice, social justice, different models of power relations, of partnership, of equity, of respect. In other words, a world that sees value of each and every human being to manifest the purpose for which they were created by God. Because I am also a believer and I know that God did not create just for the sake of creating us, and the kind of things we are trying to interrogate in Africa, it is not natural, it is not God-given. Poverty is a created scarcity, and if it is a created scarcity, it can be dealt with, and dealing with it in exactly what you have observed our ordinary women doing.

The WSF was the platform in which GCAP was articulated. Kaara was excited that she was part of the group that convinced the international organizations to come to Africa as their next convention venue. She hoped that this would give Africans a chance to contribute to the rest of the world on issues of social justice leadership, to contribute from African women's experiences of creative and resourceful leadership.

Radical Servant Leader

For Kaara, the WSF and its local manifestations were a platform to exercise what she explained as the purpose for which God created humanity—to live lives of dignity and respect. In her understanding, social justice is a divine imperative necessitated by the need to solve social inequality and scarcity problems. In the previous quote, she made that connection between theistic spirituality and social justice. The agenda of fighting for social justice also involved being a certain kind of leader, specifically, a leader whose motivation for leading is in order to serve. She explained:

> It is the heritage that we have of the preparedness of engaging with life, that heritage, the remnant is still there, just like

I am trying to tell you I watched in my grandmother and mother. The training that the fulfillment of the being is the delivery of service to humanity contradicts with the paradigm perpetuated, especially from the West, that the fulfillment of the being is how much you exploit life. . . . And it is my submission that those who make history should write it and read it, that is, let the African women tell you who they are, and why they are. Because it is what they do, let them substantiate what they do and listen to them, because they have a way forward and they have a vision about life.

Here Kaara not only defined the kind of leader needed—one who finds fulfillment in serving humanity—but also connected this to her heritage, arguing that she learned it from her mother and grandmother. This orientation toward serving others was so important that she emphasized it by saying it again and again during the individual interview as well as at the focus group. She was of the conviction that finding fulfillment in serving humanity is a paradigm shift away from Western and patriarchal models and a rebirth of traditional cultural models of leading to serve.

Kaara perceived the need to deconstruct social structures, including patriarchy's constructions of gender, arguing that only in this kind of critical exercise would scholars and practitioners alike be able to reconstruct a just society. She explained her stand by going back to Kenya's freedom struggle history, showing that those in power, the colonial and the postcolonial, have perfected the art of distorting history to leave out those who contributed the most:

Those who do not create but control have perfected mechanisms of keeping off those who create, because there would be a contradiction. And our Mau Mau history is classic of what has happened, and that's what inspires me a lot. Because you do see, when we came to independence, the freedom fighters, all the Mau Mau, are nowhere, no recognition when it came to sharing of the "national cake." And for the last 40 years there has been a deliberate effort to erase that part of our history. And this year, it was very ironic to see the Kenya National Human Rights Commission, awarding Michuki, who has very unpopular participation in Mau Mau, [a] medal for being a good fighter. He was given an award together with the widow of Kimathi. So do you see? Can you see? They are in the government. I am just validating

what I was saying, those who control. You can see Michuki,
who has a very bad record in Mau Mau.

Kaara's consternation at the turn of events where a colonial collabora-
tor was given an award by the human rights commission alongside the
widow of one of the freedom fighters who was killed by the colonial
forces was justified; it was an absurd abuse of power and, more so, an
insult to the historical authenticity of Kenya's freedom struggle. As
Kaara further explained:

> Michuki was an outrageous home guard. Even has a nick-
> name of *Kimendero,* the one who crushes. So can you see
> the irony of the Kenya National Human Rights Commission
> in the so-called second liberation victory having Michuki
> and the widow of Kimathi being awarded the same award?
> Shamelessly, that is what I am trying to say. They shamelessly
> distort or try to erase; and where they cannot erase they
> reconstruct it differently for their own expediency. . . . That
> is what we need to deconstruct to show how the essences
> of those who really sustain life are important. And with this
> redefinition and reconstruction of the world, it is so clear,
> the women, we are the people with skills to deconstruct
> and reconstruct. The men just destroy, because theirs is to
> make profit.

Kaara argued for the need for those who lead for social justice to
deconstruct these arrangements in order to speak truth to power, to
bring into the light that which is shrouded in darkness. In the previous
quote, she eloquently illustrated what she called "rule by domination,"
the dominant model that supports silencing the real freedom fighters
and awarding colonial sympathizers. The widow of Field Marshall Dedan
Kimathi, the freedom fighter who was hanged by colonial powers in
the mid-50s, being awarded the same human rights award as a colonial
supporter is the height of irony. Michuki was the minister for security
in the then current government of Kenya, while Kimathi continues
to languish in utter poverty in spite of her family's obvious sacrifice
for Kenya's freedom. It is an illustration of the social contradictions
that Kaara talked about from the beginning of my conversation with
her, social contradictions that she began to experience as a child and
continues to experience and critique to date. In this environment,
an effective woman leader cannot be anything but an outsider within
her own culture. Kaara's story illustrates this experience, because

even though she is a Kenyan African woman, her values are at odds
with those made normative by the current dispensation of leaders in
politics, business and civic society. She espoused and aptly illustrated
her values of serving humanity in contradistinction to the norms of
exploiting humanity.

Kaara has learned creative problem solving, innovative survival
mechanisms, and alternative gender relationships that she utilizes in
her own life and leadership as a tempered radical—a woman intent
on changing her society, the nation, and organizations from within.
In fact, she is so intent on social transformation that she is not afraid
to campaign in local, national, and global forums. In 2005 alone, she
campaigned for debt relief in Glen Egles, Scotland, by walking with
others in front of the resort with placards that had the faces of the
eight leaders and the message to end poverty and cancel debts; gave
speeches in the White Band campaign against poverty in London; and
gave the keynote address to the United Nations Summit in New York,
alongside President Clinton. In these forums, Kaara urged powerful
Western nations to practice justice, especially economic justice, by reducing the glaring inequalities. Her speeches are eloquent, if somewhat
blunt, in stating the difficulties that Africa faces and the possibilities
inherent in African grassroots actions and powerful Western nations'
relationships with the continent. In speeches to a gathering of world
leaders in St. Paul's Cathedral, London, in July, preceding the G8
Summit, and the 58th Annual UN Summit, held in September 2005,
she defined her position as an African woman to whom statistics bear
the faces of real people:

> In our pursuit for global justice and creating a better world
> that will uphold our heritage, we have come a long way. I
> stand before you today as an African woman, somebody
> who experiences on a daily basis the pain and indignity of
> hunger, disease, and illiteracy. For one who works at the
> grassroots level, it is a rare honor for me to be given such
> an opportunity, and I thank the organizers and all of you
> for this . . . when I see *Live 8* and *Make Poverty History*
> talking about 30,000 people dying daily, for me this is not
> a statistic. The images that go through my mind when I see
> these numbers are the faces and names of real people, my
> family, my neighbors, my friends, my community.

Beyond Kaara's identification with the social and economic problems
that plague the continent, she is also able to recognize the agency

of Africans, especially women, in pursuit of their own emancipation. In the same speech just referenced, and in the many quotes already given about the resourcefulness of Africa's women, Kaara illustrated this self-determination of African women:

> But today I want to bring to you the other Africa, the one that does not appear much on TV screens, the Africa that is waging a determined struggle against poverty, as nations and as a continent; the Africa Union and the new African parliament, led by a woman, is a symbol of this new Africa. However, the real transformation that is taking place is at the level of the individual citizens of Africa. The people of Africa are increasingly refusing to accept a life of bondage, poverty, and injustice. And our message to our governments in Africa is loud and clear: NO MORE EXCUSES. We will not tolerate corruption and inefficiency from our leaders anymore.

In the same meeting, Kaara connected the struggles in Africa to those of Katrina victims in the United States, showing the global nature of injustice and scarcity. For Kaara, even as local people in either context struggle for their self-emancipation, there is also a global call for nations and leaders to find solutions for local-yet-global problems. She said:

> 2005 has been a monumental year. We have seen bold and broad maneuvers and engagement to address the critical issue of global poverty and inequality, an inequality whose responses and backlash has been and continues to be visited on us daily . . . of course, inequality is not only between nations but within nations. As Africans, we express our deepest solidarity and condolences with the people of this country affected by Hurricane Katrina. This reality has become loud and clear . . . as much as the dominant discourse on poverty is developing world centric and sub-Saharan Africa specific, the so-called developing world too has its stake, a big stake for that matter. Please listen to your own millions of citizens who are asking you to take action against poverty. Don't tell us you don't have enough money to meet your aid commitments and cancel debts of all poor countries. You found a lot of money overnight for the war on Iraq and canceling Iraq's debts.

These quotes from Kaara's speeches at the UN in New York and St. Paul's Cathedral in London illustrate how well versed she is in both the local and global realities of social and economic injustice. To the G8 leaders, Kaara had this to say as a challenge:

> And can we have some honesty please? We no more allow African governments to pretend there is good governance when there isn't. We don't want the G8 leaders to exaggerate their announcements on Friday and then to break their exaggerated promises. Let's stop playing with words which we may not realize are in fact playing with the lives of our African people. We need aid that is truly additional new money. We need debt relief that is not based on more harmful conditionalities. We need this now, not after 10 years. And let us not forget the eighth millennium goal was not just about aid and debt, but crucially about trade. We are all a people of God, created in God's image to live and manifest God in our lives. Our God is not a God of want and fear and indignity. Mr. Secretary General, as you meet the G8 leaders, please personally tell them on our behalf: Let God's people go from bondage to freedom; freedom from want, freedom from fear, and freedom from indignity. G8 leaders: We want to see your sense of justice, your courage, and your humanity.

To say that Kaara is courageous is an understatement, yet it is hard to find a more fitting descriptor for one so imbued with boldness in agitating and advocating for social and economic justice. In the aforementioned speech, she bluntly, publicly, and pointedly challenged the UN secretary general to pass on African women's demands for freedom from bondage, want, indignity, and fear. No wonder he invited her to give the keynote address at the UN in September 2005, with the caveat that she be as honest there as she was at the London meeting. She talked about this at the focus group meeting, which was held a few days before she traveled to New York. She said:

> Leadership in Africa does not lead Africans, but it is co-opted to deliver Africa for expediency. Because 2 days ago I just received an invitation, and I am supposed to be a keynote speaker in opening the UN assembly together with former president of the United States, Bill Clinton. So how can you explain Wahu Kaara and Bill Clinton on one platform?

[It is] to make a candid position to set the process of that discussion within the civil society or the civil commons, a group that the UN can no longer ignore. It just summarizes and confirms my argument, because I am a symbol of the African woman; I am a symbol of that role that we have never absconded as African women from our grandmothers to our mothers, to me and to you, our daughters. This is because in two very important conferences, I have been saying Africa will not die for Africa anymore. Africa will now live for Africa. And this is because the African women, I being one of them, we have refused to die for Africa. And we are living for Africa, because we manage budget lines without a budget, we give health service without medical insurance, we mobilize resources with no capital, etc.

This quote illustrates Kaara's most important arguments in defense of the African woman and in elaboration of the resiliency of the African woman, that *African women are, by and large, resourceful in solving social and family problems in spite of their material limitations.* In fact, Kaara argued that the same capacities women use in the private arena are the skills required for leadership in the public arena: resourcefulness, creative problem solving, deep concern for the needs of the community, and motivation to serve those needs, ability to see the bigger picture so that the private becomes public, and the local global. And all of this is motivated and upheld by a deep spiritual spring. Kaara said: "Spirituality gives you the capacity to pursue the truth without illusion. I think as you hear me talk, you can get the courage that I have and the commitment that I have and the energy that I have. It's not because of the breakfast that I ate. No! It's because of the spirit that is inspiring me."

Future as a Leader

Kaara's vision for Kenya, Africa, and the world involves achieving social and economic justice for the world's marginalized, beginning with those in her own backyard. As a widow at an early age, she knows firsthand the struggles women face in attempting to achieve their professional, social, community, and family goals. As a mother and grandmother, she wants a better future for her grandchildren, a future that includes equal access to education, property and political rights for women, access to aid facilities without harmful conditional ties for her beloved

Kenya, and access to health services for the marginalized and poor. She hopes for a future where Africa's real economic prowess can be realized, when economic injustices pushed upon the continent by unfair trade relations with the powerful Western nations are finally eradicated, a hope that she shares with all of her fellow campaigners in GCAP. Whereas she continues her busy campaigning and speaking schedule around the globe, as well as in local assemblies, her future goal includes seeking to join political leadership. Kaara ran for parliamentary elections in 2007, 2 years after the interview, but she lost to a woman who was more recognizable to the constituents, Bishop Margaret Wanjiro, who is the senior pastor of a mega church in Nairobi. Wanjiro had the financial resources to campaign and beat the competition, which Kaara still lacks. Kaara also has the disadvantage of not being known locally, even though she has an international reputation in the economic justice movement.

Resonance

Kaara captivated me during the individual conversation and held all of us, the young, the middle aged, and the old, spellbound during the focus group. I noted in my memos how it was interesting watching the DVD of the focus group, because all of the women present seemed to be utterly mesmerized by this small but fiery speaker. When Kaara came into the meeting for the focus group, the dynamics altered drastically, from talking about a woman's place in the kitchen to the national and global positioning of women as the answer to 21st-century social problems. We could see how she would and did captivate audiences in those global conferences with her "candid position," as she enumerated African women's agency in their own emancipation and the global leaders' role in helping African people emancipate themselves. If Kaara is the symbol of the new and emerging African woman as leader, then there is hope for that desperate continent indeed.

As a well-traveled, educated woman, it was interesting to note how Kaara seamlessly moved between the local and the global, the private and the public, making important connections and showing how the different spheres interact. Of particular importance is how she explained leadership, service, courage, social and economic justice, and just about everything else that she touched upon in terms of spirituality: that the purpose for engaging in and the modus operandi for social justice leadership are deeply spiritual. Everything about her life and leadership is imbued with that critical spirituality that engages with social realities and attempts to change the status quo. For Kaara, social justice is the goal of leadership. She remarked: "That's what I am determined to do. And that will be done without fear or favor. It will be done with courage and determination inspired differently not by the gains that you are going to get. So fulfillment of life which is very spiritual is the basis for all this."

Kaara truly believed in and practiced spirited prophetic leadership, so much so that her final words to me during the individual conversation were this: "Breathe life into academics. That's the spirit. The spirit is the only one who compels life."

I hope for Kenya's sake, for Africa's sake, for the sake of the millions of people living in deprived conditions in Global South locations, and for the sake of our understanding of what it means to be a truly prophetic and deeply spiritual leader who will live and die for social justice that Waku Kaara will continue to be effective in her economic justice activism. I believe that the world is enriched by having this 2005 Nobel Peace Prize nominee serve as a compelling example of visionary, nurturing, and conciliatory leadership.

Tempered Radicals

Rocking the Boat without Falling Out

In this chapter, I explain tempered radicals as one of the themes illustrated by the women's portraits. Using direct quotes, I demonstrate how the women leaders' stories explain and expand on tempered radicalism. As described by Meyerson and Scully (1995), tempered radicals are people who are living at odds with the majority culture, and who then choose to be proactive about changing the status quo. Not all women leaders in Kenya or Africa can be described as tempered radicals. Wahu Kaara described the situation thus: "When women are co-opted in ruling as men, they are not part of us; there is a disconnect." The women selected to participate in this study were chosen because of their ability to lead as women, their refusal to become "androcentricized" or masculinized, and the fact that they have chosen to seek a more just society. What follows is an account of how some among the 16 women whom we describe as tempered radicals navigate the terrain of social, cultural, gender, religious, age, and ethnic identities as these relate to their experiences as leaders. As tempered radicals, these women leaders are invested in the institutions, organizations, and communities of which they are a part, yet they also want to transform them—they want to rock the boat without falling out (Meyerson, 2001; Meyerson & Scully, 1995; Ngunjiri, 2007).

Choosing Battles Wisely

In order for women in leadership to rock the boat without falling out, they learn through experience to choose their battles wisely—some they fight, and some they let go of in order to stay alive and keep their jobs to fight another day. Dr. Jeniffer Riria described it this way:

> If I can avoid a battle, I will avoid it. But if [I] am forced
> into a battle, I will say, let's get into it. I will fight when I
> know [I] am correct and am right. Most times I win my
> battles . . . but when I lose, I turn around and apologize.

Riria further explained that she chooses battles based on principles;
she will not engage in frivolous fighting, nor will she be malicious to
anybody. Sometimes strength of character and integrity serve women
in leadership well when they do find themselves engaged in battles for
social justice. Muthoni Wanyeki talked about being ready to stand up
and be counted in the struggle for social justice:

> I am honest in terms of if I believe something in terms of
> what can and should happen, then that is what I will stand
> up to defend. Certainly I think I do have the capacity to
> stand up and defend ideas for myself but also for other
> people.

Furthermore, Wanyeki was convinced that women must also be ready
to act: "Forcing yourself to act on an issue even when you can see
there is going to be consequences is really important. And once
you've done so, to be prepared to deal with the consequences." She
was of the opinion that activism would not be enough if all one did
was speak about justice. One must also act—that is, walking the walk.
In her case, in spite of working as the executive director of a highly
hierarchical organization, she attempted to still act according to her
values, especially collectivism and communalism. Reverend Mbugua
also discussed her own idea of choosing battles wisely:

> Once I know that something is right, nothing will stop me.
> Once I read the Bible and find the truth, I find a fighter
> spirit within me, and I say I don't want this to happen to
> my daughter.

Because of her convictions about justice and right action, when Rev.
Mbugua found out that there was no theological basis for not ordaining
women in mainstream denominations, she sought ordination through
the Reformed Gospel Church, an evangelical denomination in Kenya.
Her impetus for action is: "I have this winner or fighter spirit that we
are not going to leave this thing hanging; let's get to a conclusion."

In each instance, the women find themselves different from the
norm, or disagreeing with the organizational modus operandi. Yet

they have to belong and be a participant of the organization, culture, or community that they aim to transform. They find themselves struggling to fit in and to fight against those elements that are unjust. But whatever they do, it is not necessarily merely personal gain; rather, it is for the good of the whole. Even those battles that start out as personal struggles, such as Rev. Mbugua's desire to be ordained, became community successes. Mainstream churches now ordain women, something they were resistant to doing prior to Rev. Mbugua's pioneering act. Later on we will see how choosing battles wisely connects with spirituality, as it requires the exercise of wisdom that is gained from experience and maturity.

Meyerson (2001) gave five ways through which tempered radicals make a difference: resisting quietly and staying true to oneself; turning personal threats into opportunities; broadening the impact through negotiation; leveraging small wins; and organizing collective action.

Quiet Resistance

For those individuals who want to change the status quo without ruffling feathers, quiet resistance works. As described by Meyerson, forms of resistance may include mentoring and supporting minorities within the organization or in the community, choosing to dress in a way that is culturally relevant, using artifacts and symbols in the office to address one's cultural heritage, and channeling information to other marginal people within the organization.

I asked Professor Faith Nguru, one of the highest-ranking women at Daystar University, whether she had faced any challenges connected to her gender as she rose through the administrative ranks. She replied:

> No, not very many. I found that it was a good thing to be
> female, because there weren't very many of us. Of course,
> I remember maybe chauvinism of some sort, when you sit
> round a table; it is taken for granted if there is need for a
> cup of tea you are the one to get it. I wouldn't mind getting
> it; just that it is like taken for granted.

Nguru, rather than confront chauvinistic behaviors directly, found ways to work around them. For instance, after she returned to Daystar in 1995 as a freshly minted Ph.D., she found that a lot of tasks would be dumped on her lap. Rather than complain, she learned to delegate;

everything got done in time and done well. As such, she quickly rose through the administrative ranks, becoming dean of students and, currently, director of research and consultancy.

Another quiet resister is Shiphrah Gichaga, who, prior to becoming the national coordinator for Forum for African Women Educationists, Kenya chapter, had served as an inspector of schools in the Ministry of Education. She could not remember any overtly sexist discrimination at the Ministry of Education, but she still described it as challenging: "It is always a challenge for a woman in leadership. Maybe for men it is easier." She went on to describe how she worked extra hard to prove herself and how she rose from a high school teacher to an inspector of schools to later serving FAWE. Her biggest struggles involved those who challenged her for traveling so much, as her job as an inspector of schools took her to different parts of the country, and some were quick to point out that she should be at home raising her children! Yet interestingly, she did not regard that as sexist; she felt that that was just the way things were.

Whereas these two women leaders' challenges revolved around remaining true to themselves as women and as leaders, attempting to juggle careers with family responsibilities, the other women leaders faced overt gender discrimination and resented the gender stereotyping that resulted in their being expected, for example, to serve tea at board meetings. Most refused to accept being domesticated in their professional roles and needed to act in more drastic ways to assert their rightful position in their organizations. Dr. Esther Mombo illustrates this point:

> I remember like one time I was brought flowers to arrange, so I ask them, why should I arrange them? They said because I am a woman. And I ask, so and so, did he arrange flowers? Why should I arrange flowers? I will do flowers if I want to, but not because it's an expectation.

Turning Personal Threats into Opportunities

Unlike Nguru and Gichaga, other participants found it necessary to be a little more radical rather than tempered, to varying degrees, depending on the context and situation at hand. There was more of a need to challenge the status quo, beginning with turning personal threats into learning and action opportunities for themselves and those around them. They found that they could not merely be quiet resisters; that was not an option, because their organizational settings required more of a confrontation with gender norms and stereotypes.

Njoki Wainaina was intimately connected to the women's movement and development issues from the 70s, having attended, participated, and/or organized many of the women's rights meetings of the 70s, 80s, and 90s. However, feminism and women's rights in Kenya came with negative connotations, mainly derived from propaganda spread by a government that was resistant to change. As such, even as late as 1995, when the Beijing Women's Global Conference took place, women working on human rights and development issues were targets of both bad press and physical harm. Wainaina described some of her experiences confronting the misinformation that surrounded the Beijing conference thus:

> Beijing got very bad press here. And you know people believed a lot of the things they heard. And Beijing also created a lot of fear on the part of the men. I found that early in the period after Beijing, in the church and from the pulpit the minister would start talking about Beijing and without knowing enough about it would say all manner of ridiculous things. That gave me my opportunity. I would just wait outside the church, and I would say, by the way can I talk to you for a moment. You talked about Beijing. Have you ever seen the Beijing platform for action? Of course, they didn't even know there was such a thing as a platform. Then, I would say, you know, as a servant of the living God, you are supposed to use the pulpit to speak things that are truthful, things that will help, things that will enrich people's lives. And one of the responsibilities you have is to never, ever speak about things you don't know anything about. So I would suggest that before you speak about Beijing again, you look at the platform for action. But for a start I can tell you I was the leader of the women's NGOs to Beijing, so if you have any issues, talk to me. And I can also tell you that as a Christian woman, there isn't anything that I cannot stand for, and that I will not stand by. So let us understand what it is we are talking about. You read the platform for action, [and] you will realize that you are wrong.

Confronting men, especially ministers and preachers, is not something that women do lightly in Africa. Yet Wainaina could not let the misinformation continue, not when she was so intimately involved. So she turned a personal threat into a learning opportunity for many men. Eventually she gained such a reputation as a gender consultant and educator that men's organizations began to invite her to speak to them, especially about how to stop gender violence. Even after she had retired from FEMNET, she continued to serve as a gender consultant for men's groups, many of which began as Christian men's fellowships from various churches.

Nangurai's story is described in an earlier chapter, especially as it relates to how she moved from being a high school teacher to a primary school headmistress at AIC Kajiado, where she soon began to rescue girls from forced marriages. Her move was precipitated by a particular event, when the school board decided to remove girls from the high school in a bid to improve the performance of the school in national examinations, essentially blaming the poor performance on the girls. Nangurai, although she was still a young teacher and deeply steeped in Maasai culture, found herself needing to contravene discriminatory gender norms:

> I ask what the background is and how we got here. And the chairman of the board said, "You are just a woman. Decision has already been made . . . do you know you have no right to speak here?"

Nangurai confronted the elders and had the courage to speak up and to act in order to enable Maasai girls to acquire education. What was most surprising about the encounter and her retelling of the story is the fact that she is a shy, soft-spoken woman. I could hardly imagine her acting confrontationally. Hers is a quiet strength. She is able to stand up and act, to speak up on behalf of disenfranchised Maasai women.

Wahu Kaara is an eloquent and a strong woman, actually the opposite of Nangurai when it comes to personality. She too has found it necessary to confront injustices, to turn personal threats into educational opportunities. She is convinced that each battle a woman in leadership wins she wins not just for herself but for other women as well. As she said, "You do not buy confidence from a shop, you have to acquire it." In commenting on Nangurai's experience with the board and giving advice to younger women in leadership, Kaara said: "Deal with the board . . . ensure they understand you are there by merit not as a favor."

Kaara had her own experiences with school and community boards when she was a headmistress of a girls' school in Muranga district. She found that some of the founding elders had very different ideas about how to lead the school than she did, even though they were not educators. It had gotten so bad that the board president would hold the headmistresses at ransom by refusing to sign checks for school expenses:

> You become so frustrated and you start quarreling with him. The next day you are transferred. So in one year and a half, they had about five heads of school, the school could not run. So they took me there as a trial.

Unlike her five predecessors, Kaara would not bend. As she described it, she did not consider herself a grasshopper, and those elders were no giants. She used an Old Testament analogy to explain her situation:

> So I gave the check to be signed; as usual, he refused. So I wrote an official letter, "I am advising you to call an executive board meeting to enable me [to] be transferred from the school with immediate effect." So I gave the letter. He read, and now he didn't know what to do because I had given tentative dates for me to be transferred. So he sent a message for me to go. And nobody ever entered his house. I entered his house. I wasn't going to talk from outside. I didn't know there was a tradition that nobody enters the house. So when I went and now he wants to speak to me outside, and I said, *ndirona ta itari mugeni wa guku ii, ririia urienda twarie ni urinjita,* [which means] I see perhaps you are not ready for me; when you are ready, call me; so he now took me inside the house and we talked. And I told him, I appreciate that you are a founder member, you are senior, but you cannot be the head of the school. I am young and a woman for that matter, but I head the school. I am the face of the school, without me there is no school. So it is for you to appreciate the technical skills that I bring. Because I go from school a to school z all over the country; you are only a board member here. Do you know what that old man told me? "*Haiya, na nyina wa Kiama wi muthamaki,* [which means] Kiama's mother, you are really a leader."

Kaara refused to bow out of the school because of resistant board members/community leaders, but, more importantly, by firmly but respectfully showing the elders their role and demonstrating hers, she was able to develop excellent relationships with them. In fact, later on, when she got into trouble with the old regime for her involvement in the second liberation movement, that elder stood up for her, saying she was not a political agent but rather an effective leader of the local girls school. That saved her from the fate that befell her husband, who had to live in exile for 6 years.

Broadening Impact through Negotiation

Broadening impact through negotiation necessitates the courage to step out and act or speak up against injustice (Ngunjiri & Lengel, 2007). Meyerson (2001) felt that it was imperative to proactively transform problems and reframe meaning, to use negotiation strategies to help transform issues and open avenues for constructive action. For these women leaders, broadening impact is a prerequisite to achieving their stated goal for being leaders in the first place: social justice for various marginalized populations. Negotiation is an important strategic tactic in achieving progress toward social justice, and it is a strategy that many of the participants constantly referred to as they described their leadership communication strategies. According to Meyerson, "To think in terms of negotiation is to think in terms of competing interests, differing positions and concerns, distinct sources of influence, and alternative framing of issues. Negotiating requires discipline and action: people must participate in shaping how problems unfold" (p. 79).

One of the best examples of broadening action begins with the story that Wainaina told about her experiences after Beijing, where she confronted misinformation by reeducating men and later became a gender consultant for men's organizations. She further explained:

> Women's leadership is the most political work. First of all, we are fighting for rights. We are fighting for something some- body else has [that belongs to us]. So we have to fight them, persuade them. Trick them. So it is so political. You need to be very confident to just be able to continue and to say you know, yes, I understand what you are saying, but . . . and to be able to keep your head and not to get angry.

In her experience, angry outbursts would not lead anywhere; rather, learning to negotiate with those who withheld women's rights was the

more effective strategy. This strategy, however, was not just one employed
by women in contemporary leadership situations; rather, it has been
in use since colonial times. Muthoni Likimani explained this well as
she historicized women's agency in their own and the community's
emancipation during the first liberation movement. She explained how
during the guerrilla warfare that freed Kenya from colonial domination,
most men were either in detention or fighting in the forest. Women
were left to their own devices to take care of the homes, participate
in forced labor daily, and serve the fighting forces:

> One such woman was working for me later. She told me,
> "I used to fill bullets in my market basket. Then I would
> put maize floor or beans and carry it. I would meet these
> armed forces, and I would say, Habari Watoto! (Hello, young
> people), and they would respond "Habari Mama." And she
> will go and will take the stuff to the safe place they had
> agreed with the forest fighters. Without that bare-footed
> woman who has never been in a classroom, they would not
> have survived.

Likimani told other stories about prostitutes in Nairobi who would hide
bullets stolen from their patrons in their skirts and pass them along to
the freedom fighters. In other words, women used whatever resources
were at their disposal and found ways to participate in the freedom
struggle, figuring out ways to negotiate with the adversary, nay, even
to trick them in order to emancipate themselves.

In her lifetime, Kaara has been actively involved in agitating for
political freedom, beginning with when she was a university student.
Having received what she described as education that facilitated critical
thinking and active engagement, she continued that legacy by helping
her own students, in addition to engaging her children sp that they have
all grown up to become activists for social and economic justice. To
further broaden her impact, she has been an institutional entrepreneur,
helping to set up economic justice organizations such as Kenya Debt
Relief Network and World Social Forum, organizations that engage in
negotiations with the Breton Woods Institutions and Global 8 leaders
on behalf of Kenya and the developing world. Sometimes however,
leaders agitating for social and economic justice ideals may feel help-
less in the face of insurmountable odds. That is when leveraging small
wins, building from minute successes, helps to both restore hope and
keep them focused on and energized about their goals.

Leveraging Small Wins

Small wins are those seemingly minuscule successes that result in concrete, measurable, and visible progress in the process of organizational transformation (Meyerson, 2001). Small wins become an impetus for further and broader action down the line. They encourage social justice leaders to keep fighting the good fight. Nangurai illustrated the utility of small wins when she talked about her experience with rescuing Charity, the first girl who came to her escaping forced marriage. When the struggle became especially intense with fathers threatening her life and coming to the school to take their daughters away (the school was under police protection for a long time), watching Charity's success as she progressed through her education and career helped put things into perspective. She declared: "When we succeeded with Charity, now I thought to myself, no other girl will be given away if we can help it."

Similarly, Ole Marima, who also works among the Maasai community, knows how to begin small and to expand from there. When she worked at World Vision, she had a lot more resources to expend on her community for water projects and other development activities. Upon her retirement, she was determined to continue serving her community, as she explained:

> I retired from World Vision in 1992, so I have been on my own since then. I have been a farmer, I have gone back to do awakening of my people both in politics and community development programs. I have involved women a lot, and I started to sell to them the idea of micro-enterprise, including farming and small- scale entrepreneurship. I said, Lord, help me to appreciate what you have given me. He has given me land, [so] I went into wheat farming and cattle trade. I encouraged the women to keep goats and to do subsistence farming, starting with kitchen gardens. We also started [educating them on] nutrition and personal cleanliness. So I have been with those women, which was very easy, because I was giving them knowledge, which they appreciate, because I believe in lifting them up. That was not so much of a challenge, because the only thing I was encountering was the illiteracy rates.

Marima began with very small lessons on personal hygiene and kitchen gardens. Both she and Nangurai also illustrated the insider/outsider experience of tempered radicals who are involved in the cultural transformation of their own communities, as educated and economically advanced Maasai women who work to advance the status of their illiterate womenfolk through agriculture, education, and community development.

Organizing Collective Action

Meyerson (2001) provided three preconditions that were necessary for effective collective action, as evidenced in the literature on social movements: (1) the presence of immediate political opportunities or threats; (2) available structures for members to organize themselves into a collective; and (3) the framing of collective identity, opportunities, and threats (p. 124). All of these preconditions exist in the African context, in what Abuom called "the collective mass of the oppressed." That is, particularly in Kenya, colonialism and neocolonialism have provided the political threats that necessitated women's collective action in order to survive. Secondly, communities traditionally collectivized to help each other with farming responsibilities, even before the colonialists disrupted the agrarian economy. Land was held by the clan, and clan members would all gather and help each other during planting, weeding, and harvesting. It wasn't so far fetched, then, that women would collectivize during the colonial struggle, or that they would form women's rotating credit and savings groups for social and economic support in the current economy. Economic disenfranchisement, inadequate educational access, and limited access to credit facilities all serve as reasons for women to collectivize. Likimani helped put this phenomenon in historical perspective by describing women's agency during the emergency period in Kenya:

> The woman would be caught up in communal forced labor from 7:30 in the morning to 4:30; by the time she walked back to her hut, it is dark. And mzungu were asking, these maize and beans, when were they planted? Because these women who planted the gardens spent all day at communal forced labor . . . they would organize themselves: the one would give wood, the other will give some water, and the other will have collected some food from the garden and dug around a few rows of potatoes. That's what an African woman will do.

In contemporary Kenya, women have found it necessary to collectivize to solve social, economic, and political problems. For instance, Marima discussed some of her political engagements:

So I am called Honorable Marima, women's shadow parliament, Nairobi North. But that's the kind of thing we have
decided to be, the alternative parliament. When we get
empowered and all this, these are the people who are the
voice of reason. That's what we have decided to call ourselves, voice of reason.

Similarly, Mombo has found it necessary to work with other women in
theological circles. She is actively involved in the Circle of Concerned
African Women Theologians, which conducts research and writes
and publishes issues related to women in the church. In addition to
women's issues, the circle has published and provided leadership in
the African church on matters relating to the pastoral care of those
affected or infected by HIV/AIDS. At her institution, Mombo brings
women together to discuss gender socialization in the African church
and society and its impact on women's status:

I need the support of women because it's an isolated environment; I just have to have the support of women. So I have
groups of women, I tell them, you are socialized in a certain
way. And something else, when I do workshops, like I bring
together a hundred women and we talk about this socialization. I ask them, why do you think you are [perceived] as
a bad boss as a manager and not the man?

Kaara has found that becoming actively involved in organizations that
support social and economic justice ideals for Kenya, Africa, and the rest
of the developing world is an effective, collective tool. She explains:

The World Social Forum is involved in looking for another
world, building a just world because in the current world
everybody is quite unjust. And, the Social Forum tries to
critique the liberal paradigm as it exists and tries to engage
in alternatives that people creatively are coming up with;
the Social Forum is keen in trying to build synergy of the
emerging alternatives for sustenance of life.

Kaara further talked about the necessity for building alliances among
people, groups, and organizations, because individuals by themselves
may have a limited impact, but collectives can pool resources and have
both a broader and deeper impact.

In addition to these five methods of actualizing tempered radicalism that Meyerson (2001) conceptualized, African women leaders utilize several other tools at their disposal in negotiating their social identity as African women leaders and members of a particular ethnic community, in a specific nation, under the current global capitalist arrangement.

Intercultural Boundary Spanning

All of the women in this study have at least an associate's degree; most of them have a master's degree or higher, making them part of a small elite in Kenyan society. Their education and global travels have afforded them a social status that puts them way above their illiterate sisterfolk in the villages and slums. Yet rather than merely enjoy their class privilege, these women articulated a leadership that is akin to that described by African American scholars—lifting as they rise. In order to be effective in lifting marginalized women, children, and the poor, these women had become adept at spanning cultural, social, and educational barriers, building bridges, and closing gaps. They bridge the gaps between young people and the older generations in dealing with cultural malpractices, poor, marginalized, illiterate communities in need of legal and educational literacy, and women in need of economic emancipation.

Marima closed the gap between literacy and illiteracy by working in women's development activities in her rural community. She related:

> First of all, when I was in World Vision, I was able to register an all-women development organization called Reto [Maasai for self-help] organization. I brought in the aspect of self-sustenance. At Reto, we address issues of health and education. . . . That's what I was visualizing, that if I bring the level of education to these people, they will be able to do a lot for themselves. I was already accepted through Maasai land by everybody, because even while I was in World Vision I managed to make the Reto women go back home. And they made money and materials; I made water the key thing, so we are so easily accepted because we came to address the issues that were affecting them. . . . Now there is another big issue that we need to deal with, that is FGM. It's a sensitive issue. It takes mad people to talk about it, because first of

all it's a taboo. You never even mention it. When you dare
to talk about it, they are either thinking you abuse them, or
they think you are mannerless, that kind of thing. But I find
that we have already managed to change a few. And even if
we don't change them completely, we have given them the
opportunity to come to be taught their basic rights. Because
we believe FGM is a human rights violation, then we look
at the health issues related to that. . . . We have a rescue
center in Kajiado, it's called Tasaru Rescue girl's center. I
do it with Agnes Pareiyo.

Here Marima discussed how she continued to be involved in the
development of the Maasai woman, beginning with issues of health,
education, and economic empowerment, and using the social capital
she has acquired through the years, beginning to tackle the taboo
issue of female genital mutilation. Realizing that Maasai women in the
rural setting have no comprehension of women's or human rights, she
approaches FGM from the perspective of health in addition to rights,
something that they can now understand based on previous training
received through her other development activities. Marima does not
work alone; she collectivizes with other educated Maasai women both
in the development of Reto and in the rescue efforts at Tasaru.

Nangurai also believes in bridging the knowledge gap between
her young charges and their elders, and between the literate and the
illiterate. One of the areas on which she has recently begun to embark
is education relating to HIV/AIDS, having realized that Maasai women
were ignorant about how it is spread.

In the course of talking to the ladies, you know we are
very close so sometimes I bring them to my house and we
watch videos together. I was talking to a group of them. I
talked to them about AIDS in urban centers. But they were
laughing that they are safe, they don't go to urban centers.
Forgetting that their men go to sell cattle in the urban
centers and when their pockets are full and there are the
women/prostitutes waiting for those heavy pockets. [Maasai]
women call them skirt wearers. Because they wear shukas
(sarongs). And the husband will come home and say I slept
with a skirt wearer. They didn't realize their husbands will
bring the disease home.

For a woman who grew up in a comfortable, middle-class family, Judy
Thongori was surprised by the amount of illiteracy and poverty that

most women in Kenya live with when she started working at FIDA. She described her experience thus:

> I came face-to-face with poverty. It occurred to me how legal illiteracy had affected people's lives. And how gifted we were; we had all this knowledge in our heads, and it didn't cost anything to give it to others. But that knowledge given to someone who really needed it helped a lot. I remember driving to Embu and meeting a client waiting outside the court—she started jumping with excitement. Having a competent lawyer was more than she could imagine. Having a lawyer from Nairobi was like a miracle. So you can imagine the way it affected her confidence and everything. Now children who almost couldn't go to school could go back to school. I could hardly believe I was the same person who used to practice commercial law. I was a changed person.

Through her encounter with poverty and legal illiteracy, Thongori found her calling: educating the public through the media on family law, engaging in public debates about the same, and helping every woman (or man) who needed legal knowledge to fight for their rights. She provided legal education in community centers and churches and through television and in the newspapers, even as she also helped construct family law in the country. She found, like most women in this study, that their knowledge and networks provided them with the resources necessary to solve social, legal, economic, and educational problems. Bridging those gaps of knowledge and resources provides the women leaders with avenues for leadership through service.

Resourcefulness and Creative Problem Solving

In each of the 16 narratives, the women discussed the ways and means that they had utilized to solve the problems they had encountered on personal, professional, and community levels. They also described what they considered an African woman's trait: that of being a resourceful and creative problem solver wrought upon the crucible of poverty and challenges. Micro-credit, women's merry-go-rounds (savings groups), legal know-how, and networks were all resources that women could creatively employ in solving the problems that they and other womenfolk encountered.

For Kaara, the growth of micro-credit was one example of women solving their own problems. She related:

We are the engines of our own societies. Look at the micro-credit thing emerging from the women's groups, which is not anything that anybody came to energize; it is the creativity and innovativeness as we look to meet these budget lines without any budget, and people come up with a very viable way of mobilizing resources, out of goodwill. And we are living for Africa, because we manage budgets lines without a budget, we give health service without medical insurance, we mobilize resources with no capital, etc. Poverty is a created scarcity, and if it is a created scarcity, it can be dealt with and dealing with it in exactly what you have observed our ordinary women doing.

Kaara eloquently explained how women manage family finances when there is actually little money, send their children to school, provide health care, and meet their families' needs with minimal tangible resources. That is because women in Africa, and Kenya especially, have learned how to "create something from nothing," to work with the little they have, stretching it to meet their basic needs. That, for Kaara, makes African women the engines of their society.

Mombo was resourceful in dealing with the problem of having few women in the pipeline for church leadership. She said:

I found about 10 women students, but now there [are] about 60. That has taken raising money for their support. I also have a conviction that we have to bring women such as single mothers who are left out within the church hierarchy, who are never given an opportunity; I have been admitting them for theological education. The church has criticized me for that, but for me it's okay.

Mombo recognized that as academic dean, she had the opportunity to change the status quo by ensuring that a steady stream of women would receive a theological education. To make that happen, she made use of her networks locally and abroad to source scholarships for women students, because the churches refused to sponsor them. Rev. Mbugua, who is all too familiar with the struggles of women in the church, discovered that women found ways to deal with family problems. Some of the problems women were dealing with were brought on by the fact that some men did not sufficiently contribute to the upbringing of their children. She related:

> I feel that necessity is the best teacher. Just that necessity and knowing that this drunkard will never build me a house, he will never educate my children, he will never do this or that. So the issue then is, do I follow him drinking, do I look at my children as they suffer, or what do I do? So for me, necessity has become a great teacher. And even the people, it is true the African women are very resilient. And I guess it is because of their poverty. So necessity and, in a way, poverty and problems have their own blessings in disguise.

Rather than wallow in self-pity, these women found ways to creatively solve their problems, as individuals or in collectives. As Mbugua observed, rather than wait for a drunkard husband to provide, the woman would simply fill in the role of father and mother and provider and sustainer for the family. This experience is what both Wahu and Abuom criticized, saying that it is socializing boys to grow up into irresponsible men, because they watch their fathers being irresponsible, and girls to take on too many family responsibilities, because they watch their own mothers doing the same. Both of them were convinced that a resocialization needed to take place, by first encouraging men to rise up and be responsible fathers and husbands. In the meantime, women and women leaders found resourceful ways to handle their problems. In addition, women leaders talked about their maturity through experiences.

Maturity in Leadership

Meyerson and Scully (1995) theorized that tempered radicalism may look different at each stage of a person's development, with some persons becoming more tempered with age and others becoming more radical. Many of the participants talked about the mistakes they had made in their earlier leadership experiences because they were too bold, too radical, and too independent minded to be effective. For example, Mombo talked about her experiences when she was still teaching in a diocesan college and attempting to bring about changes in policies. She said:

> While in this diocese I initiated the whole dialogue on the ordination of women. Between 1985 and 1995, I spoke about it in every synod. And at first they would chase me and tell me to go away and get a husband. I made a lot of mistakes

back then, coz I was young and didn't know how to play the game. I began politicking, coz I realized you had to find ways to gain the men's trust. By 1990 they had agreed in principle that they would ordain women, so it was working. By the time I was leaving to go and study for my Ph.D. I knew they would never go back.

Learning how to play the game meant several things for Mombo, one of which was approaching issues with care and choosing battles wisely in order to survive long enough to see some change. Whereas she would not give up the fight, she learned how to agitate more effectively, lessons she would utilize later as an academic dean in an institution where she was the only female in a leadership position when she began working there. Similarly, Wainaina talked about learning interdependence with age, having discovered that too much independence was not a good thing. She related:

I found that even in the home where you have grown up in very different environments and we have children jointly with somebody who doesn't have your values. I mean someone who can tolerate who you are and the things you stand for, but they do not necessarily go along. Then when you disagree, that becomes a real challenge, because either you have to give up your position or you have to defy. And for me, I chose to defy a lot of things, and obviously that creates conflicts; and over the years, looking back now 30, nearly 40, years of that, I can see that perhaps had I been a little bit more better prepared, or better mentored. There are certain things I could have persisted on, and negotiated. Because in the beginning, my thing was independence. I wanted to be independent; I didn't want ever to ask for this, and so on. But looking back now, we need to grow out of dependence, into independence, to a higher level of interdependence. And that is something that I have only now learnt a little bit later in life. It would have been very good had I had that frame of mind. Then when I became independent, I would have started working towards interdependence. What I found is that in my independence, I sort of just said, well, I don't need you. I can get on without you. If I were to live my life all over again, I would really negotiate a little bit more to move out of the independence frame faster.

At 65 years of age, Wainaina could look back at her life and realize the mistakes she had made. She felt that she had passed on some of those streaks (especially fierce independence) to her children and wished she had learned early enough to seek interdependence at home and in her work. In this illustration, she is talking about some of the struggles she had as a married woman over gender constraints and expectations. Luckily for her, even though she had some regrets, her marriage had survived all of those years. The lessons she learned throughout her life and work helped her better navigate the changing terrain of feminist organizing, especially as African women begin to actively engage in lesbian and abortion debates.

Mbugua also found herself reflecting back on relationships between men and women and how learning to temper her approach has enabled her to prevail. She said:

> Another lesson I have learnt is tolerance. Because before I would get very impatient with men and feel like they were being inconsiderate about women. But now I realize that they too are ignorant. They, too, were brought up in the same circumstances like us that women are inferior and men are superior. So this has enabled me to have the patience to work sometimes behind the scenes to ensure that men are trained. Coz I realize that there are so many trainings for women, but men are not being trained.

Learning tolerance, perhaps better explained as learning that both men and women are socialized within the same gender norms and stereotypes, helped Mbugua rearrange her outlook, giving her the patience necessary to find solutions to those problems rather than merely blaming men for patriarchy. In the maturity process as leaders, women also found that they could make good use of what Patricia Hill Collins (2004) calls the outsider/within positionality.

Leverage Outsider/Within Positionality

Outsiders/within are people who belong to a certain social group or organization but who, because of their social identity and/or different value system, find that they cannot fully fit into those organizations and communities. They exist on the margins as they attempt to both fit in and stand out. Mombo aptly described this positionality in her experiences at St. Paul's University. She said:

I realized that I rubbed shoulders with the hierarchy. I will
open my mouth at the meetings. I will interrupt, because
I realized that when I waited for the opportunity to speak,
it would not be given to me. So sometimes I will jump in
and say, "Mr. Chairman, this is what I want to say," and I
would say it. Very interesting experiences, because this is
an institution which is charged with, which is supposed to
stand for, fairness and justice. Yet there are gender inequities;
they are oppressive, [and] it's basically an unfair institution.
The good things they are doing I support, the things that
are bad I critique.... The ladies had been told [I] am a
feminist, so they did not want to associate with me in case
they are called feminists too. So if I become assertive, I am
not motherly, if I become motherly, I am not assertive. And
remember, when I came they said "she is just a woman."

Mombo found out through her experience what researchers have
proven through their studies—that women in leadership and management positions are evaluated utilizing different standards than men
(see, e.g., Carli & Eagly, 2001). When she showed assertiveness, she was
judged as not being motherly enough, and if she displayed motherly
tendencies, then she was not considered assertive enough. Whereas she
was not surprised by the gender inequities at St. Paul's, having been
in church-related institutions her entire professional career, she was
determined to do something about it. She learned to assert herself at
board meetings and to actually use that which was thrown at her to her
advantage (such as the label "feminist"). She later talked about realizing that since they already called her a feminist, she could articulate
certain policy positions fearlessly, because a feminist is one who refuses
to be a doormat! She might as well have been following Kaara's advice
to young leaders: "In the boardroom, you have no apology to say you
have forgotten me. Sort them out so that they will never dare to forget
you, because you are there by right and merit, not as a privilege."

Mombo was not alone in finding out that assertiveness was not
rewarded in women, or the contradictions inherent in being a woman
in leadership in the African context. Riria found similar challenges
in the financial management/banking sector and the development
arena. She said:

But let me tell you, there is a price. When you see me here,
let me assure you there is a price. And one of the prices you
pay is how people view you. So a lot of women will shy away

so that they are not construed a certain way. I am construed as a rebel, because I stand for what I believe, and I will not let any man mess with me. That I don't do. Feminine I am, but don't mistake it to mean I will let anybody walk on me. Now, assertiveness has not been taken very kindly by men. You have got to work double hard; you have to be a different person. I don't want to be taken for a man. I start by telling people I am a mother, I am a grandmother, and then on top of this I am this [professional]. Because women think that you have to behave like men. I can tell you I am very feminine.

Riria felt the need to defend her femininity even as she asserted herself as a leader. She told many stories about her experiences in boardrooms, where men would be attempting to reduce her to "just a woman" by commenting on her dress, hair, and makeup rather than treating her as an equal partner. She had learned how to take their "compliments" and then go straight ahead into the content and substance of the meeting, without ever getting angry or complaining about sexual harassment. However, she recognized the fact that she had to work doubly hard to ensure her credibility as a leader in the financial world, merely because she was a woman. It was part of the price to pay for being a woman in leadership within the African culture and in fields dominated by men. But, as Wainaina advised:

In fact, one of the other things about the strengths is that as [a] leader, you must be prepared to be different. Never be afraid of being different. If you are afraid of being different, you are not going to get far. If you are afraid of being called names, of being called a bad girl, of being used as [a] bad example, you are not going to get anywhere. I am prepared to take all that, because in my village now there are certain things I have done that young girls can do, but what will the villagers say, they have learnt bad manners from Njoki. That's a sacrifice I am willing to make for the rights of women.

Throughout this chapter, African women leaders have articulated the various ways in which they survive and thrive in a patriarchal society, having learned to become tempered radicals intent on rocking the boat without falling out. They not only utilized the five strategies articulated by Meyerson (2001) but further expanded upon the notion

of a tempered radical by demonstrating other context-specific strategies that they utilize. These strategies are similar to those expressed
by African American women in leadership,[1] suggesting that the fact of
their oppression under racism, sexism, and other intersecting forces
might be eliciting similar survival strategies in the two groups. Both
groups leverage their outsider/within positionality in organizations.
They are resourceful problem solvers, and they talked about learning
how to choose battles wisely as they matured in their leadership—they
have to rock the boat, yet remain in it.

In order to be successful, these women leaders are not only
tempered radicals intent on bringing about social transformation, but
they are also servant leaders; they earn credibility by demonstrating to
their constituents that the goal of their leadership is to serve them, to
help them achieve social justice.

Critical Servant Leadership

Finding Fulfillment in Serving Humanity

Servant leadership is often considered a revolutionary concept that operates counter-culturally. "Since the time of the industrial revolution, managers have tended to view people as objects; institutions have considered workers as clogs within a machine" (Spears, 2002, p. 2). However, the African women in this study illustrate the fact that servant leadership is not counter-cultural from the traditional African worldview. In fact, they argue that the clash between modernity and tradition is what has altered the attitudes of the leaders due to the emergence of capitalism and its antecedents of individualism and competition. These women leaders argue that the notions of leadership as gendered male and the practices that emanate from modern conceptualizations of leadership are alien to their sensibilities as Africans and as women. For them, serving ought to be natural, inherent in a cultural genetic makeup—African women serve others, in their immediate family, their communities, and their nations, as will be demonstrated henceforth. That is not to say that traditional African society was not patriarchal—those in Kenya and most of eastern Africa were patriarchal but tended to have dual-gender complementary roles. Colonialism and Christianity, as already described in previous chapters, disrupted that dual-gender complementariness, creating a situation where the emergent norms were neither traditional nor modern, and competition rather than cooperation became the modus operandi between men and women. In this chapter, African women leaders describe their leadership as service oriented and help define exactly what servant leadership means to them.

A Redefinition

Many of the African women leaders in this study were quite comfortable using the term *servant leader* or talking about ideal leadership being service oriented. For Wahu Kaara, though, servant came with the connotations of "beneath, subjugated, emaciated" that she did not feel comfortable using, so she redefined the terminology thus:

> I don't want to take servant because of the connotations in how it is used, but fulfillment in serving humanity; leadership that provides [the leader] with a sense of fulfillment in serving others. That is the greatest strength we have as African women in leadership. I learnt how to serve and lead by observing my grandmother and mother, so this is a heritage that we have, the training that the fulfillment of the being is the delivery of service to humanity. This, of course, contradicts the paradigms perpetuated, especially from the West, that the fulfillment of the being comes from exploitation!

In spite of her discomfort over using the term *servant leader*, Kaara was convinced that those who would be effective as women in leadership needed to learn how to serve, and she talked at length about those who did not do so, as will be demonstrated later. However, that discomfort is the paradox that makes servant leadership unique, that those who choose this modus operandi do so intentionally, having first felt the nudge to serve, and then in the process of becoming leaders, as described by Greenleaf (1977). Whereas Greenleaf did not confess to having "discovered" servant leadership from the Christian scriptures, servant leadership is the method of leadership that Jesus taught his disciples to use. The disciples were uncomfortable with having their master serving them, in that context, taking on the most menial and humiliating tasks that the house servant had to do for guests—washing their feet. However, Jesus was eloquently putting common understanding of leadership on its head by demonstrating to his disciples the model of leadership he wanted them to emulate. Greenleaf ascribed his discovery of servant leadership to a story where the person who served a team of sojourners later turned out to have been the leader of the monastic group (see "The Servant as Leader," in Greenleaf, 1977). This book demonstrates the practice of critical servant leadership, as the women are able to lead and serve by breaking down barriers and deconstructing unjust social arrangements aided by the wisdom they have acquired from critical spirituality and a servant's orientation to leading (McClellan, 2006, 2010). McClellan coined the term "critical servant leadership" to capture the merging of critical spirituality.[1] Whereas the African women leaders were quick to point out that serving others in their families, communities and nations cam naturally to them, they were also cognizant of sometimes being perceived as merely beasts of burden (Ngunjiri, 2009). this chapter demonstrates how they deconstruct those perceptions and social arraignments aimed at disenfranchising them and/or their constituents, instead working at perpetuating social justice ideals.

In the political field, Ngilu expressed her dismay at the brand of leadership demonstrated by those in elected office. She was convinced that if there were more women in parliament, especially women who were willing to serve, they could make a difference. She said:

> I hope that someday soon those in elected office will not be the masters but instead will humble themselves to be servants of the people. This is where women come in, because women have always been servants, right from their kitchens, their churches, their communities, and their schools. Women are born servants, always ready to serve the family, the community, and soon the nation too. We haven't seen leaders yet because women have yet to arise.

Whereas I do not necessarily agree with the way some of the women in the study ascribed servant leadership to "being born to serve," I understood what they meant—in the African context, women served everyone else. In fact, part of the reason there is a disparity in literacy rates between girls and boys is because parents send their boys to school, while girls are made to stay home and look after their siblings, help on the farm, or perform domestic chores. In this scenario, the women leaders were ascribing positive characteristics to the training they received as young girls that they articulated in their leadership—that they are born to serve. Rather than serve in a subservient, subjugated sense—the reason many of them are in leadership is to attempt to emancipate womenfolk from this subjugation that places women in a second-status position in society—these women found a way to make good use of their cultural heritage. They explained the various ways that their leadership had to be from this servant orientation.

To wrap up their explication of leadership as service, Abuom explained how African women's resiliency adds to their capacity to thrive in spite of nearly insurmountable challenges. She said:

> I was saying that when you look at the continent and in this country in particular, I can see the resilience of the African women in terms of economic survival and ensuring that in spite of all the bartering of the family structure, she holds

the unit together. She becomes the pillar. To leave her at the
pictorial image of a beast is not telling the whole story.

Here Abuom demonstrated what I will discuss in a later chapter, the
contradictions inherent in the women's social position—beasts of
burden versus servants/leaders by choice. She argued that African
women, because of the context in which they live out their lives, have
to be resilient, to persevere in the face of insurmountable challenges,
because they have to hold the communities together. They are the glue
that binds individuals and groups into feasible communities. Yet at the
same time, she recognizes that they do pay a high price, akin to being
beasts of burden. Her contestation, however, is that women in Africa
are not merely beasts of burden but, rather, are also the source of the
communities' strength and sustenance.

In the text that follows the women leaders articulate their choice
to lead from a servant leader perspective, something they explain that
they have acquired through experience and by observing their mothers,
grandmothers, and *Othermothers*[2] in the community, something deep
within African traditional cultures, especially in regard to women—that
women were first and foremost service givers, and that this is partly
how they fulfilled their purpose for being. Kaara was convinced that
whereas modernity has washed over these traditional notions of providing service, a remnant can still be found among some women leaders,
not all, because many have been co-opted into ruling like men:

> Those women in parliament have to take a deliberate move to
> practice politics in the new dispensation which I am arguing
> is the pedestal of women, constructive way[s] of doing things.
> But if you go on the politics of maneuver, of exploitation,
> of corruption, like many of our men, and we know many
> women who have perfected that—that is a misnomer.

Kaara illustrated that the real, the authentic, African women's leadership that is respected and honored and credible is the one that is
service oriented. When women in parliament forget their origins as
mothers and as servants of the community, they quickly lose credibility
with their constituents. In discussing the servant as leader, Greenleaf
prophetically observed the following:

> The signs of the times suggest that, to future historians, the
> next thirty years will be marked as the period when the dark
> skinned and the deprived and the alienated of the world

effectively asserted their claims to stature, and that they were
not led by privileged elite but by exceptional people from
their own kind. (1977, p. 34)

The women leaders discussed here are a fulfillment of Greenleaf's apt
prophecy—they are the dark skinned and deprived and alienated who
have arisen to serve their own kind in their search for social justice. I
will illustrate the various ways in which the women articulated servant
leadership as their chosen and culturally relevant leadership style.

Empowerment

Greenleaf conceptualized servant leaders as leaders who are committed
to the growth of people (Greenleaf, 1977). Spears (2002) talked about
servant leaders as leaders who "believe that people have an intrinsic
value beyond their tangible contributions as workers . . . deeply committed to the growth of each and every individual . . . to nurture the
personal, professional, and spiritual growth of employees" (pp. 7–8).
Kaara demonstrated this when she argued that it is time for women to
take the reins of leadership in Africa, in order for there to be reconstruction and rebuilding after 4 decades of corruption and exploita-
tion. She further said:

> They [men in power] must exit and give us [the] way, oth-
> erwise we will all perish, but women refuse to perish. It is
> game short for men, not that I have a problem with men
> per se, but with the brand of leadership, nay, rulership with
> an iron fist. The new leadership must be about what each
> person can contribute to humanity, and history is showing
> us that this is the moment where women have the greatest
> opportunity to make their known and not-acknowledged
> contribution to humanity. We build, we nurture, and we
> have constructive skills.

Similarly, Abuom argued that women should be able to articulate their
particular brand of leadership skills and practice, acquired on the
hearth and in their private spheres of influence:

> So when I look at women and leadership, I am saying there
> are traits and skills in women arising from both nature and
> nurture; the roles that women play in the home that involve

multitasking, these have led to skills of inclusion, negotiation, and to care ... we have to turn around a leadership
that is holistic, that is inclusive of all, that recognizes and
upholds everybody.

Here Abuom posited that women's leadership derives from their
socialization as nurturers, sustainers, and life givers, and the cultural
mandate to serve the community, resulting in experiences that might
cause women to become servant leaders. But as Kaara contended previously, not all women in leadership are necessarily servant leaders who
provide holistic, inclusive leadership. Rather, some choose to take on
this paradoxical notion of leading to serve and serving to lead.

To demonstrate practical ways in which women leaders nurture,
build, and reconcile in order to empower others, Mombo, in a previous quote, spoke about increasing the number of women undertaking
theological education at St. Paul's in order to ensure a pipeline of
trained women for ecclesial positions.

Finally, Nguru talked about her own leadership and what she felt
distinguished her at Daystar University:

I think an important one is a serving attitude. How best
can I serve these people? And then a willingness to play a
coordinating role, recognizing the potential of the people
you are working with and utilize the potential that I see in
other people. And affirm the various gifts that you see around
you and work with them to the best of your abilities.

Other women leaders talked about empowering others through facilitating their access to resources, including credit facilities, education and
training, and opening doors for women to participate in organizational
leadership. They demonstrate the cultural roots of women's leadership
as servant leaders intent on empowering others through inclusion,
negotiation, and an ethic of care.

Healing and Reconciliation

Spears (2002) posited that one of the greatest strengths of a servant
leader is the ability to heal the self and others. Servant leaders want
"to make whole" both themselves and those they serve. As Greenleaf
(1977) conceptualized, "There is something subtle communicated to
one who is being served and led if implicit in the compact between

servant leader and led is the understanding that the search for whole-
ness is something they share" (p. 36). These African women leaders'
purpose for engaging in social justice leadership is to heal the wounds
of social injustice. Thus they seek to heal individuals, communities,
societies, and nations in their work and words as leaders.

Kaara talked about the work of the World Social Forum as an
organization involved in critiquing existing economic structures and
advocating for alternatives that help heal nations:

> The World Social Forum is keen in trying to build synergy
> of the emerging alternatives for sustenance of life. Because
> the current paradigm, it's clear, is serving the interest of
> finance capital only for profit, and at the level we are in, it
> is actually a great danger to life sustenance.

Abuom proposed a leadership that is based on pooling resources, or
in Kenyan language, pulling together (Harambee), one of our national
mottos:

> Bring what you have, and I bring what I have, so that we
> are in relationship. Because I don't have what you have, and
> you don't have what I have, so we are brought together so
> that you partake of mine and I partake of yours. This is a
> powerful way of thinking about it. My worry, and my real
> wish and prayer, is that God will give me grace and health
> to work with these churches on the issues of resolving con-
> flicts; conflicts fueled by people who flag ethnicity during
> national elections.

Like previous elections, the 2007 national elections precipitated violence in various locations in the country, as parliament aroused ethnic
animosities, creating conflict where people had coexisted peacefully for
generations. In fact, the chaos that erupted was the worst the country had experienced since independence. It is this kind of behavior
that Abuom was decrying here, and hoping that she would find ways
as a national and Pan-African Christian leader to help resolve such
conflicts.

Nangurai expressed her desire to not only take girls away from
their parents in order to provide them a safe haven to acquire education but also to seek reconciliation with those parents once they began
to understand the benefits of educating their children. She illustrates
this point thus:

But when you see Charity and others like her, it's very
encouraging. Charity is now an orphan, as her parents are
both dead. But reconciliation had already taken place with
her parents. With her first salary she took her father a blan-
ket seeking his blessings. Now she is the one who is taking
care of her sisters and brothers. So when you see that you
get that strength.

Other than being a source of encouragement when she was feeling
down, Nangurai was excited by the fact that Charity had been able
to reconcile with her parents. Whereas rescue from forced marriages
often meant that the girls and their parents were at loggerheads, she
worked hard to help them reconcile in order to maintain familial and
community relationships.

Achieng, whose tales of the impact of war in southern Sudan were
heartrending, to say the least, talked about how women had initiated
peace efforts in their country:

We want [the] war stopped, because the war is killing people
who were not involved in the decision. We know that there is
a problem, but that problem does not need to mean killing
people who are not involved. And those who question who
are we, *we are not victims, we are actors* [emphasis added]. That
is the story of Sudan Women's Voices for Peace formed in
1994 with the background of peace building and advocacy
for human women rights. We want to speak for ourselves.
We are not speaking only for women and children; we are
speaking for the families here. We are speaking for security
at home. . . . We developed a program called seeds of peace.
It's a counseling program to promote emotional healing for
victims of war.

Achieng was quite adamant that she and her fellow Sudanese womenfolk were not victims but, rather, had chosen to become active agents
of their own emancipation. Part of that agency involved instituting
Sudanese Women's Voice for Peace and similar organizations that gave
women a collective voice against the violence and war in their countries.
In each case, the women articulated how their personal experiences,
professional exposure, and community needs interacted and led to
their practice of healing as reconciliation, conflict resolution, trauma
counseling, gender mainstreaming, and peace building. The stories
further demonstrate how women engage in institutional entrepreneur-

ship with the purpose of providing alternative institutions that meet social justice ideals for the common good.

Stewardship

Servant leadership assumes a commitment to serving the needs of others by using the tools at the leader's disposal (Spears, 1995, 2002). Stewardship implies holding something in trust for another. Kaara was convinced that Africa's strength lies in the commitment her people have toward human solidarity:

> So that is the strength that Africa has, that together we can make it; that spirit of human solidarity, that commitment to not just exist[ing] but living, because living is participating and making your life practical and the essence of being. And for me, Africa will decide what becomes of it, because Africa is the only continent and to some extent Asia, where you find that the bedrock of the human spirit has not been defiled, that has not been broken, *that is determined to see future generations have something to inherit* [emphasis added]. Not for purposes of consumption, but for propagating the purposes of creation and the continuity of humanity.

This strength in solidarity is behind African philosophies such as *Ubuntu* (individual-in-community identity and the essence of humanness), *Harambee* (pooling/pulling together), and *Umoja* (oneness, united we stand). African philosophies such as these three empower women to collectivize as stewards of their communities and to pool their resources in order to, for example, send children to school, build decent and safe houses, and install safe water in their homes. Through collective action, women develop their local communities and ensure that their (communal) children have a future. Without safe housing, clean water, and education, there would be no future generation to speak of.

In historicizing the notion of stewardship, Likimani talked about how women in colonial times contributed to the freedom movement yet were left out of the discourse in the existing canon as recorded in textbooks. She explained:

> My interests are in women and development, and it is what I write most about, women, because I feel they have been ignored. . . . When I was young, we had emergency [as our]

people were fighting the colonialists. [They formed guerrilla warfare as] the Mau Mau,[3] the forest fighters. . . . You read so many books. You never see the name of a woman who fought. Have you ever read any?

In Likimani's case, stewardship involved putting women back into history by writing about their involvement in the struggle for freedom. Her 1985 book *Passbook Number F 47927: Women and Mau Mau in Kenya* was written for this purpose. In it, she explicated women's participation in the freedom movement, helping younger generations gain a better understanding of both gender relations in that time period and how women helped to sustain their communities in the midst of calamities.

Mombo's notions of stewardship include providing a home to children needing one, in spite of the fact that becoming a foster parent as a single woman made tails wag incessantly. As she said, "I have fostered three sons, I am being asked to consider fostering a girl. Maybe I will. For me, they are my family, although sometimes as a single parent you are seen as a monster. I give them an education and a home." Mombo was convinced that providing a home for three children, ensuring that they had access to food, shelter, clothing, and quality education, was part of her stewardship as one who had been blessed with resources. She did not have to wait until she got married, if ever, to play that role, even though it brought with it challenges as a single woman in a community that privileges marriage.

Each of these stories demonstrates the women's articulation of serving others through stewardship, ensuring that future generations would have hope through education, learning about their history, and engaging in the creation of a just society.

Building Community

Greenleaf (1977) felt that much had been lost in U.S. society through the institutionalization of services that in prior generations would have been provided through local communities. As such, he conceptualized servant leaders as people who helped to build community within the institutions that they led. Community has not yet been lost in most African contexts, even though with the advent of urbanization, globalization, and the impact of armed conflicts it has disintegrated in certain contexts. African women leaders work to strengthen existing communities as well as to recreate a sense of community where this may have been eroded or damaged.

Nangurai, in her role as headmistress of a girls' boarding school that also serves as a rescue center, talked about creating community between the girls and their estranged parents. She was of the opinion that reconciliation was imperative to maintaining family relationships, that educating the girls should not mean taking them away from their communities without the hope of a return. For Nangurai, this was particularly critical to the success of her mission, because community is especially crucial among the Maasai who, as a pastoralist group, live in transitory villages. She explained:

> We hold meetings with the parents to bring them on board to our programs. We also have programs where we try to help them reconcile, and recognize that she is still their daughter. It is very difficult. We hold culture talks where old women come and talk to the girls about their culture. And sometimes we hold debates whereby we go through the cultures and say which ones are good, which ones are not, and some of them [old women] walk out in protest. Especially when we touch on [female] circumcision, yet it's important for them to know what is expected of them.

As a parent herself, she felt it was necessary for the girls and their parents to maintain their familial relationships during the girls' schooling and beyond. As such, even though she faced a lot of resistance, some of the parents had begun to support her after they came to recognize the positive impact education was having on their villages.

As a survivor of the war in Sudan and a peace builder, Achieng talked about not only working with women but also with men because of the need to rebuild their war-ravaged country and to recreate a sense of community in southern Sudan. Here she reiterated her conviction that they are not merely victims but have become actors in the rebuilding process:

> As we said, we are actors, we are not victims. We want to speak for ourselves. We are not speaking only for women and children; we are speaking for the families here. We are speaking for security at home: Who is the main victim of war? It's that woman out there. Nobody cares for this woman. We do spend time on men's care, but nobody is caring for the women. If we are talking about politics and about this war, we don't sleep . . . keeping peace, providing peace, that is our identity. We also advocate that we are

women, daughters, mothers, wives; we don't belong to any
tribe, because we can marry anybody.

With the strong sense of ethnicity being part of the cause of conflicts
in most of Africa, Achieng's mantra was that women belong to no
tribe and that every tribe served as part of her organization's (Sudan
Women's Voice for Peace) method of reaching out to all Sudanese in
engendering the lost sense of community.

For African contexts, building community can be more about
developing an already existing community by empowering women
economically in order for them to provide for their families, such as
what Riria does. Such women engage in small-scale entrepreneurial
undertakings, including community schools and small-scale businesses.
In other contexts, it means building peace in order to rebuild community, where years of war have left people displaced and disenfranchised. Yet in other cases, such as Nguru's, it means utilizing available
resources for community building and service—above and beyond
the call of duty as an organizational leader. Whatever the case, the
women illustrate servant leadership as community restoration in their
various ways. Critical to their understanding of service is the notion of
rebuilding or strengthening families in order to rebuild or strengthen
communities and, in that way, to strengthen the nation as a whole.
As such, Achieng, who is from the Sudan, talked about representing
entire families in her work as a peace builder.

The importance of community in the African context cannot
be overemphasized. *Ubuntu,* that African worldview that regards individual identity in terms of community identification, continues to be
strong (Mbigi, 1996; Mbiti, 1969). Ubuntu, or being fully human, is
derived from the Bantu languages of eastern and southern Africa. As
described by Archbishop Desmond Tutu, "A person with ubuntu is open
and available to others, affirming of others, does not feel threatened
that others are able and good, for he or she has a proper self-assur-
ance that comes from knowing that he or she belongs in a greater
whole and is diminished when others are humiliated or diminished,
when others are tortured or oppressed." So when Africans say, "I am
because we are, and because we are, I am," it is not simply a mantra
but a complete worldview that recognizes community as being pivotal
to individual identity.

To further elaborate on the sense of Ubuntu, or the essence of
being human in the African worldview, it is important to talk about
kinship. As Mbiti (1969) contended, kinship "largely governs the behavior, thinking and whole life of the individual in the society of which

he [*sic*] is a member. . . . The kinship system is a vast system stretching laterally (horizontally) in every direction . . . everybody is related to everybody else" (p. 104). An individual's identity is tied up with her or his sense of community—I am because we are, and because we are, I am. Furthermore, it becomes particularly important to protect those kinship ties by rebuilding communities, by enhancing the sense of community. It is no wonder, then, that the women leaders actively engaged in building and restoring community; they were articulating what it meant for them to be women and leaders in the African context. In addition to building community, the women referred to their leadership as service that is compelled by a spiritual source.

Humility

Humility is a prerequisite to a leader's ability and propensity to become a servant leader, one who, in spite of her or his positional power, chooses to serve. For these African women, becoming humble and becoming servant leaders go hand in hand. They explained how they find fulfillment in serving humanity, otherwise they would not do the kind of work they do that requires so much thankless effort and struggle (Ngunjiri, 2006b). Some learned to serve by observing other leaders; for others, servant leadership and humility came from their Christian upbringing, education, and familiarity with biblical stories. Gichaga talked about her servant leadership in terms of both Judeo-Christian terms as well as recognition of the worth of each individual:

> One is to emulate Jesus, who was the best teacher and the greatest leader of all. As a leader, he was also a servant. I try to utilize some of his teaching[s] [as a] servant leader. And a little earlier I said [I] am a people person, and that again has impacted on me, because for me as a God-fearing person, every person is important. And it has created peace in the office. . . . The other thing is just humility.

Riria also talked about humility as being part of what makes up her leadership, humility that she learned through her Catholic schooling:

> And we were also taught humbleness, because you get to a point that you think you can't then get somebody to do it for you at that point. So it taught you to trust yourself but also to trust the input of others.

Similarly, Thongori talked about having learned humility from her mentor, and being able to use that in her practice of law for the marginalized:

> Lee taught me the humility that ought to attend to the practice of law. When we came from law school, we were not taught to serve. We graduated so that we could come to the city, make money, and actually be served as it were. I learnt about service, and service for me is basic.

Nguru also connected humility and service, in her case utilizing Christian scriptures and terms:

> By using biblical terminology, one would say *not to lord it over the people.* You come around a table, people want to be affirmed to reach their potential, and in that way, they perform to their best. Currently at Daystar I am coordinating a program of training in the region, and I see that I still use tools and skills of working with people. Recognizing them, helping them maintain their dignity, and helping them to do their best.

In the various ways described in this chapter, the women leaders demonstrate some of the elements of servant leadership described in the literature. More importantly, they illustrate how they practice servant leadership as the approach to leadership that is culturally relevant and that enables them to find fulfillment in serving humanity. Their approach to servant leadership is guided by their ability to deconstruct existing social arrangements and to engage in constructing alternatives, either through transforming existing institutions or as institutional entrepreneurs. For them, servant leadership is a bold assertion aimed at transforming the status quo, guided by practical wisdom from their spiritual center.

Spirituality and Leadership

In listening to, observing, and reading materials about and by these African women leaders, it became increasingly clear that spirituality is the modus operandi and the raison d'être for their leadership and life. Spirituality seemed to permeate everything they thought about, pursued, and talked about, so much so that more often than not, it was an unspoken understanding. This would illustrate what Professor John Mbiti, one of the premier African theologians and philosophers, asserted 40 years ago: that Africans are notoriously religious/spiritual (Mbiti, 1969). Oftentimes in analyzing the transcripts, it was clear that the same quotes that illustrated servant leadership also illustrated spiritual leadership. In the same way, many of the quotes that illustrated tempered radicalism also pointed forward to a spiritual foundation for action. In the following pages, I demonstrate how the African women leaders in this study talked about and illustrated their personal spirituality and its connection to their leadership for social justice.

Spirituality as a Source of Direction and Purpose for Life and Leadership

Prior research cited in chapter 2 indicates that African American women utilize spirituality as a source of direction and purpose for their lives and their professions (Jones, 2003; Mattis, 2002). The quotes that follow illustrate how the African women leaders in this study used theistic spirituality to explain why they do what they do—spirituality was the foundation upon which they built a purpose for life, and a sense of direction as leaders. Judy Thongori, now a renowned expert on family law in Kenya, talked about discovering her purpose in life after graduating from the University of Nairobi with an LLB and landing her first job in the attorney general's chambers. She was dissatisfied with that job because she felt it was not challenging enough, nor did it feel purposeful to her. As she explained it:

> I remember praying to God many mornings that God give
> me a purpose for life. . . . So I like to give encouragement
> or direction to people's projects. So what am I saying? Yes,
> I actually don't have to be involved everywhere in every
> board that exists . . . and I know that I am accountable to
> your God. I know whatever it is God I have done, even in
> court, when someone comes and talks to me about cases,
> I will never ever shut them out. I give free advice, family
> advice; I get so excited and am walking on air because I
> have been able to help somebody.

For Thongori, purpose for life meant stepping down from her corporate law job to advocate for the underserved women through the
Federation of Women Lawyers, and even after she had left FIDA, she
continued to tithe a portion of her private practice to giving pro bono
services. In addition, as recounted in her personal narrative, Thongori
educates the public on legal matters through the media, community
settings, and every other avenue that opens up to her.

In the political arena, the often misunderstood but arguably the
most powerful woman in Kenyan politics also talked about finding her
purpose through her relationship with God. In the quote that follows,
she explains why she fought so hard for the Health Bill that failed in
parliament, in which she had proposed a national health insurance
similar to that found in Canada and the United Kingdom. She was
convinced that it was the only effective way to provide health care to
all persons in Kenya, not just the rich and the middle class. However,
her bill failed, because the president did not sign it into law, arguing
that the government did not have the resources for a national health
insurance plan. Hon. Ngilu was not willing to give up completely, though
she changed her tactics to ensure that government hospitals and dis-
pensaries, especially those in rural and marginal areas, were revamped
and refurbished with the necessary resources. As she explained: "God
knows that [I] am on the right track. It is not the masses that are
right . . . I may be alone, but it is right."

Mombo felt a sense of calling to teach adults in church institutions,
but she struggled with the call, particularly in attempting to explain it
to her parents. They were hard pressed to understand how and why a
single, young woman would choose to join a theological institution as
a student. Mombo related:

> I felt that God was calling me, but I couldn't be exactly
> sure where. I wanted to teach adults not children. But I

felt that there was a whole area of struggling to convince my father.

Mombo not only joined St. Paul's as a student but also continued to further her education, to the great delight of her parents. Additionally, she was able to provide financial support to her family. For her, spirituality provided her with a sense of calling that required her to engage in theological education first as a student and then as a professor and an administrator in a Christian university.

Reverend Mbugua dropped out of school at age 16 and 2 years later was married with two children. Even though those early years were extremely difficult, she felt that they served as a training ground for her life's calling later on:

> You will read in my book that I left school as a very young girl, at 16, got married at 18, and so I had not finished school. I had to finish my secondary school by private education. But that transition was very difficult. I had come from a very good family, very rich family. My dad had gone to Alliance High School, believe it or not, in those early years. I think he said he was student number 36. So I had the opportunity of going to school. But falling in love and whatever, it was a very vulnerable time of life where I become a mother when I was too young and had responsibility when I was very young. And that gap, I thank God for that gap, because had I remained in that sheltered life, I would not have taken life very seriously. I would not have identified my own purpose of life. I see that God wanted me to work with women, so he had to give me an opportunity to suffer, and really suffer. . . . So back to the question of how did I get here. It started with a need. God made me realize that need, and God made me answer the question, what will you do about it? And my whole life that is what it has been . . . women know that if I know what it means to shed tears, I can identity.

Reverend Mbugua began a ministry to serve women because she could identify with their struggles, and she became one who leads by identification. She could look back and see her struggles as preparation for her life's work—empowering women through Christian fellowship, financial education, life skills training, and the like.

In each case, the women explained their life journeys and career choices in terms of being God directed. They felt a sense of calling and discovered their purpose in life through experiences that they described as being "God-ordained," so that even negative experiences served as preparation for leadership later on.

Spirituality as a Source of Leadership Practices

According to some scholars, people of African descent, especially those whose work involves social justice, explain their leadership and professional practices in moral, ethical, and spirited terminology (Dantley, 2003a, 2003b; Dillard, Abdur-Rashid, & Tyson, 2000; Jones, 2003; Mattis, 2002). Similarly, African women leaders in this study described a divine compulsion to engage in transforming leadership through service. Professor Faith Nguru talked about her leadership practices and behaviors thus:

> I get fulfillment from knowing that I have touched somebody's life, that somebody's life will not be the same because of a certain encounter. Like the work I am doing with the house helps [domestic help], and with the students in the [primary] school. I am excited that they are able to have a Christian context in which they are learning. . . . So that's where I get fulfillment, that lives are being changed as I interact with them. And that [I] am doing God's will.

For Nguru, her life's work was not only her leadership at Daystar University but also in her rural community where she and her husband (Rev. Dr. Nguru, vice chancellor of Daystar University) had established a Christian elementary school and provided resources such as water and wheelchairs to the villagers.

Anisia Achieng also described her peace building, conflict resolution, and reconciliation work, relating it to her personal spirituality:

> I think one of the areas in leadership is having convictions about what you are doing. In leadership, to sustain being vision, to sustain being tolerant, to sustain being strong, you have to have faith. When your faith is increased by what you are doing, not by just going to the church and praying. My outside work and outside activity must not relate differently from my beliefs. My conversations must relate with my faith.

It does not mean I cannot relate with non-Christians, but
it must mean that they have to be seeing from me that my
faith is my strength.

For Achieng, leading from a position of convictions, being a person of
integrity who walks her walk, and finding strength in her faith were part
of what enabled her to thrive as a leader. Spirituality was not just about
praying and attending services but about being a person of integrity
and courage in spite of the challenges inherent in peace building in
the context of war in the Sudan. Similarly, Wahu Kaara described the
connection between her leadership and her spirituality, saying:

It is the spirit that moves mountains. This is the time of
spirituality . . . because it gives you the capacity to pursue
the truth without illusion. I think as you hear me talk, you
can get the courage that I have and the commitment that
I have and the energy that I have. . . . It's because of the
spirit that is inspiring me. Then I am emboldened within
the parameters of my Christian faith. I confess Christ as
my savior, and if he could die for our liberation, we are
only being asked to act upon our liberation. That's what I
am determined to do. And that will be done without fear
or favor. It will be done with courage and determination
inspired differently not by the gains that you are going to
get. So fulfillment of life which is very spiritual is the basis
for all this.

Kaara's courage, determination, and ability to speak truth to power
came from her spiritual foundation, one she explained in reformed
evangelical Christian terminology. As far as she is concerned, her
leadership has everything to do with enacting the liberation that she
believes she has through her relationship with God/Christ. That too is
the conviction of liberation theologians,[1] who agitate for the kingdom
of God on earth and the preferential treatment of the poor. Kaara's
education and experiences place her as a practitioner of liberation
theology as she works on the local, Pan-African, and global scene agitating for debt relief and poverty eradication.

Ole Marima also described the correlation between her spirituality and her leadership:

Without being spiritually strong, I would not be able to make
it. I seek divine intervention, and am not a fundamentalist,

actually am not even a charismatic. I worship at Nairobi
Baptist Church and Africa Inland Church, but I draw my
strength from God. I would be dry, absolutely dry, if I
remove him from all that [I] am doing. I grow every day,
[and] he is the one who renews my strength, he renews
my brain, because on my own [I] am not able to do that.
When I tell people [I] am 53, they say, Mom that's a lie.
If you see my first-born he is going on 36. So, it is a direct
link. That's the basic line in my life. And that's why I have
come this far.

Marima credits her faith in God with helping her succeed as a leader
as well as a woman and a mother. She felt that God renewed her and
gave her strength to lead in various capacities.

Spirituality as a Source of Strength in the Midst of Challenges

Mattis (2002) and Jones (2003) found that African American women
utilized their spirituality to cope with the challenges from racial discrimination, structural injustices, personal problems, illnesses, and
professional struggles. Similarly, the African women leaders interviewed
talked about how they dealt with leadership and personal challenges
in terms of prayer, finding supporters, and getting help when feeling
weak. For example, Riria constantly mentioned the place of prayer in
her personal and professional life:

When I can't go on, I pray, and God hears my prayers so
much. Once I do that I see a way out. I never get desperate.
I get depressed, get really challenged, but never desperate,
and I have never felt alone. Because I really have never felt
I am desperate to a point where I don't find value in life. I
may feel so challenged that I don't know what to do . . . [if]
I am really discouraged, I feel that I can stay in bed the
whole of the next day. But I pray, and I am telling you,
prayer is so powerful.

For Riria, the power of prayer worked in her personal and professional
life, to the point where she had encouraged her staff to inculcate prayer
into their own lives. As an organization, KWFT began all of its meetings
with prayer members prayed when one of their own was thrown in jail
unjustly, which happened often, when a client who did not want to
pay would bribe police to harass the debt collector! Riria could attest

to the fact that prayer had helped her through many a dark night of the soul, through many trials and tribulations as a woman, a mother, a grandmother, and a professional.

For Nangurai, strength came in the form of people who would show up just when she needed someone to encourage her to keep on keeping on:

> I get encouraged when someone from the community comes and tells me "thank-you for what you did. My daughter is now helping me; she is the one who took me to hospital." I keep telling people that God keeps sending me angels, coz you have to work through people. Like if I talk about Rev. Joyce (my liaison for the study), she just came. She just came, and when she came here we talked and I was strengthened. So there are people who support me, even if they are not able to give financial support, they give moral support.

Achieng also found strength through her spirituality, in practical as well as more metaphysical ways, as she explained:

> I had a very bad accident. Normally when you work as a volunteer you are not insured. But I was fortunate that many friends from Europe paid [my bill] in Nairobi hospital. But I believe my healing was based on God's grace. Just 2 months [later] I was back to my peace work; nobody could believe it.

As far as she was concerned, Achieng's healing from the accident (which happened in a very remote area of northern Kenya on her way to Sudan), through a confluence of events, convinced her that God was at work in her life. People volunteered and paid her bills at Nairobi Hospital (the best but also the most expensive hospital in Kenya), and she got better faster than anyone would have expected, proving to her that God's grace was at work. Her explanation for her healing is actually quite common among many Kenyans and Africans, who find not only a physical cause for disease but also a spiritual one, therefore, healing must also be both physical and spiritual. For example, when an African falls ill, she may see a doctor, but she might also seek the counsel of a pastor, or if she is still connected to African traditions, a traditional healer/medicine person who helps her reconcile with God or spirits or the living dead, as the case may be.[2]

Mombo found strength in the conviction that God had called her to work in Christian higher education, and she was able to persevere through many years of sex and age discrimination because of that conviction:

> Even when I was being treated as a child and my morality [was] being scrutinized, my focus was that God had called me here. I served for 8 years. . . . It's lonely to be a woman leader, because you can't enter fully the male world, as much as you try to work within it. Because they still have their own clichés and phrases that you might not understand. Your fellow women mistrust you. So you are hanging in the middle, without support of the men or the women. It's a lonely exercise. But for me, that's where my faith comes in, because at the very hour of need when I feel God I am alone, then I realize that God's grace is sufficient for me when I have no one else.

For Nguru, when she felt weak or lacking in wisdom, God was there to uplift her and provide what she needed to keep going. Furthermore, she could draw on that relationship to empower herself:

> I think it [spirituality with leadership] connects in the way that there are times when I feel weak, I don't feel like I have the strength, and then I call on a strength beyond mine in prayer as a Christian. I ask God to fill me with his power, with his wisdom and with his strength. . . . And then I draw on, avail myself to, that power so that all these things can flow through me.

For these women, spirituality helps them deal with the loneliness that comes about as a leadership and personal challenge, giving them strength when they are weak, and helping them when their authority as leaders is questioned. In addition, spirituality gives them the power, wisdom, and courage to stay the course, to persist rather than give up when the challenges seem insurmountable. As such, their ability to be effective tempered radicals and/or agents of change is rooted in the strength, power, and courage derived from their spirituality. Spirituality enables them to love those they work with or for, a challenge when those are the same people making life difficult for the women as leaders. These quotes thus illustrate two elements of Africana spirituality that Paris (1995) discussed, namely, beneficence and forbearance. One of the greatest virtues that an African person can exemplify is beneficence, or altruistic love,

because it exemplifies the goal of community as it is inter-
nalized by individual persons and community leaders. That
is to say, the individual's disposition is so shaped by the
ultimate goal of community that he or she finds content-
ment in facilitating the well-being of others. (Paris, 1995,
pp. 136–137)

Paris argued that Africana people developed forbearance out of the
multitude of sufferings that they have had to endure in their history,
such as dehumanizing racial oppression, economic injustice, and political disenfranchisement. In this continuing context, African women have
developed a resiliency and persistence necessary for survival. African
women leaders in this study have acquired the capacity for silent,
subversive activities or radical, overt action, and their spirituality gives
them the wisdom to do so.

Practical Wisdom/Critical Spirituality

Dantley (2003a) coined the phrase "critical spirituality" to describe a
spirituality that combines two radical perspectives, thus:

The element of critique and deconstruction of undemocratic
power relations is blended with spiritual reflection grounded
in an African American sense of moralism, prophetic resistance, and hope in order to form the viscera of this hybrid
theoretical construct called critical spirituality. (p. 5)

Similarly, Paris (1995) conceptualized an element of Africana spirituality that is similar to critical spirituality thus:

Practical wisdom is excellence of thought that guides good
actions. This virtue pertains to the measure of cognitive
discernment necessary for determining what hinders good
action and what enables it . . . the fully developed capacity
of a free moral agent. (p. 144)

Here African women leaders demonstrate how they have deconstructed
social constructs such as religion, culture, gender roles, and leadership; they did not merely deconstruct unjust social arrangements;
rather, they were also able to postulate alternative, just, and humanistic
arrangements. Beginning with Reverend Mbugua, religion has been

one of the arenas of contracted contestation for African women, as
they came to realize it as a tool for their disempowerment, however,
they can articulate a religious sensibility that helps them emancipate
themselves. Mbugua said:

> One of them is God's faithfulness and God's desire for women
> to rise up. Because I have seen all these openings that he
> has given us which shows for sure it is his desire for us to
> rise up, and then another lesson I have learnt is tolerance.
> Because before I would get very impatient with men and feel
> like they were being inconsiderate about women. But now
> I realize that they too are ignorant. They too were brought
> in the same circumstances like us that women are inferior
> and men are superior. So this has enabled me to have the
> patience to even work out sometimes behind the scenes to
> ensure that men are trained. . . . I said, if you stand there
> and start telling men you don't know so I want to teach
> you, they will refuse. So we have worked behind the scenes
> and encouraged pastors to be trained.

Mbugua deconstructed religion, realizing that Christianity came
entrapped in Western patriarchy, which combined with existing African
patriarchy, so that men are socialized to believe in their superiority and
women in their subservience to men. Rather than overtly attack the
norms, Mbugua has found a way to work behind the scenes to ensure
that men are re-socialized through training, beginning with the pastors.
As one who works in the religious hierarchy, she is well placed to impact
the training that both men and women receive. She is not alone in
her ability to deconstruct unjust arrangements, though. Wanyeki also
found traditional cultures and Christian religion to be instruments of
domination and discrimination against women. She related:

> The first question you have to ask, for example, in FGM,
> is what exactly about it was supposed to be cultural, [and]
> then you come to the fact that maybe not necessarily the
> physical pain, but the teaching; then you are like, okay, so
> what are the teachings, and then you are like, oh my God
> this is so sexist. Can we have a different rite of passage that
> flips the script around? I think some of the most interesting
> work in Africa is being done by people who are willing to
> do that kind of exploration and reinterpretation of culture
> and religion and so on.

Wanyeki was cognizant of the fact that rites of passage are deeply entrenched in African traditions, particularly those of Eastern African nations, and take on traditional religious connotations. A reinterpretation of culture was called for to salvage the good from those rites and to discard the harmful and unhealthy aspects.

As a player on the global platform, Abuom apprehended the necessity for alliance building across differences in dealing with the oppression that women faced in just about every corner of the globe. She explained:

> So, alliance building is very critical. For me, the future leadership is first to draw from the historical biological processes and attributes that women have evolved for surviving the onslaught of oppression. And structuring that into coherent leadership models, and then applying those models in the various positions. Because we will go a long way in doing that, you can't lead without alliances. You can't lead without support and without the feedback, because you need to know where you stand . . . be a woman. The world needs caring and nurturing leadership. It doesn't want this killing, cutting each other's feet off. The world needs the consultative kind of leadership, not the solo approach or the hero. We have gone beyond the stage of heroism.

Abuom conceived of the leadership that is required in the current global, national, and local scene as the type that is consultative, not the lone-ranger style of earlier times. She was convinced that consultative leaders would be better placed to include everybody—men and women, young and old—from the northern hemisphere and the southern hemisphere, and so on.

Kaara also advocated consultative leadership, the type that brings about positive transformation to nations and communities. She felt that while men are in control, women are the real leaders in homes and communities, especially in the African context. During our focus group discussion, she explained her position vis-à-vis the domination of leadership by men:

> Of course I go straight to leadership. The first thing I read here is that leadership is dominated by men. And leadership to me, I understand it from the point of view of service to humanity. We confuse leadership and control, because what we experience is domination by control, rule by iron hand,

which is not feminine at all. And, I thank God our role is very clear on what we need to do. We need to nurture life, and I think that is what is holding African nations, because the African women have been able to play that role seriously, consciously, or even sometimes unconsciously. We are in leadership, we lead at home, and we lead in communities. I say this because our men are co-opted by the leadership that controls and dominates other people to deliver us for labor and to deliver our resources. Therefore, they are anti their society, they don't serve their society. And therefore, that's why we have gaps and that's why we are still very dissatisfied on the question of leadership in Africa. . . . As women we have to liberate leadership first from rulership, just as we are saying here, that how we lead in the kitchen is very important. It is that model that we need to bring into the public domain.

Kaara explained her conviction that women do lead, only that they lead from the background, in the private domain and in grassroots organizing, such as funerals, weddings, and other community events. However, she was convinced that women needed to be leaders in the public domain, where they could help neutralize the harm that has been caused by those of Africa's political leaders who have sold Africa to the slave master economically. She felt that women's nurturing capacity would place them in good stead as leaders, helping them sustain a legacy for future generations. Furthermore, Kaara expounded on the need to deconstruct the current structures:

We are doing an operation of our society, and we are putting item by item there, which is a malignancy, and look for a cure. Actually it's very ironical that patriarchy dictates that the man is the one to protect and give security, but in actuality it is the mothers who provide and who give security. So you see the contradiction, and I think that is how currently we need to deconstruct, and I hope you can do it, deconstructing the patriarchy arrangement.

Kaara was quite clear about the injustice and irony of the patriarchal arrangement; she called on women to collectivize to overturn it and bring about a revolution in leadership. This last quote also echoes what Achieng was saying about women being the peace builders and the ones who provide security in their communities.

Mombo talked about her own efforts at disrupting patriarchal arrangements at St. Paul's University by attempting to educate women, to help them understand how they have been socialized to believe in harmful gender arrangements:

> So I find the support of women. I look for women who can buy the feminist view. Because I realize that feminism is refusing to be a doormat. And I refuse to be a doormat. Trying to invite people like Professor Wangari to come and talk to my students has proven an impossible hurdle. Because "here she is inviting other feminists to talk to the students." It's a very narrow conception of feminism. Trying to move way from those narrow conceptions is very hard because of the socialization of both men and women into patriarchy.

Mombo attempts to help her students understand what feminism is in a way that supports the emancipation of women from their subjugation under men. It is a tough battle to fight, though, owing to the aforementioned negative connotation of feminism in Kenya.

These quotes illustrate the various ways in which the women leaders articulated well-thought-out critiques of social structures. Not only did they offer critiques to demonstrate what is wrong with such structures, but they also sought to reconstruct them to be socially just. Their reinterpretations of culture, gender roles, leadership, and religion are tools that aid them in their activism and advocacy for change as tempered radicals and servant leaders.

Dissonance

Whereas 15 women leaders, plus the liaison, all talked about their leadership being impacted by their spirituality, Wanyeki did not. She was uncomfortable with being regarded as a leader and even more uncomfortable with any discussion of spirituality. She talked her social positionality and its impact on her credibility as a leader. She related the following:

> The idea of being single and young, I am always seen as young particularly because I am not married and don't have children and so on. And to finally accept that and to see that is the context from which they come from but it doesn't mean we can't exchange ideas and that happened after a

while. I guess the trick is to leave your anger at the system
and to find a way out of crossing that divide.

Wanyeki felt that her single, child-free status was a barrier to her credibility, particularly in her work at FEMNET, where the older women
regarded her as merely a child. Perhaps this contributed to her discomfort over questions about her leadership:

> First, I think there is something wrong with the idea of
> attempting to lead. I don't think I have ever attempted to
> lead. I think I have attempted to find a way that I can con-
> tribute in some way my ideas to bear on a situation. And that
> has meant trying to maneuver to find a way to live materially,
> but also all the other kinds of social capital, like contacts
> and so on. Yeah, and in the end I think your beliefs and
> your commitments show through your work, and eventually
> that does count for something. So, for me, I don't see it as
> a generational battle or something; we have to find space
> to make our ideas live in this context, and in the process
> of doing that you can [go] up against all these dynamics,
> generational, class, and you try and deal with it. Here again
> I am kind of resistant to the idea that I am a leader.

As our discussion progressed, Wanyeki explained her discomfort over
considering herself a leader, and she had a hard time describing the
source or cause of her discomfort. However, when I pointed out that
she did have a position as an executive director that gave her a platform
from which to speak, including her weekly byline in *The EastAfrican*,
a regional, weekly paper, she began to realize that she was indeed a
leader. Wanyeki was the executive director of a Pan-African organization,
African Women Communication and Development Network (FEMNET),
a position she had held since 1999. However, the older women who
made up the board were still in control, so that she felt somewhat
limited in her capacity to truly lead as opposed to playing a managerial role. In addition, as a woman who had grown up in a home where
religion was neither encouraged nor discouraged, and who had since
developed a distaste for organized religion, Wanyeki was not comfortable with any terminology that reeked of religious overtones, such as
service. Yet when she described her work in her position as executive
director, she talked about being honest, being willing to die for the
cause, standing up for what she believes is right, being able to work
alongside semi-literate rural women effectively, even though she herself

was born and raised in the city, and attempting to be a change agent in the organization, as well as in society. All of these descriptions fit both the servant leader and the tempered radical who are guided by spiritual, rather than necessarily religious, values. Although Wanyeki is barely 40, single, and childless, she fits in with the rest of the women in that she too is fighting for social justice, and even though she is not religious, her values are deeply spiritual, actually deeply African and spiritual.

As such, it becomes clear that Wanyeki is internally motivated to seek social justice, a spirituality that is a blend of values learned from various religious and indigenous traditions rather than a single religious faith. She, however, felt that whereas she is interested in religion as a matter of course in her work of gender, development, and human rights, she does not follow any one religion. Hers is a syncretistic spirituality, a blending of values that she said resonates with who she wants to be as an African woman keen on social justice issues. She fits better with being regarded as following a spiritual, values-based leadership—values such as commitment, courage, conviction, and compassion for marginalized people. Her position as executive director of FEMNET has given her credibility and access to other human rights organizations in Africa and abroad. Her current position as the executive director of the Kenya Human Rights Council gives her the authority and credibility to speak and write about human rights abuses in the country. Whether she thought of herself as a leader or not, other women did—the four or five (older) women leaders who recommended that I speak to her. Her humility only helped further endear herself to me as a leader who did not let her position go to her head!

Summary

In this chapter, I explored how African women leaders expressed and explained their version of spirited leadership. They explained that the Spirit gives them courage to act, the wisdom to choose their battles, and the energy and inspiration to keep fighting for justice, and that it is the compelling force behind their tempered radicalism as well as servant leadership. Spirituality is both a source of personal strength as well as a raison d'être for the women's leadership. It is infused in everything they say and do, in their critiques of current structures of leadership or rulership, in their lifestyles of both boldness and humility. It is so deeply embedded in their psyche that it is inseparable from who they are and what they do, serving as part of their self-identity. It was refreshing to see how these African women leaders have blended their traditional spirituality, Judeo-Christian values, and educational experiences to exhibit a profound spirituality that is relevant and contextual, personal and collective, and private, yet engendering public engagement. Whereas they explain a lot of their spirituality in terms of Christian values and biblical terminology, it was also possible to perceive their *Africanness*. More importantly, it was evident that their spirituality was also influenced by their experience as women in Africa who have undergone intersecting oppressions from their geographical location in a third world nation, their gender in a neopatriarchal culture, their positions as leaders in a male-dominated public sphere, their ethnicity, and sometimes even their age and marital status. Their practical wisdom or critical spirituality enabled them to deconstruct several social arrangements, including culture and religion and leadership, as they looked at how each of these impacted upon their existence and leadership experiences. In the next chapter, I will further elaborate on the interconnectedness between the elements of the conceptual framework, as I seek to reframe it. As well, I will explain my personal journey and provide suggestions for further study.

15

Convergence

Spirited Leadership

As I was working on the themes expounded upon in the previous three chapters, it became increasingly clear that the three main components of the conceptual framework intersect in practice. As such, even though I separated them in discussing my findings and presented them here as separate chapters, in reality the women are both tempered radicals and servant leaders, and their spirituality impacts, and is impacted by, both. This is an important redefinition of the relationship among the three elements of the conceptual framework. Increasingly as I codified and recodified the constituent themes, I found that several of the quotes illustrated two or all three of the elements of the conceptual framework, thus the conclusion that they are all somewhat related. As such, the three—spirituality, servant leadership, and tempered radicalism—are distinguishable, but in the experiences of these African women leaders, they are inseparable elements that create a unified whole that I henceforth refer to as *spirited leadership*. To my way of thinking, *spirited* is an apt descriptor of the holistic leadership of these women. Spirited means several things: forceful, feisty, brave, determined, strong-willed, vigorous, energetic, lively, and animated, all words that describe the lived experiences and expressions of leadership for these 16 women. In looking at the definitions of spirit, several prominent words and phrases aptly describe these women leaders themselves, and their beliefs as well as practices. Spirit is: (1) an animating or a vital principle held to give life to physical organisms (Dantley, 2003a, b); (2) a supernatural essence or conviction about the existence of a higher authority/God (Fairholm, 1997); (3) the activating or essential principle influencing a person to act in a specified way; and (4) a lively or brisk quality in a person as well as a mental disposition characterized by firmness or assertiveness (*Merriam-Webster's Collegiate Dictionary*, 11th ed.). A person's spirituality is the "essence," the depth, of who the person is, defining the self, including the ways that a person thinks and feels (Fairholm, 1997). "Spirituality is the quality of being spiritual, of recognizing the intangible, life-affirming force in self and all human beings" (Fairholm, 1997, p. 29). These descriptors appropriately depict the women leaders in this study, defining their personalities as spiritual and spirited personalities, their beliefs as spiritual beings, and their leadership as spiritual and spirited leadership.

Making Meaning

As the elements of the conceptual framework and their constituent themes intersected, so did the enterprise of undertaking this study. I found that in terms of literature, especially in attempting to construct a conceptual framework, I was dependent upon the literature on Black women's experiences in the United States as a template upon which to theorize and understand continental African women's experiences. Similarly, in explaining the spirituality component, the literature base was mostly African American, with a few African sources. However, as was evident from the descriptions of spirituality, people of African descent share certain characteristics beyond mere skin color. The most important of these is a history of oppression, whether through slavery or colonialism, and the consequent dislocation and identity politics. As such, it should not be surprising that the stories of African women leaders told herein will find resonance in the African American experience and could be described in those terms.

One of the most important themes that emerged in this study and that contributed to holding together the three elements of the conceptual framework was the ability of the women to deconstruct history, culture, religion, leadership, and other social constructs, as described in chapter 14. Greenleaf (1977) noted that critique without offering solutions breeds hopelessness. These women leaders not only critiqued social constructions of gender, culture, leadership, religion, and the dominant discourse on history, but they also reconstructed these to make them more just, more inclusive of different, or gendered and ethnic, points of view. They illustrate what Oduyoye (2001) argues in explaining African women's theology, that African women theologians critique both Africans' and Christianity's patriarchal constructions that disparage the humanity of women. "The search for an empowering anthropology begins with a probe into African myths of origin, asking fresh questions in order to untangle the thread which has tied women to iniquity. In Africa, the injustice done to the humanity of the woman is linked also with biblical narratives and their interpretations of the entrance of sin into biblical affairs: hence, the need to take into account both traditions" (p. 68). This ability to deconstruct and reconstruct social realities aids women leaders in becoming tempered radicals and servant leaders, in articulating their position vis-à-vis gender, leadership, and social justice. This ability is connected to their traditional African values of practical wisdom, the ability to observe keenly, to perceive correctly, and to utilize limited knowledge to make perspicacious decisions regarding the realities they face today. This ability is also connected to their acuity in historicizing the status of women from the colonial period to the current era, showing how the intersections of culture, traditional religion, Christianity, colonialism, Westernization, and market economy combine to create hegemonic structures that are acutely oppressive to women (Oduyoye, 2001). But it is noteworthy that these women do not consider themselves victims. In the words of Anisia Achieng, they are not victims but active agents of their own emancipation.

Tempered Radicals

Courage, determination, initiating change, and more courage are terms that describe well the experiences of these African women as leaders. Their life stories demonstrated the five points on a continuum of strategies that Meyerson (2001) had conceived of as being utilized in making a difference: (1) resisting quietly and staying true to oneself, (2) turning personal threats into opportunities, (3) broadening impact through negotiation, (4) leveraging small wins, and (5) organizing collective action. In addition to these strategies, the African women leaders also utilized other strategies relevant to their particular contexts: (1) intercultural boundary spanning, (2) resourcefulness and creative problem solving, (3) learning to be tempered with age and experience, and (4) leveraging their outsider/within positionalities. The last four strategies arise from the cultural and socioeconomic realities within which African women enact leadership. Tempered radicalism connected with spirituality—the women talked about becoming emboldened and being persistent because of their spiritual convictions and their relationship with God and other human beings. Critical spirituality/practical wisdom aids the women in deconstructing and reconstructing dominant discourses, a necessary prerequisite to coming up with alternative structures and becoming actively engaged in fighting injustices (Dantley, 2003a). All of the aforementioned strategies were also useful in their agency as servant leaders.

Servant Leadership

Several of the women leaders explicitly stated that they believe and practice servant leadership, as something they have learned through their Christian beliefs or as something they have acquired from their cultural heritage as African women. Wahu Kaara helped redefine servant leadership in terms of "finding fulfillment in serving humanity" in order to connect it explicitly with that African heritage. She felt the need to avoid the use of the term *servant* because she felt that it has certain connotations for the oppressed; the notion of servant is not one the oppressed are comfortable ascribing to themselves, in her opinion. The women leaders illustrated several strategies of servant leadership: (1) empowerment, (2) healing, (3) stewardship, (4) humility, and (5) community building. According to these women leaders, as African women, their credibility in their local communities or organizational settings was dependent upon their constituents recognizing them as serving their needs, as meeting the felt needs of the people. Servant leadership connected with spirituality along the lines of being something the women had acquired through their spiritual foundations, as well as themes such as humility and healing. Theirs was a version of servant leadership that can best be described as "critical servant leadership"—intentional about seeking solutions toward human rights, women's rights, girls' rights, the political participation of women, the economic rights of women, and war and national debt problems encountered in Kenya, Sudan, and the Continent.

Spirituality

The spirituality that these women leaders articulated and expressed is what Paris (1995) referred to as Africana spirituality, or what Dantley (2003a) conceptualized as critical spirituality resulting in prophetic leadership. In addition, as Mbiti (1969) and Paris (1995) persuasively argued, the spirituality expressed by African peoples is one where all of life is sacred: there is no distinction between the sacred and the profane (Oduyoye, 2001). As such, those who utilize this spirituality as the foundation upon which their lives and leadership are built are likely to view their leadership in terms of service to humanity and realizing social justice ideals.

Spirituality is intricately connected to both tempered radicalism and servant leadership, but it is also distinguishable as an element by itself. For these African women leaders, spirituality serves several purposes: (1) a source of direction for life and leadership, (2) a source of leadership practices, and (3) a source of strength in the midst of oppression and challenges. In these three broad themes, I found that spirituality is a source of courage to act, a divine inspiration to lead for social justice, a source of fulfillment in the face of performing thankless work, and the impetus for action. As Kaara stated, spirituality gives one *the capacity to pursue the truth without illusion.* Spirituality also enabled these women leaders to be committed to a vision in spite of all of the challenges and barriers they faced, the vision of a more just society. As such, they were willing to sacrifice their personal comforts and to go without community commendation when necessary in order to achieve that vision. In these ways, spirituality enabled these women leaders to become tempered radicals: courageous, visionary, committed social justice activists and change agents. In addition, it enabled them to become and behave as critical servant leaders, because it is credited with giving them fulfillment in serving humanity and the boldness to speak truth to power. Several women employed *Christianese,* that is, the repertoire of words and values inherent in the Judeo-Christian tradition of which they have their early training and exposure. A few, especially Anisia, Abuom, and Kaara, were better able to make the connections to their traditional belief system from their ethnic cultures. In addition, spirituality and servant leadership connected upon the foundation of humility—the ability to not lord it over others but instead to put their constituents' needs first.

As mentioned elsewhere, practical wisdom or critical spirituality describes the element of spirituality articulated by these African women leaders, which enables them to deconstruct and reconstruct social realities, critiquing, analyzing, and redefining social constructs to make them socially just. Whether the spirituality was described in theistic terms or in terms of values, as Wanyeki did, the ability to offer a profound critique of the status quo, and then to offer possible alternatives and solutions toward recreating a just society, connected all of these women.

When all three elements and their defining characteristics are put together, what emerges is spirited leadership, the kind of leadership that combines servant leadership, tempered radicalism, and critical spirituality in agency for social justice. The women's identities

Boldness   Wisdom

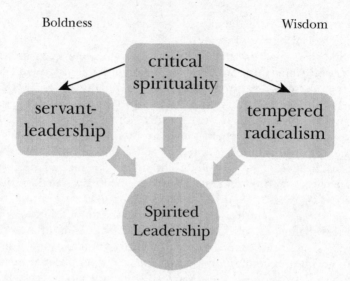

Figure 15.1. Spirited Leadership

as women, as Africans, as leaders, as Christians, and as members of
particular communities combined and intersected in producing this
form of spirited leadership.

Contesting Womanhood and Leadership

So what would be the portrait of an African woman in leadership? This
book demonstrates that women do serve in leadership roles—the 16
included here are invested in achieving social justice ideals. They have
no common demographic denominator—the 16 ranged from ages 40
to 80. They have no common marital status—every status is represented
here in this small sample, and even though their leadership experiences are impacted by their status, especially being single versus being
married, for the most part, they lead irrespective of that social status.
Additionally, though they face more questions about their credibility,
those who have no children are just as likely to be involved in social
justice leadership (Mombo and Wanyeki) as those who do have children.
Women in leadership are also likely to come from any ethnic group.
Even though only about seven are represented here, there are women
leaders in local communities in every one of the 41 people groups in

Kenya. And, Achieng assured me, there are women leading grassroots organizations from every region of her native Sudan as well.

These 16 women share many commonalities, as demonstrated through the thematic chapters: they are tempered radicals ranging from the mild tempered to the gregarious radical; they are servant leaders who believe in healing, reconciliation, empowering, and building communities. They lead because of a spiritual compulsion, and they are spirited—animated, energized by spirit. These 16 women also share the social contradictions that come with being women and leaders in the African context.

Beasts of Burden or Servant Leaders

Whereas Abuom was quick to point out that depicting African women as beasts of burden was not appropriate, and instead argued for looking at them as sustainers of the community, it is also possible to argue for a both/and conclusion. That is, women, as depicted by these 16 leaders, are heavily burdened with the cares of their communities; they have to balance between the needs of their families (husbands, children, parents, extended families), the needs of their communities, and their own professional growth/development (see Mabokela, 2003a, for a description of women in South African universities). The refrain heard from almost all 16 women was: *I have no time for myself!* As such, as they serve everybody else, these women leaders are struggling with finding time to replenish their energies, to look after themselves. As Gichaga asserted, "I no longer have the time to just catch coffee with the girls or attend weddings, bridal showers, baby showers, and all those other activities women attend socially. I have no time to socialize . . . in fact, some of my friendships have died off because I do not have the time to spend with friends." Similarly, Thongori talked about realizing the need to expend energy on her husband and their relationship as much as she did her work and her children, because she did not want her marriage to suffer the effects of her crazy schedule, this too in a society that demands that women serve everybody, as these women leaders attested to in their descriptions of their leadership as servant leadership.

Culture, Tradition, Modernity, and Change

Another contradiction that the women leaders face daily is culture and traditions, and the changes that have come about due to Western education, a capitalist economy, and missionary Christianity. As was evident in both the individual portraits and the thematic chapters, these women had the ability to deconstruct traditions that had played a punitive role in women's status. Women in Kenya and in many parts of Africa cannot inherit property from their fathers and/or husbands. Those who are widowed are often left landless and hapless when their in-laws invade their homes and take off with the family property (Muteshi, 1998). Those who either have never gotten married or have ended up divorced find that they cannot expect to live out their lives peacefully in their natal homes—their brothers are likely to push them out, this in spite of the fact that in traditional societies, divorced women were readily reabsorbed into society and remarried easily. In some traditions, single women were not buried in the homestead but would be buried on the periphery, marking their marginal status in the community (Mbiti, 1969). The contradictions inherent in living out their lives in a context where modern and traditional norms coexist as uncomfortable bedfellows impact their leadership experiences and expressions. On the positive side, these women are able to draw from their cultural heritage and values articulated in their leadership practices, such as servant leadership, Ubuntu, and Africana spirituality. On the other hand, traditions and cultural malpractices form the bulk of the activism in which many women are involved—wife inheritance, inheritance rules, cultural "reconstructions" of womanhood (Oduyoye, 2001), and the place of girl children. The women leaders showed their acuity at picking the best out of traditional cultures and throwing out the rest. Unfortunately, the context of leadership has not been as effective in doing so. This clash between cultures, where the norms now in operation are neither supported by authentic traditions nor by changes in modernity (Gyekye, 1997), continues to be an expansive arena for women's leadership in Kenya, as in most other sub-Saharan African countries, as they advocate for change for more equitable social arrangements and the recognition of the humanity of all, irrespective of race, ethnicity, gender, or social class.

Wife/Mother and Career Woman

As is common with women managers, leaders, and professionals in the West, African women in leadership struggle with the dilemma of managing their "biological" roles versus their professional roles. Not only do they struggle with the contradiction, indicated earlier, that overburdens them but also with the daily grind of managing their personal and familial roles with their professional careers. As Riria put it, they are caught between their biological roles of motherhood and/or wifehood, with their need to be competent and credible career professionals. One of the differences between African women in Kenya and women in the West is the social structure. In Kenya, women can be mother and leader and wife and career professional, because of the wide availability of domestic helpers who take care of the cleaning, cooking, and general house care. However, like their counterparts elsewhere, African women find that gender socialization that dictates that leadership is male, and that women "should be in the kitchen," is much harder to deal with than the physical demands of managing a home and career. Whereas they can be excellent at delegating, prioritizing and planning when dealing with the physical/material issues of a work-life balance, the social and emotional issues cannot be delegated or prioritized away—the higher these women climb, the higher the probability that their marriages will fail, as Riria so aptly illustrated. Whereas Thongori could attest to her maternal needs with her assertion "we get completed by our babies," motherhood was a site of contestation for these women. For those who are mothers, it provided them with social credibility, because of the high status ascribed to mothers in African society. But it worked as a double-edged sword, in that those who were not mothers (biologically) were then considered unsuitable for leadership, again, as Thongori argued when telling the story about the media article—that women can be competent leaders, irrespective of whether or not they have children. Yet in looking at the portraits of the mothers, it was quite clear that they ascribed some of their leadership practices to their roles as mothers. They felt that they were better leaders because they were mothers. They also talked in terms of fighting for social justice because they were invested in leaving a legacy for their children. In that kind of environment, women like Wanyeki and Mombo were regarded as "mere children" because they did not have children of their own. The same tool that worked for the majority of women in leadership in this context served as a hegemonic oppressor for the minority.

Thongori exemplified the paradox within which women leaders in the African context must exercise their leadership:

> I am not a rebel, I cannot be a rebel. Even though patriarchy
> is very high in this country, I need the sense of belonging
> and respectability that comes with certain social structures,
> such as marriage, in order to be credible in fighting for
> women's rights as human rights. I respect such structures

and remain in them even as I challenge them and seek to
change them.

It seems plausible, then, to say that, for African contexts, the sociocultural setting demands that women be *all things to all men*: mothers,
wives, leaders, servants, sustainers, healers, community and institutional
builders, and everything else in between Oduyoye, 1995a, b, 2001). It is
no wonder, then, that for at least 14 of these women, spirituality played
such a significant role in helping them cope, giving them direction,
and sustaining them personally, assisting them to thrive and succeed
as leaders in context.

Personal Sacrifices: The Blight of Divorce

In reflecting on divorce in Kenya, I sought to apprehend why women
who are divorced are treated with such disrespect in the society. Professor John S. Mbiti, who wrote one of the pioneering books on African
religions and philosophy, placed his discussion of divorce within a
chapter on marriage under the section on procreation. That is because
marriage had the purpose of extending the family name through procreation. He observed that

> divorce is a delicate accident in marital relationships. In the
> African situation, what constitutes a divorce must be viewed
> against the fact that marriage is a "process." In many societies
> that "process" is complete only when the first child is born,
> or when all the marriage presents have been paid, or when
> one's first [*sic*] children are married. Marriage involves many
> people, and not just the husband and wife, and the transfer
> of gifts in [the] form of livestock, money or labor. Once the
> full contract of marriage is executed, it is extremely rare to
> dissolve it. If a dissolution does come about, then it creates .
> a great scar in the community concerned. (1969, p. 145)

In the traditional setup, divorce was possible only in very limited circumstances, the greatest single cause being sterility or barrenness on
the part of the woman (if the husband is impotent, then his brother
can perform sexual duties to fertilize the wife for him and save the
marriage from breakdown; sometimes the husband can take a second
wife without divorcing the barren one). Other allowable causes of
divorce are cruelty from the husband and the effects or suspicion of

engaging in witchcraft. Remarriage after divorce was common, especially when the woman had children she retained after the dissolution of the first marriage. This was all true in pre-independence African societies, and some of these norms have remained intact. However, the women we are talking about in this particular book, except for Likimani, who got divorced before independence, divorced over the last 2 decades. As such, there seems to have been a change where divorced women may find it difficult to remarry, and whatever the cause of their divorce might have been, society treats them as failures for having "failed" to secure their marriages. At least that was the experience that Riria described, where she felt that she was being judged as having failed in spite of the fact that she is successful professionally. What remains clear from this exchange is that there needs to be more studies examining divorce, particularly from the perspective of the women (the men always remarry), to comprehend the social and cultural norms that place women at a disadvantage in marital relations in this way.

Thongori also talked some about this issue of divorce from the perspective of a women's rights advocate. She felt that society tended to portray all "strong" or "radical" women as either single or divorced. As such, when the media asked to interview her, she was happy to oblige to demonstrate that there are strong, radical leaders who also happen to be married with children. The social implication was that strong women end up divorced, thus blaming women for the breakup of their marriages.

Another explanation given for the breakup of marriages is that African societies have moved from their traditional norms of complementary and dual-gender roles to competitive, combative roles where men and women are in constant conflict. Abuom explained that she grew up in a family where gender complementarity was the norm, involving flexible gender roles. She argued that this is no longer true in most African communities, partly due to the disruption of those traditional norms by missionary Christianity and colonial labor policies. After independence, it was not possible to revert to those traditional norms, as society had been irrevocably disrupted. Similarly, Nkiru Nzegwu describes dual-sex roles to have been the norm in Onitsha, Nigeria, but like in Kenya, those flexible gender roles were disrupted and dismantled by missionary Christianity with its Victorian gender roles (Nzegwu, 2001). As such, one of the other causes of divorce is apparently the competitive nature of marriage relationships in contemporary African societies (Kuria, 2003). That translates into competitive relationships, even in organizations and institutions, creating a situation where men perhaps feel that women should be domesticated and should therefore not be in leadership roles, particularly if that leadership involves authority over them. It is quite clear from this short discussion of divorce in Kenya that research is needed to better understand the issues surrounding women's roles, marital relationships, divorce, and leadership in Kenya, and quite possibly in other sub-Saharan African countries as well, particularly because I could not find literature dealing directly with divorce and the status of women and their ability to be effective and credible leaders.

Personal Resonance

Storytelling forms the bulk of cultural transmission; the primary storytellers are elder-sage women, the mothers and grandmothers of the community (Kolawole, 1997; Likimani, 1985, 2005; Ngunjiri, 2006a). Beyond passing on cultural history from generation to generation, these sages also inculcate moral values, norms, and the expectations that society has from the younger generations. In conducting this study, I listened to the elder-women as they taught me through their stories, engaging in culturally expected inquisitive responses and questioning to delve further and deeper into the women's experiences. In the African culture, children and youth are encouraged to be learners, to be curious about how the world works, and this knowledge is to be gained not only through book-type learning but especially by listening to elders. As an unmarried and a child-free woman, I am still regarded as a child by African standards. The women leaders took seriously their roles as educators and mentors, enthusiastically passing on their lived and tested wisdom, to both guide the audience that my written work would eventually reach and me. As one leader in my study expressed it, "You are the academic; it is your responsibility to write the books and inform a wider audience . . . [go and] imbue spirituality into academe."

I went into fieldwork as a *supplicant learner*, as necessitated by the cultural context of the study. A supplicant learner is one who is willing to put aside, at least for the moment of interaction with the participant, her or his "expert" stance and instead adopt a "childlike" persona in that researcher-participant relationship, that is, becoming an interested learner who recognizes that the participants are experts of their own experiences, and, as an African, regarding the participants with the respect due to elders. In describing their work, Lawrence-Lightfoot and Davis (1997) talked about the respect with which they entered and encountered each new context, a respect that enabled them to relate authentically to the participants and involve their participants as co-creators of the portraits. A common feminist critique of traditional social science research has often been that it is undertaken from the perspective of the researcher as expert (Allen, 1998), neglecting the participants' own expertise embedded in their lived experiences. Such neglect would have been counterproductive in my context, because the African cultural element of reverence for elders demands that younger people regard their elders with honor and respect (Gyekye, 1997). I therefore entered the field as a supplicant learner, one who felt humbled by the knowledge that these busy women were willing to spend time with me, telling me their stories, letting me observe their lives, and learning from their experiences.

Additionally, as mentioned previously, in the African culture, a 30-something unmarried and child-free woman is still considered a child/youth. Humbling myself as a "child researcher," then, was a way to honor the cultural heritage of my community and open up space for the women to engage in the role of cultural educators and experts of their own experiences. Furthermore, the African patronage culture demands that a younger person be introduced to people in authority or to older people by another older person or person in authority (Gyekye, 1997). To this end, I utilized the services of a liaison—my maternal aunt, who introduced me to some of the women leaders. Because my aunt is an ordained minister, a university lecturer, and a community leader, the women leaders were cognizant of her status and were willing to speak with me. I did not completely give up being an expert in both leadership theory and research process; I exercised my expertise as I analyzed and composed the final product, having been the witness, active listener, and interpreter to the events that I was describing (Lawrence-Lightfoot & Davis, 1997). However, in the field, I engaged in culturally mandated normative behavior, such as utilizing a liaison and taking the stance of a supplicant learner in order to maximize my learning and honor my participants. That process became part of my learning process—learning to do research in culturally appropriate ways. My aim was to produce research that would be emancipatory for the participants by engaging them as active co-creators of knowledge, in the production of narratives about their experiences (Lawrence-Lightfoot & Davis, 1997).

Intersectionality is a term used to describe the multiple oppressions that women and people of color face (Crenshaw, 1991). Critical feminist research enabled me to interrogate the intersectional oppressions that arise from social context, gender, culture, political economy, educational attainments, and the women's chosen vocation as social justice leaders. I was invested in conducting research in a manner that did not *objectify* my participants or create exploitative relationships with them; instead, I attempted to engage in a research journey that was transformative for both participants and me (Collins, 2000; Tillman, 2002).

My Transformative Journey through Research

One of the personal results of this research journey has been my growth and transformation in the area of cultural self-awareness. My participants ranged from ages 40 to 80, thus serving as a reservoir of history. I learned the history that does not appear in textbooks—women's roles in social transformation, including their involvement in Kenya's freedom movement and their activism toward achieving peace in Sudan and other parts of Africa. It was particularly inspiring and informative for me to learn the kinds of skills that women utilized as "underground" leaders, such as negotiation, peace building, and *Othermothering*, that is, bringing up the community's children (Beauboeuf-Lafontant, 2002; Murtadha-Watts, 1999). In terms of ethical leadership, the participants demonstrated leadership that included the ethics of care, justice, and critique (Starratt, 1991). These ethics were evident particularly as they engaged systems of injustice in governance, health care, education, law, and the abuse of traditions relating to females, such as female genital cutting and forced early marriages.

Additionally, several of the women also engaged in leadership that included an ethic of risk as they challenged unjust social, cultural, and legal systems—they talked about being threatened and losing their jobs and their marriages as part of the price that they paid for their commitment to social justice (Beauboeuf-Lafontant, 2002; Ngunjiri, 2005, 2006c; Welch, 2000). There was a sense of relief in discovering that among the 16 participants there were 16 different kinds of people—some loud and boisterous, others quiet and seemingly demure, yet all were able to be effective social justice leaders. Through this discovery, that leaders need not conform to some ideal behavioral makeup, I came to the realization that I too could achieve success as a leader by being true to myself and committed to my calling.

Critical Encounters

One of the limitations inherent in a qualitative approach that requires intimate engagement with the context is that I often felt rushed because I had only 3 months in which to conduct the fieldwork. Additionally,

I sometimes felt overwhelmed by the number of women willing to be interviewed, and I could not say no to those who recommended still other women leaders to be interviewed. My original proposal stated that I would interview just five women, but by the end of the fieldwork, I had interviewed 16 participants, including those who had been too busy to speak with me when I first arrived. Their enthusiasm to participate, and their willingness to open up the core of their lives, even about issues that were painful and difficult, came as a surprise to me. Even more surprising were the resiliency and strength they displayed, in spite of challenging leadership environments. As one woman leader asserted, "We are not victims. No, we are victors as we strive to bring justice to our society."

This research journey has stretched me academically and transformed me in intimate ways. Academically, I was fortunate to work with a dissertation committee that challenged and supported me, enabling me to create a final product about which I, and committee members, could be proud. These members have become mentors in the academy who continue to encourage and guide me, even after my graduation. Culturally, I reconnected with a part of myself that I took for granted—the reverence for age and veneration of elders that demanded that I become a child researcher or supplicant learner. I knew that my culture rewarded inquisitive behavior from the youth, especially when that inquisitiveness was directed toward learning from those elders. However, never before had I used this cultural heritage to inform my academic pursuits. My relationship with the women elders/leaders was positively impacted by my stance as a supplicant learner. They constantly talked about how they felt honored and respected by being actively engaged in the research process (Ngunjiri, 2006a, 2006c).

These women leaders taught me by their example what it means to be a woman and a social justice advocate in spite of, rather than in the absence of, oppressive forces. I saw resiliency personified in each of the women as each had chosen a difficult path in order to serve her local communities, institutions, nations, and the continent of Africa as a whole. The women were willing to suffer the consequences of their radical actions, the indignities of being regarded as cultural traitors, and sometimes even foregoing the comforts of marriage in order to emancipate marginalized people. They challenged me to view my status as a Black-African-woman-academic as a tool for the emancipation of marginalized persons, whether in my teaching, research, and/or service within and outside of the ivory tower (Freire, 1970; hooks, 1994). Many of these women utilized scarce resources to advance their social justice agendas with varying degrees of success. The challenge for me, then, is to use the resources at my disposal to agitate and stand up for social justice ideals. These resources include my position as a junior faculty member, my location in North America, my voice as an alien in the United States, and my status as a cultural ambassador for my native land. The resources and opportunities to stand up for social justice ideals may also arise through my writing, research endeavors, and any speaking opportunities that come my way. That is, my life in academe needs to be guided by the principles that I learned from the women leaders—how to allow spirituality to guide me, how to become a servant leader, and how to stand up and be counted as a tempered radical.

The women leaders also challenged me to imbue spirituality into academe, urging me to use my voice and to critically engage with injustice. By spirituality, the women leaders were urging me to be true to the calling that I have received, to listen to my inner voice, to remain spiritually tuned, to seek authentic relationships with students and colleagues, and to realize purpose and meaning through my work ((Murtadha-Watts, 1999; Paris, 1995; Tisdell, 2003). Listening to them, I could hear echoes of Paulo Freire, as he urged professors to engage in emancipatory teaching and research (1970) and Michael Dantley, as he challenged professors to utilize African American prophetic/critical spirituality in training leaders for social justice (Dantley, 2003a, 2003b, 2005).

The women leaders in this study exemplified servant leadership, that is, engaging in leadership because of the compulsion to serve (Alston, 2005; Greenleaf, 1977). As Greenleaf prophesied:

> The next thirty years will be marked as a period when the dark skinned and the deprived and the alienated of the world effectively asserted their claims to stature, and they were not led by a privileged elite but exceptional people from their own kind. (Greenleaf, 1977)

Greenleaf perspicaciously foresaw what these women leaders manifested in their exemplary lives: the dark skinned, deprived, and alienated leading their own kind toward emancipation. Studies of other dark-skinned, deprived, and alienated folk have yielded similar themes of spirituality, servant leadership, resiliency, and courage in the face of struggles (Beauboeuf-Lafontant, 2002; Dove, 1998a; Jones, 2003; Mabokela, 2003b; Mbugua-Muriithi, 1996; Meyerson, 2001; Murtadha & Watts, 2005; Reid-Merritt, 1996). The dark skinned and deprived from this study, and those mentioned earlier, have a collective mentality, a social consciousness, derived from their Africana culture and their social location in communities of people who have historically endured much oppression. My research journey put me in touch with that collective consciousness and with the spirited mentality that demands action against injustice in ways that surprised me, moved me, stretched me, and molded me into what I am becoming: a socially conscious, ethically engaged scholar, researcher, leader, and practitioner, all rolled into one. As such, I stand on the shoulders of giants.

This research and writing journey has been a personal, emotional, cultural, and spiritual process for me. I have been transformed, challenged, and stretched in ways I did not know were possible from something that began as an academic exercise. Culturally, I was forced to reconnect with a part of myself that I took for granted, and to use it to my benefit and for the edification of the participants. Here I am referring to the process of conducting research as a child researcher/ supplicant learner. I have known for a long time that curiosity that leads to learning is highly regarded in my culture, but this was the first time that I utilized that cultural knowledge to undertake a study. My relationship with the elders who participated in this study was deeply impacted by my choice to go in as a child researcher rather than the norm in social science inquiry, where the researcher is an expert. The elders/women leaders appreciated my high regard for them, the honor and respect that I showed them by approaching them in this manner. It was partly the reason the eldest one, Muthoni Likimani, was willing to not only participate but also to recommend and sometimes even approach other possible participants on my behalf. Similarly, Wahu Kaara declined to attend an important regional meeting in order to participate in the focus group. Each woman leader with whom I had the privilege to converse had to make certain sacrifices in order to make time for me, and for that I was deeply appreciative.

Through my interactions with these elders, I learned what it means to be an African woman and to lead for social justice in spite of, rather than in the absence of, oppressive forces. I saw resiliency personified in each of the women, as each chose to take a difficult path in order to serve humanity in local communities, institutions, the nation, and the Continent. They were willing to suffer the consequences of their radical actions and stance, to suffer the indignities of being regarded as cultural traitors, and sometimes even the comforts of a marital status in order to live out what they believed to be just and right, for themselves and for all those they attempted to help emancipate. This was a challenge to me, to realize that even though my own life has had its share of challenges and experiences of oppression because of my gender, skin color, national origins, and marital status, I have a role to play in the emancipation of my people—my people broadly defined as African peoples wherever they may be found, as well as any people who suffer the indignities of oppression due to their social identities. These women leaders illustrated for me action at the family, local, national, continental, and global levels, eloquently demonstrating that one such as myself can act toward alleviating injustice from wherever I am located, starting in my own neighborhood and continuing to the ends of the earth, literally and figuratively. Many of these women have engaged in activism for social justice with minimal resources, yet they have succeeded to various degrees in bringing about a more just social order, whether in one small location or as the agitate on global platforms. The challenge for me is to use whatever I have, to creatively and innovatively harness the resources at my disposal, including but not limited to my position in academia, my location in North America, my voice as an alien in this land, my written word, and the many avenues for speaking that come my way to agitate for social justice.

Spiritually, the women leaders challenged me to "put spirit in academia," a tough nut to crack, to say the least. They felt that I had a certain perspective as an African/woman/Christian/educated/youth that should be visible. They insisted that spirituality should be part of my voice in academe in any study in which I engage, in any paper I write, and in any teaching I will ever undertake. They demonstrated those elements to me by telling me their stories, including how they led when they were younger, the lessons they have learned, and the pitfalls to avoid, but, most importantly, the fact that Spirit energizes, directs, propels, and should be the guide for my life and leadership. Should I fail to emulate these women leaders, I will have no one to blame but myself. In addition, the women decried the lack of mentors; they felt that they had struggled to lead without much direction and hoped that my own life and leadership would not be the same. That was part of the reason they insisted I bring a few of my friends to the focus group to begin mentoring relationships with them. They were intent on changing the course and direction in which they practiced personal leadership, by beginning to engage in intergenerational relationships to create a pipeline of prepared leaders who would take positions of responsibility as those positions arose. This was the one area in which they felt they had not done enough, and they used the opportunity that this study afforded them to begin to change that. In that sense, I felt that I had served a purpose beyond my academic achievements, a reciprocal role by bringing my friends along to begin that process.

Future Directions

I recommend that leadership studies be undertaken in different locations, especially among those who have been historically left out of the academic debate on leadership, because such studies would provide a much-needed broader perspective to the study and practice of leadership. The more journal articles, academic and popular press books, and other media we have available to teach us about leadership from different perspectives, the richer our understanding of the theory and praxis of leadership will be.

In addition, studies specifically about African peoples are necessary, especially if these are conducted along the lines of celebrating diversity, learning from the "Other" in order to understand the self. African peoples have been misrepresented and pathologized for several hundred years. It is about time to begin to celebrate their resiliency and strength, and how that can contribute to "mainstream" theory and praxis of leadership. As demonstrated in this book, African women are a particularly resilient lot, having had to become strong in the midst of a myriad of calamities. As such, they provide for us, men and women, African and non-African, powerful lessons about surviving and thriving in spite of the circumstances that we face personally or professionally. They are powerful lessons around social justice agency and activism and resourceful problem solving to rebuild broken *communitas*.

Perhaps my word to future researchers of African realities is that they should consider reconnecting with African culture when undertaking their studies. If there is one thing that hit home for me, it was the fact that entering the field in a culturally responsive way helped make this study more doable, whereas attempting to reduce the amount of jargon in the text made it possible to communicate my writings to a broader audience. As such, I recommend for those undertaking research on African realities to consider conducting it and writing it in such a way as to be culturally responsive and to be able to communicate with the people they purport to represent. Respect and honor go a long way toward enhancing this kind of journey and enabling the researcher to authentically represent her or his participants, even when communicating with the audience.

Today, African women have made a lot of progress as far as achieving milestones in political participation, attaining education, engaging in entrepreneurship, and serving their communities in various ways. Women such as those presented here, and others leading in rural communities, urban sprawl, or privileged to be heads of state, such as

President Sirleaf, present us with worthy lessons for leadership praxis. They demonstrate persistence and perspicacity and the privilege that comes with serving the needs of others. Considering the struggles that women encounter getting to and staying at the top, their stories are helpful in demonstrating a "stick-with-it" attitude. In addition, some of the voices here demonstrate how women lead effectively without necessarily taking a "fighter" stance, rather, wisely finding ways to bypass the glass ceiling, as the context dictates.

Conclusion

As I have quoted elsewhere in this book, Greenleaf (1977) prophesied that

> the next thirty years will be marked as the period when the dark skinned and the deprived and the alienated of the world effectively asserted their claims to stature, and they were not led by a privileged elite but by exceptional people from their own kind. (p. 34)

How perspicacious of Greenleaf to foresee and foretell what was to come in the arena of leadership. The African women leaders who participated in this study are excellent examples of the dark skinned, the deprived, and the alienated leading in order to serve the cause of social justice. By being spirited servant leaders and tempered radicals, these women leaders illustrated the various ways in which they have attempted to change cultures, communities, and organizations. Studies of other dark-skinned, deprived and alienated women have provided similar stories of resiliency and courage in the face of struggles that are sourced from a deep well of spirituality, and a serving attitude aimed at lifting up their constituents (Beauboeuf-Lafontant, 2002; Dove, 1998b; Jones, 2003; Murtadha-Watts, 1999; Reid-Merritt, 1996). The dark skinned, deprived, and alienated in this study and from the authors just cited have a *collective mentality*, a social consciousness bred from their Africana (Continental and Diaspora) culture and their positionality in communities of people who have historically endured tremendous oppression. Their spirituality and social consciousness make the women leaders toughened and wizened agents for socially just causes. They pay a high price for their activism, yet they continue to speak out, to stand up and shout when necessary to bring about much-needed changes.

The African women leaders whose stories illuminate our understanding of leadership here join their sisters in North America and other places, those women who are struggling to bring about social justice in its various manifestations.

Notes

Chapter 10

1. See Nkiru Nzegwu (2001), who illustrates how the dual-sex system, whereby men and women had separate but complementary roles to play in society, operated. These kinds of systems were destroyed by the twin cultural systems of colonialism and missionary Christianity that imposed foreign, Western, and Victorian norms as part of the "civilizing" activity.

2. Kwame Gyekye (1997), in *Tradition and Modernity*, argues that the impact of colonialism and Christianity on culture has produced a state of flux in which the current norms and practices are neither traditional nor modern/Western/Christian. Instead, such norms and practices have neither the support of (real) traditional cultures nor those of modernity, thus creating a climate that is ripe for excesses, abuses, and the corruption that is so prevalent in African states.

3. See Tabitha Kanogo's (2005) incisive critique of the impact of colonialism and Christianity on women's lives, especially during the period 1900–1950.

Chapter 12

1. See, for example, Bell and Nkomo (2001), Beauboeuf-Lafontant (2002), and Jones (2003), who describe the experiences of African American women within U.S. institutions and organizations. Patricia Hill Collins's (2004) work on outsider/within also further expounds on the strategies that African American women utilize to survive in majority-White institutions and society.

Chapter 13

1. As stated, critical servant leadership is an amalgamation of critical spirituality and servant leadership. This construct is an extension of both servant leadership and critical spirituality. It is all encompassing of the underlying foundations of servant leadership and the overarching goal of critical spirituality. In this regard, critical servant leadership is more than a leadership theory; it is

a way of being, a connection to communities and people who are marginalized, frowned upon, and separated by the mainstreams of society. A critical servant leader is guided by a willingness and commitment to promote and sustain equity and social justice. One merely does not practice critical servant leadership; one is a critical servant leader. Those who commit themselves to becoming a critical servant leader must begin a journey of personal reflection and a recommitment to social justice by incorporating the characteristics of critical servant leadership into his or her daily life (McClelland, 2010, p. 98).

2. *Othermothers* is a term used within African American literature to refer to women who serve as mothers to children other than their own, children who find themselves destitute, or simply women who extend their mothering beyond their own blood families to other children in the community (Beauboeuf-Lafontant, 2002). The term is an apt descriptor for the roles that many African women play as mothers to many children—"it takes a village to raise a child" would be the practical application of that notion. In most African communities, legal adoptions and fostering are rare, but women will take in children who need a family and look after them as if they were their own, and this is expected, and even encouraged, as part of African culture.

3. Mau Mau stands for Mzungu Arudi Ulaya, Mwafrika Apate Uhuru, which is Swahili for "Colonialist/Briton go back to your country so that Africans can have freedom." This was the name that the freedom fighters gave themselves. Mau Mau freedom fighting took place between 1950 and 1960; a state of emergency was declared in 1952.

Chapter 14

1. See, for example, one of the preeminent voices in liberation theology, James Cone's (1990) *A Black Liberation Theology*. Liberation theologians came from the marginalized, Black, Latin American, and Asian communities. They conceptualized a hermeneutic of freedom for the oppressed, those oppressed by racism, poverty, economic disparities between nations, and so on.

2. See John Mbiti's (1969) *African Religions and Philosophy*, where he explains the African worldview and its impact on health, kinship, cosmos, and so on.

References

Adler, N. (1999). Global women leaders: A dialogue with future history. In D. Cooperrider & J. E. Dutton (Eds.), *Organizational dimensions of global change: No limits to cooperation* (pp. 320–345). Thousand Oaks, CA: Sage Publications.

Allen, B. J. (1998). Black womanhood and feminist standpoints. *Management Communication Quarterly, 11*(4), 575–586.

Alston, J. (2005). Tempered radicals and servant leaders: Black females persevering in the superintendency. *Education Administration Quarterly, 41*(4), 1–10.

Alston, J. A. (2000). Missing in action: Where are the black female school superintendents? *Urban Education, 35*(5), 525–531.

Alston, J. A. (2005). Tempered radicals and servant leaders: Black females persevering in the superintendency. *Educational Administration Quarterly, 41*(4), 675–688.

Amadiume, I. (1997). *Reinventing Africa: Matriarchy, religion and culture.* London: Zed Books.

Anthias, F. (2002). Where do I belong?: Narrating collective identity and translocational positionality. *Ethnicities, 2*(4), 491–514.

Astin, H. S., & Leland, C. (1991). *Women of influence, women of vision: A cross-generational study of leaders and social change.* San Francisco: Jossey-Bass.

Bakare-Yusuf, B. (2003). *Beyond determinism: The phenomenology of African female existence.* Retrieved March 23, 2004, from http://www.feministafrica.org/02-2003/bibi.html.

Baker, A. (1998). *Voices of resistance: Oral herstories of Moroccan women.* Albany: State University of New York Press.

Bandura, A. (2001). Social cognitive theory: An agentic perspective. *Annual Review of Psychology, 52*, 1–26.

Bass, B. M. (1990). *Bass & Stogdill's handbook of leadership: Theory, research and managerial applications* (3rd ed.). New York: The Free Press.

Bass, B. M. (1999). Two Decades of Research and Development in Transformational Leadership. [Article]. *European Journal of Work & Organizational Psychology, 8*, 9-32.

Beauboeuf-Lafontant, T. (2002). A womanist experience of caring: Understanding the pedagogy of exemplary black women teachers. [research]. *The Urban Review, 34*(1), 71–86.

Bell, E. L. J. E., & Nkomo, S. M. (2001). *Our separate ways: Black and white women and the struggle for professional identity.* Boston: Harvard Business School Press.

Berdyaev, N. (1960). *The origin of Russian Communism.* Ann Arbor: University of Michigan Press.

Berger, I., & White, E. F. (1999). *Women in Sub-Sahara Africa: Restoring women to history.* Bloomington and Indianapolis: Indiana University Press.

Bloom, C. M., & Erlandson, D. A. (2003). African American women principals in urban schools: Realities, (re)constructions, and resolutions. *Educational Administration Quarterly, 39*(3), 339–369.

Burns, J. M. (1978). *Leadership* (1st ed.). New York: Harper & Row.

Carli, L. L., & Eagly, A. H. (2001). Gender, hierarchy, and leadership: An introduction. *Journal of Social Issues, 57*(4), 629–636.

Chavez, C. (2008). Conceptualizing from the inside: Advantages, complications, and demands of insider positionality. *The Qualitative Report, 13*(3), 474–494.

Chisholm, L. (2001). Gender and leadership in South African educational administration. *Gender and Education, 13*(4), 387–399.

Collins, P. H. (1996). The social construction of black feminist thought. In A. Garry & M. Pearsall (Eds.), *Women, knowledge and reality: Explorations in feminist philosophy* (pp. 222–248). New York and London: Routledge.

Collins, P. H. (1998). *Fighting words: Black women and the search for justice.* Minneapolis: University of Minnesota Press.

Collins, P. H. (1999). Moving beyond gender: Intersectionality and scientific knowledge. In M. M. Ferree, J. Lorber, & B. B. Hess (Eds.), *Revisioning gender* (pp. 261–284). Thousand Oaks, CA: Sage Publications.

Collins, P. H. (2000). *Black feminist thought: Knowledge, consciousness, and the politics of empowerment* (2d ed.). New York: Routledge.

Collins, P. H. (2004). Learning from the outsider-within: The sociological significance of Black feminist thought. In S. Harding (Ed.), *The feminist standpoint theory reader: Intellectual and political controversies* (pp. 103–126). New York and London: Routledge.

Cone, J. H. (1990). *A Black theology of liberation* (20th anniversary ed.). Maryknoll, NY: Orbis Books.

Coquery-Vidrovitch, C. (1997). *African women: A modern history* (B. G. Raps, Trans.). Boulder, CO: Westview Press.

Crenshaw, K. (1991). Mapping the margins: Intersectionality, identity politics, and violence against women of color. [Review, conceptual]. *Stanford Law Review, 43*(6), 1241–1299.

Cubillo, L., & Brown, M. (2003). Women in educational leadership and management: International differences? *Journal of Educational administration, 41*(3), 278–291.

Dantley, M. E. (2003a). Critical spirituality: Enhancing transformative leadership through critical theory and African American prophetic spirituality. [review/conceptual]. *International Journal of Leadership in Education, 6*(1), 3–17.

Dantley, M. E. (2003b). Purpose-driven leadership: The spiritual imperative to guiding schools beyond high-stakes testing and minimum proficiency. [theoretical, conceptual]. *Education and Urban Society, 35*(3), 273–291.

Dantley, M. E. (2005). African American spirituality and Cornel West's notions of prophetic pragmatism: Restructuring educational leadership in American urban schools. *Educational Administration Quarterly, 41*(4), 651–674.

Denzin, N. K., & Lincoln, Y. S. (Eds.). (2000). *Handbook of qualitative research* (2d ed.). Thousand Oaks, CA: Sage Publications.

Dillard, C. B., Abdur-Rashid, D., & Tyson, C. A. (2000). My soul is a witness: Affirming pedagogies of the spirit. *International Journal of Qualitative Studies in Education, 13*(5), 447–462.

Dolphyne, F. A. (1991). *The emancipation of women: An African perspective.* Accra: Ghana University Press.

Dove, N. (1998a). African womanism: An Afrocentric theory. [research]. *Journal of Black Studies, 28*(5), 515–539.

Dove, N. (1998b). *Afrikan mothers: Bearers of culture, makers of social change.* Albany: State University of New York Press.

Drath, W. H., & Palus, C. J. (1994). *Making common sense: Leadership as meaning-making in a community of practice.* Greensboro, NC: Center for Creative Leadership.

Eagly, A. H., & Johannesen-Schmidt, M. C. (2001). The leadership styles of women and men. *Journal of Social Issues, 57*(4), 781–797.

Fairholm, G. W. (1997). *Capturing the heart of leadership: Spirituality and community in the new American workplace.* Westport, CT: Praeger.

Freire, P. (1970). *Pedagogy of the oppressed* (30th anniversary ed.). New York: Continuum.

Giesler, G. (2000). "Parliament is another terrain of struggle": Women, men and politics in South Africa. *The Journal of Modern African Studies, 38*(4), 605–630.

Greenleaf, R. K. (1970/1991). *The servant as leader.* Indianapolis, IN: The Robert R. Greenleaf Center.

Greenleaf, R. K. (1977). *Servant leadership: A journey into the nature of legitimate power and greatness.* Ramsey, NJ: Paulist Press.

Gyekye, K. (1997). *Tradition and modernity: Philosophical reflections on the African experience.* New York: Oxford University Press.

Hartsock, N. C. M. (2004). The feminist standpoint: Developing the ground for a specifically feminist historical materialism. In S. Harding (Ed.), *The feminist standpoint theory reader: Intellectual and political controversies* (pp. 35–54). New York and London: Routledge.

Heilman, M. E. (2001). Description and prescription: How gender stereotypes prevent women's ascent up the organizational ladder. [research]. Journal of Social Issues, 57(4), 657–674.

Hersey, P., Blanchard, K. H., & Johnson, D. E. (2001). *Management of organizational behavior: Leading human resources* (8th ed.). Upper Saddle River, NJ: Prentice Hall.

hooks, b. (1994). *Teaching to transgress: Education as the practice of freedom.* New York and London: Routledge.

Hudson-Weems, C. (1997). Africana womanism and the critical need for Africanan theory and thought. [conceptual/theoretical]. The Western Journal of Black Studies, 21(2), 79–84.

Jones, S. N. (2003). *The praxis of black female educational leadership from a systems thinking perspective.* Unpublished doctoral dissertation, Bowling Green State University, Bowling Green.

A journey of courage: Kenyan women's experience of the 2002 General Elections. (2004). Nairobi: AWC Features.

Kabira, W. M., & Ngurukie, P. (1997). *Our mothers' footsteps: Stories of women in the struggle for freedom.* Nairobi: The Collaborative Centre for Gender and Development.

Kamau, M. N. (1996). *The experiences of women academics in Kenya.* Unpublished doctoral dissertation, University of Toronto, Toronto.

Kamau, M. N. (2004). Outsiders within: Experiences of Kenyan women in higher education. *JENDA: A Journal of Culture and African Women Studies,* 6. Retrieved from http://www.jendajournal.com/issue6/kamau.html.

Kanogo, T. (2005). *African womanhood in colonial Kenya 1900–1950.* Oxford, Nairobi, and Athens, Ohio: James Currey Ltd., East African Educational Publishers, and Ohio University Press.

Koestenbaum, P. (2002). *Leadership: The inner side of greatness* (2d ed.). San Francisco: Jossey-Bass.

Kolawole, M. E. M. (1997). *Womanism and African consciousness.* Trenton, NJ, and Amsara, Eritrea: African World Press.

Kouzes, J. M., & Posner, B. Z. (2002). *The leadership challenge.* San Francisco: Jossey-Bass.

Kouzes, J. M., & Posner, B. Z. (2003). *Encouraging the heart: A leader's guide to rewarding and recognizing others* (1st ed.). San Francisco: Jossey-Bass.

Kuria, M. (Ed.) (2003). *Talking gender: Conversations with Kenyan women writers.* Nairobi: PJ-Kenya.

Kuzwayo, E. (1985). *Call me woman.* San Francisco: Spinsters/Aunt Lute.

Lawrence-Lightfoot, S. (1983). *The good high school: Portraits of character and culture.* New York: Basic Books.

Lawrence-Lightfoot, S., & Davis, J. H. (1997). *The art and science of portraiture.* San Francisco: Jossey-Bass.

Likimani, M. (1985). *Passbook number F.47927: Women and Mau Mau in Kenya.* New York: Praeger.

Likimani, M. (2005). *Fighting without ceasing.* Nairobi: Nonis Publicity.

Lipman-Blumen, J. (1992). *Connective leadership: Female leadership styles in the 21st-century workplace.* Retrieved March 23, 2004, from http://www.achievingstyles.com/article_female.asp.

Mabokela, R. O. (2003a). "Donkeys of the university": Organizational culture and its impact on South African women administrators. [empirical]. *Higher Education, 46,* 129–145.

Mabokela, R. O. (2003b). Reflections of Black women faculty in South African universities. *The Review of Higher Education, 25*(2), 185–205.

Masinjila, M. (1997). Patriarchy and women's participation in politics in Kenya. In W. M. Kabira & M. Masinjila (Eds.), *Towards gender responsive politics* (pp. 2–12). Nairobi: The Friedrich Ebert Foundation in association with The Collaborative Center for Gender and Development.

Mattis, J. S. (2002). Religion and spirituality in the meaning-making and coping experiences of African American women: A qualitative analysis. [research]. *Psychology of Women Quarterly, 25*, 309–321.

Maynes, M., & Pierce, J. L. (2005). Making positionality visible in feminist research: Some methodological considerations for personal narrative analysis. Paper presented at the annual meeting of the American Sociological Association, Philadelphia, PA, August 12. [Online].

Mbigi, L. (1996). *Ubuntu: The African dream in management.* Randburg, South Africa: Knowledge Resources (Pty).

Mbiti, J. S. (1969). *African religions and philosophy.* Nairobi: East African Educational Publishers.

Mbugua-Muriithi, J. T. (1996). *Strategies for survival: Women, education and self-help groups in Kenya.* Unpublished doctoral dissertation, Ohio University, Athens, Ohio.

McClellan, P. (2006). Wearing the mantle: Spirited Black male servant leaders reflect on their leadership journey. Unpublished dissertation, Bowling Green State University, Bowling Green, KY.

McClellan, P. (2010). Toward critical servant leadership in graduate schools of education: from theoretical construct to social justice praxis. In S. D. Horsford (Ed.), *New Perspectives in educational leadership: Exploring social, political, and community contexts and meanings.* New York: Peter Lang Publishing.

Meyerson, D. E. (2001). *Tempered radicals: How people use difference to inspire change at work.* Boston: Harvard Business School Press.

Meyerson, D. E., & Scully, M. A. (1995). Tempered radicalism and the politics of ambivalence and change. [Empirical]. *Organization Science, 6*(5), 585–600.

Morrison, A. M., & Glinow, M. A. V. (1990). Women and minorities in organizations. [conceptual, theoreticla]. *American Psychologist, 45*(2), 200–208.

Murtadha, K., & Watts, D. M. (2005). Linking the struggle for education and social justice: Historical perspectives of African American leadership in schools. *Educational Administration Quarterly, 41*(4), 591–608.

Murtadha-Watts, K. (1999). Spirited sisters: Spirituality and the activism of African American women in educational leadership. In L. T. Fenwick & P. Jenlink (Eds.), *School leadership: Expanding the horizons of the mind and spirit* (pp. 155–167). Lancaster: Technomic.

Murunga, G. R. (2002). African women in the academy and beyond: Review essay. *Jenda: Journal of Culture and African Women Studies, 2*(1).

Muscarella, T. S. (2004). *A qualitative and quantitative investigation of barriers for women attaining leadership positions: The effects of role expectations, gender stereotyping and role incongruity of being female and a leader.* Unpublished Ph.D. Diss., Capella University, Minnesota. UMI no. 9315947.

Muteshi, J. K. (1998). "A refusal to argue with inconvenient evidence": Women, proprietorship and Kenyan law. *Dialectical Anthropology, 23*(1), 55–81.

Ngunjiri, F. W. (2009). Servant leadership and motherhood: Kenyan women finding fulfillment in serving humanity. *Gendered Perspectives on International Development.* Working Paper #294.

Ngunjiri, F. W. (2005, October 13–16). *Tempered radicals and servant leaders: Women and leadership in the Global South.* Paper presented at the Organization for the Study of Communication, Language and Gender Annual Conference, Reno, Nevada.

Ngunjiri, F. W. (2006a, March 12–14). *Gender and power: Deconstructing the positioning of African women leaders.* Paper presented at the 2nd Women as Global Leaders Conference, Abu Dhabi, United Arab Emirates.

Ngunjiri, F. W. (2006b, August 12–15). *Spiritual leadership: Portraits of courage, compassion and service for community transformation.* Paper presented at the Academy of Management Annual Meeting, Atlanta.

Ngunjiri, F. W. (2006c). *Tempered radicals and servant leaders: Portraits of spirited leadership amongst African women.* Unpublished doctoral dissertation, Bowling Green State University, Bowling Green.

Ngunjiri, F. W. (2007a). Banking on women for poverty reduction: Portrait of Kenya Women's Finance Trust. In J. A. F. Stoner & C. Wankel (Eds.), *Innovative approaches to reducing global poverty* (pp. 93–108). Charlotte, NC: Information Age.

Ngunjiri, F. W. (2007b). Rocking the boat without falling out: Spirited tempered radicals as agents of community transformation. *UCEA Review, XLVI*(3), 4.

Ngunjiri, F. W., & Lengel, L. B. (2007). Tempered radicals: Organizational and intercultural communication practices of Kenyan women leaders. [empirical, referred]. *International and Intercultural Communication Annual xxx,* 117–145.

Ntiri, D. W. (2001). Reassessing Africana womanism: Continuity and change. [review]. *The Western Journal of Black Studies, 25*(3), 163–167.

Nzegwu, N. (2001). Gender equality in a dual-sex system: The case of Onitsha. *Jenda: Journal of Culture and African Women Studies, 1*(1), 1–32.

Oduyoye, M. A. (1995a). Calling the church to account. *Ecumenical Review, 47*(4), 479–489.

Oduyoye, M. A. (1995b). *Daughters of Anowa: African women and patriarchy.* New York: Maryknoll.

Oduyoye, M. A. (2001). *Introducing African women's theology.* Cleveland, OH, and Sheffield, England: Pilgrim Press and Sheffield Academic Press.

Ombati, V. F. O. (2003). *Women's participation in educational leadership in Kenya: The case of Nairobi and Thika municipal primary schools.* Unpublished doctoral dissertation, State University of New York at Buffalo.

Otieno, T. N. (1995). *A study of Kenyan university and post-secondary women students: Challenges and strategies to their educational advancement.* Unpublished doctoral dissertation, Ohio University, Athens, Ohio.

Otieno, W. W. (1998). *Mau Mau's daughter: A life history.* Boulder, CO: Lynne Rinner.

Oyewumi, O. (1997). *The invention of woman: Making an African sense of Western gender discourses.* Minneapolis: University of Minnesota Press.

Oyewumi, O. (2002). Conceptualizing gender: The Eurocentric foundations of feminist concepts and the challenge of African epistemologies. *Jenda: Journal of Culture and African Women Studies, 2*(1). [Online article].

Oyewumi, O. (2003). Introduction: Feminism, sisterhood, and other foreign relations. In O. Oyewumi (Ed.), *African women & feminism: Reflecting on the politics of sisterhood* (pp. 1–24). Trenton, NJ, and Amsara, Eritrea: African World Press.

Paris, P. J. (1995). *The spirituality of African peoples: The search for a common moral discourse.* Minneapolis, MN: Fortress Press.

Parker, P. S. (2005). *Race, gender, and leadership: Re-envisioning organizational leadership from the perspectives of African American women executives.* Mawhah, NJ: Lawrence Erlbaum Associates.

Parker, P. S., & ogilvie, d. (1996). Gender, culture, and leadership: Toward a culturally distinct model of African-American women executives' leadership strategies. [research, theoretical]. *Leadership Quarterly, 7*(2), 189–214.

Pounder, J. S., & Coleman, M. (2002). Women—Better leaders than men? In general and educational administration it still "all depends." *Leadership & Organizational Development Journal, 23*(3), 122–133.

Reid-Merritt, P. (1996). *Sister power: How phenomenal black women are rising to the top.* New York: John Wiley & Sons.

Ridgeway, C. L. (2001). Gender, status, and leadership. *Journal of Social Issues, 57*(4), 637–655.

Rigg, C., & Sparrow, J. (1994). Gender, diversity and working styles. *Women in Management Review, 9*(1), 9–16.

Romero, P. (1998). *Profiles in diversity: Women in the new South Africa.* East Lansing: Michigan State University Press.

Rosenbach, W. E., & Taylor, R. L. (Eds.). (2001). *Contemporary issues in leadership* (5th ed.). Cambridge: Westview Press.

Rosenberg, P. S. (1992). *Race, class, and gender in the United States: An integrated study* (2d ed.). New York: St. Martin's Press.

Shorter, A. (1974). *African culture and the Christian church: An introduction to social and pastoral anthropology.* New York: Maryknoll.

Shum, L. C., & Cheng, Y. C. (1997). Perceptions of women principals' leadership and teachers' work attitudes. [research]. *Journal of Educational Administration, 35*(2), 165–184.

Spears, L. C. (1995). Introduction: Servant-leadership and the Greenleaf Legacy. In L. C. Spears (Ed.), *Reflections on leadership: How Robert K. Greenleaf's theory of servant-leadership influenced today's top management thinkers.* New York: John Wiley & Sons.

Spears, L. C. (2002). Introduction: Tracing the past, present and future of servant leadership. In L. C. Spears, M. Lawrence, & K. H. Blanchard (Eds.), *Focus on leadership: Servant leadership for the 21st century* (pp. 1–18). New York: John Wiley & Sons.

Starratt, R. J. (1991). Building an ethical school: A theory for practice in educational administration. [conceptual]. *Educational Administration Quarterly, 27*(2), 185–202.

Strobel, M. (1995). Women in religious and secular ideology. In M. J. Hay & S. Stichter (Eds.), *African women south of the Sahara* (pp. 101–142). New York: Longman Scientific & Technical.

Sweetman, D. (1984). *Women leaders in African history.* Oxford: Heinemann International.

Thomas, L. E. (1998). Womanist theology, epistemology, and a new anthropological paradigm. *Cross Currents, 48*(4), 488–499.

Tillman, L. C. (2001). Mentoring African American faculty in predominantly white institutions. [research]. *Research in Higher Education, 42*(3), 295–325.

Tillman, L. C. (2002). Culturally sensitive research approaches: An African-American perspective. [conceptual]. *Educational Researcher, 31*(9), 3–12.

Tisdell, E. J. (2003). *Exploring spirituality and culture in adult and higher education.* San Francisco: Jossey-Bass.

Turner, R. L. (2008). *Embodiment, positionality, and self-presentation: Informant perceptions and qualitative data.* Paper presented at the APSA 2008 Annual Meeting, Boston, MA, August 28. [Online].

Walker, A. (1983). *In search of our mothers' gardens.* New York: Harcourt Brace Jovanovich.

Weiss, A. E. (1999). *The glass ceiling: A look at women in the workforce.* Brookfield, CT: Twenty-First Century Books.

Welch, S. D. (2000). *A feminist ethic of risk* (Revised ed.). Minneapolis, MN: Fortress.

Wilson, M. C. (2004). *Closing the leadership gap: Why women can and must help run the world.* New York: Viking Penguin.

Yaverbaum, E. (2004). *Leadership secrets of the world's most successful CEOs.* Chicago, IL: Dearbon Trade Publishing.

Yoder, J. D. (2001). Making leadership work more effectively for women. *Journal of Social Issues, 57*(4), 815–828.

Young, M. D., & Mcleod, S. (2001). Flukes, opportunities, and planned interventions: Factors affecting women's decisions to become school administrators. [research]. *Educational Administration Quarterly, 37*(4), 462–502.

Yukl, G. (2001). *Leadership in organizations* (5th ed.). Upper Saddle River, NJ: Prentice Hall.

Yukl, G. A. (2006). *Leadership in organizations* (6th ed.). Upper Saddle River, NJ: Pearson/Prentice Hall.

About the Author

Faith Wambura Ngunjiri, Ed.D, is an assistant professor in the Ph.D. program in organizational leadership at Eastern University. Prior to her current position, Dr. Ngunjiri served as associate director for the program on Ethics and Spirituality in the Workplace at Yale Center for Faith and Culture, Yale Divinity School. Prior to that, she taught at Indiana University-Purdue University, Fort Wayne (IPFW) in the Organizational Leadership and Supervision division. She graduated with a master's degree in organization development (2005) and a doctor of education degree in leadership studies (2006) from Bowling Green State University. Her research focuses on the intersections of gender, spirituality, and leadership among Black and African women, demonstrated through critical servant leadership, tempered radicalism, and spiritual/spirited leadership. Her articles have appeared in the *Journal of Research Practice, Journal of Business Communication, Intercultural and International Communication Annual, The Other Journal,* and MSU's *Gendered Perspectives on International Development Working Papers.*

Index

233